War and Faith

Ikkō Ikki *in Late Muromachi Japan*

Harvard East Asian Monographs 288

War and Faith

Ikkō Ikki *in Late Muromachi Japan*

Carol Richmond Tsang

Published by the Harvard University Asia Center
and distributed by Harvard University Press
Cambridge (Massachusetts) and London, 2007

Printed in the United States of America

The Harvard University Asia Center publishes a monograph series and, in coordination with the Fairbank Center for East Asian Research, the Korea Institute, the Reischauer Institute of Japanese Studies, and other faculties and institutes, administers research projects designed to further scholarly understanding of China, Japan, Vietnam, Korea, and other Asian countries. The Center also sponsors projects addressing multidisciplinary and regional issues in Asia.

Library of Congress Cataloging-in-Publication Data

Tsang, Carol Richmond.

War and faith : Ikkō ikki in late Muromachi Japan / Carol Richmond Tsang.

p. cm. -- (Harvard East Asian monographs ; 288)

Includes bibliographical references and index.

ISBN 978-0-674-02509-7 (hardcover : alk. paper)

1. Ikkō uprisings. 2. Shin (Sect)--History. I. Title.

BQ8712.6.T73 2007

952'.023--dc22

2007002976

Index by the author

♾ Printed on acid-free paper

In memory of my mothers,

Elizabeth Richmond and Shingyō Kazuko

Acknowledgments

I wish to thank Harold Bolitho and Albert Craig, who supervised the dissertation on which this book is partially based. In Japan, Fujiki Hisashi, Minegishi Sumio, and Shingyō Norikazu gave generously of their expertise and themselves and welcomed me with the most gracious hospitality. For reading and providing suggestions for improving the manuscript at various stages, I am deeply indebted to Harold Bolitho, Phil Brown, Nelly Gupta, Joan Piggott, Conrad Totman, and two anonymous reviewers. My husband James asked insightful questions that helped improve the clarity of the text and quality of the logic. Many thanks to William M. Hammell of the Harvard University Asia Center, whose diligence saved me from many *bêtises*. All errors and inconsistencies are, of course, the responsibility of the author alone.

Several associations and foundations provided financial support. The Japan–United States Educational Commission and the Japan Foundation supported my research in Japan. The Reischauer Institute of Japanese Studies provided me with generous support during a postdoctoral fellowship. The Institute for the Humanities at the University of Illinois at Chicago also supported a year for developing the manuscript. I thank them all for helping make my work possible.

Many other people helped me in various ways at different stages of research, and I cannot possibly thank them all in this space. They include, in alphabetical order: Mark Brewer, Jim Cracraft, Wayne Farris, Higashiyotsuyanagi Fumiaki and the staff of the Ishikawa Prefectural Library Research Group, Hisada Yukako, Imai Masaharu, Ishida Haruo, Kinryū Shizuka, Kitanishi Hiromu, Kokaze Mariko, the Murata family, Robert Rhodes, Sakai Kimi, Yasutake Tomoko and Hide, and the staff of the University of Tokyo Historiographical Institute. Among my former colleagues at the University of Illinois at Chicago, Michael Alexander, Jim Cracraft, Carolyn Edie, Steven Fanning, Laura Hostetler, Mark Leichty, and Marion Miller stand out as especially helpful as I completed the manuscript.

Special and warmest thanks are due to Fujiki Kayoko, Minegishi Tatsue, and Shingyō Kazuko—for everything.

Contents

Maps and Figure

Maps

Figure

Maps

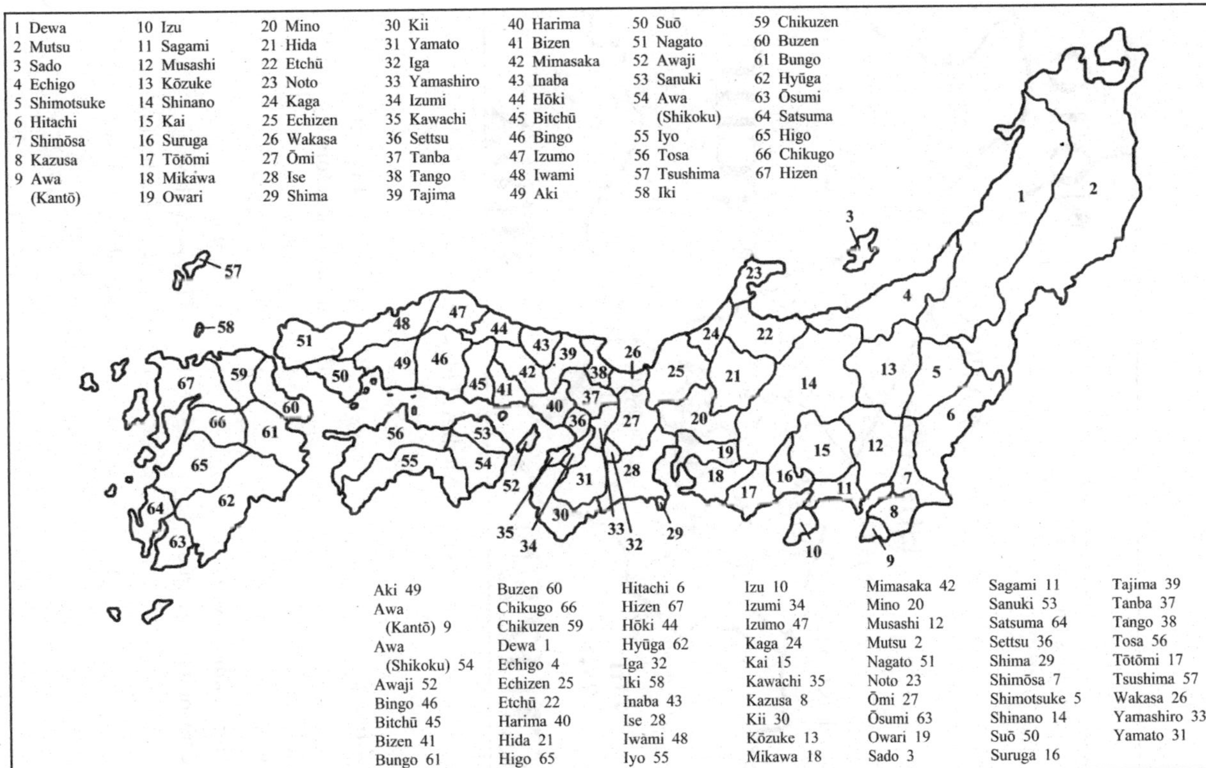

Map 1 Provinces of medieval Japan

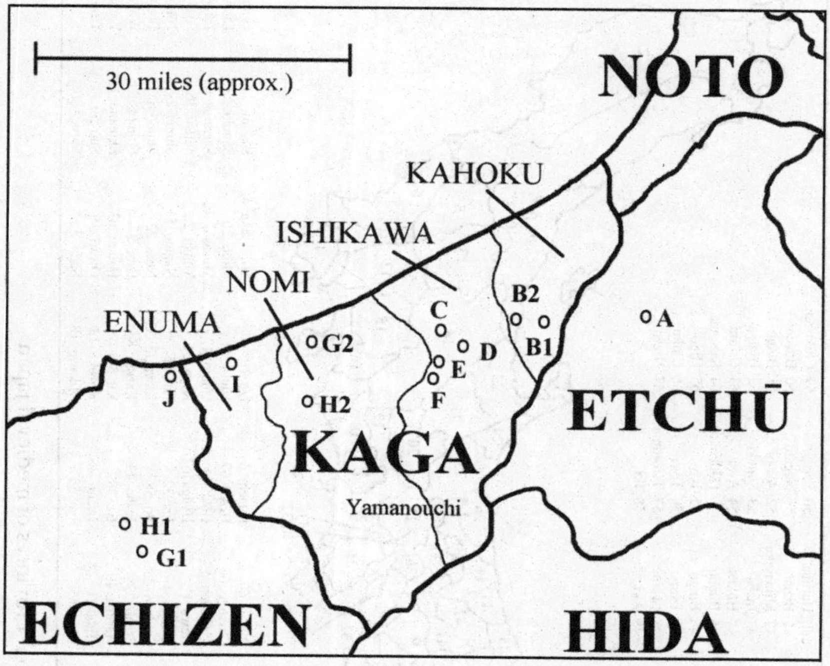

Map 2 Medieval Hokuriku

ETCHŪ

A	Zuisenji

ECHIZEN

J	Yoshizaki
G1	Hongakuji before 1506
H1	Chōshōji before 1506

KAGA

B1	Honsenji after 1531
B2	Honsenji before 1531
C	Honrenji
D	Takao Castle
E	Gantokuji
F	Hakusan Shrine
G2	Hongakuji after 1506
H2	Chōshōji after 1506
I	Kōkyōji

War and Faith

Ikkō Ikki *in Late Muromachi Japan*

Introduction

In the autumn of Tenshō 3 [1575], a Buddhist priest visited the military commander Oda Nobunaga during one of the latter's campaigns of conquest. His temple had economic interests in the province Nobunaga had just absorbed, and the priest hoped to safeguard them by being on the spot. His diary of the stay mentions some of Nobunaga's forces returning to camp after a "mountain hunt," which usually referred to tracking wild boar, a common samurai pastime. This time they did not hunt wild boar or the like, however, and the priest noted a new definition of the term: "a mountain hunt means killing members of the *ikki* (league) and cutting off their noses to bring back as an indication of the number killed. Also, more than two hundred were taken alive and beheaded in the rice fields to the west of camp."[1]

The soldiers' prey was human. In sixteenth-century Japan, rewards for warriors depended largely on the number and status of those they killed, and their commanders required proof. Noses sufficed as trophies from low-status enemies.

In this case, the noses belonged to members of the Honganji branch of True Pure Land Buddhism (Jōdo Shinshū), whose leader, the Patriarch, relished the sect's administrative, economic, and military independence, which Nobunaga sought to destroy. The sectarians had responded to the Patriarch's calls to protect their religion against the commander's attempt to subjugate it. The resistance to Oda Nobunaga occupied Honganji members from Etchū in the northeast to Harima in the southwest, and lasted ten years (1570–1580) before the Patriarch accepted a settlement that amounted to a defeat.

This prolonged war against Nobunaga, the first of three successive military leaders who tried to unify Japan under one rule, was not the only time Honganji followers took to the battlefield. The first such occasion took place in 1465, when another religious group attacked and destroyed the original Honganji temple in Kyoto. In the intervening century, Honganji members throughout central Honshu fought for various causes, and not always with the Patriarch's blessing. Collectively, historians call these battles *ikkō ikki*.

Samurai, especially military commanders, or daimyo, dominate most people's understanding of Japan prior to 1870. Although the imperial court continued to exercise some powers, the samurai dominated government beginning in the twelfth century. Thus, they have garnered the most attention;[2] their stories are dramatic and colorful. This is especially true of the period between 1467 and 1573, which comprised roughly the last century of the Muromachi shogunate, a military government that had ruled since 1338. The shogunate's national effectiveness declined steadily beginning in the 1440s, as power devolved to provincial military commanders. As a result, warfare became rampant, leading historians to dub this the era of *sengoku*, which can be translated roughly as "warring provinces."[3]

Yet villagers also played strong, active roles in this period, as did warriors of more humble station than daimyo, not to mention artisans and merchants who populated the towns and cities. Their individual lives are obscure, and often they made their impact as faceless members of groups. Indeed, since they risked the displeasure of and repercussions from those with more power, sometimes the facelessness was crucial.

Politically active groups of villagers, samurai, or townspeople, usually called *ikki*, or leagues, characterize pre-modern Japan as much as warriors do. Scholars writing in English have explored many aspects of the leagues formed by peasants in the years between 1600 and 1870, but the earlier leagues have received less attention in the English-language literature. Of these earlier instances, the *ikkō ikki* had the greatest impact over the longest period of time.

Ikkō ikki literally means leagues, or a league,[4] of Honganji sect members. *Ikkō* (lit., single-directed) refers to the beliefs of the sect, which taught only one way to achieve salvation: the worship of Amida, a Buddha who had vowed to save all sentient beings by having them reborn in his Pure Land. Once there, believers would reach Buddhahood effortlessly, and so be freed of the cycle of birth, death, and rebirth that kept returning them to suffer in this world.

The word *ikki* literally means to be "of one mind," opinion, or will. In the fifteenth and sixteenth centuries, it applied to leagues, which consisted of people "of one mind" about a given purpose. It also came to mean the actions of such leagues, often but not always violent ones. *Ikki,* then, means either a group of people, or an event that presupposes a league behind it.

During the era of Tokugawa government (1600–1868), peasants formed *ikki* many times, mostly as protests against heavy taxation. As temporal successors to *ikkō ikki,* one might expect there to be a strong connection between the two. Instead, leagues and the actions they pursued changed so much that one is tempted to say there was no continuity, that *ikkō ikki* simply died out (or were destroyed) with no legacy left to village protesters. This would be incorrect, however.

The actions of *ikkō* leagues and ultimately their defeat contributed greatly to the shape of a new governing system in Japan. Under the new system, the character of *ikki* actions changed because the context had changed so much. Thus, the influence of *ikkō ikki* on later *ikki* was profound, but not direct. For these reasons alone—their prominence and their legacy—*ikkō ikki* deserve extensive treatment. Still, they are not the only reasons.

Political histories of *sengoku* usually deal only glancingly with religion, yet the lack of attention hampers our understanding of *sengoku* polity. Many religious institutions exercised considerable political power,[5] and religious beliefs contributed to actions taken by leagues, and not just ones formed by Honganji members. This study of *ikkō ikki* and their relationship with Honganji will help fill in this vital part of the picture.

Finally, Honganji leagues drew their strength from a shared religious identity and perspective. The contribution of religious belief to both the motivation for and the intensity of fighting comes up repeatedly in both history and current events. A study of *ikkō ikki* shows one way religion and religious belief played out in a society in conflict, and expands our perspective on the force of religion in people's lives.

Ikkō ikki overall defy simple characterization. The only common feature of the numerous *ikkō ikki* events was the dominance of Honganji followers in activities that often involved non-members as well. Otherwise, as one might expect from a series of actions that spanned more than a century, the sectarians joined with each other for different reasons at different times in different places with different kinds of opponents. In two cases, in 1506 and 1531, groups of Honganji sectarians even fought against each other.

Usually, members would accept orders from the leader of the Honganji sect, the Patriarch, but sometimes they might not.[6] Often, the sectarians acted on their own, without the Patriarch's leadership or advance knowledge, and occasionally against his wishes. Predictably, the members always acted in what they perceived—rationally or not—to be their own best interests, which naturally varied depending upon time, place, and circumstances.

Any generalization about the composition, organization, size, or geographical coverage of Honganji leagues is impossible to make, and often even the specifics for an identifiable league are beyond documentation. The use of the term *ikki* in *sengoku*-era documents is loose; in most cases, the word *ikki* for league seems to characterize a group of commoners who band together to participate in some kind of battle. As for structured *ikkō* leagues, no evidence that speaks to their practices or composition exists, which brings up another unanswerable question: to what extent were most *ikkō* leagues formal, as opposed to *de facto*? The reader must be cautious about seeing institutional structures, however temporary, in every group that is labeled a league. The structures may not be there.

Despite those occasions when members responded to orders from the Patriarch, the members' *ikki* and the Honganji institution were distinct entities. The memberships overlapped, but at no time were formally constituted leagues an official part of the Honganji sect's structure, nor were they permanent. Groups formed for the purpose of concerted action; they were not simply there, ready-organized for the Patriarch to call on. Rather, he would issue a call to arms, and the members who responded became a league in one sense, a group of men "of one mind."

Honganji leagues consisted primarily of merchants, artisans, and village leaders, despite the common impression of their members as peasants. Village leaders did not command the peasants in *ikki,* but rather they did the fighting themselves. They were peasants in the sense that gentlemen farmers were farmers: locally prominent men who nevertheless seemed low and boorish to the real elite. Some village leaders belonged to a class of warriors known as *jizamurai* (lit., samurai of the soil), men with some training in weaponry who both farmed and fought, but whom warriors did not fully accept as part of their number. So whereas the equation of *ikkō ikki* events as actions of peasant leagues holds true in one sense, the reader must beware of conceptualizing those peasants as the poorest members of society.

The Patriarch's willingness and ability to send his followers into battle grew over time but never became absolute. When the sect's most powerful sponsor requested military help in 1506, the then-Patriarch at first resisted, and when he finally issued the order, the members on whom he called refused to fight. By 1570, the Patriarch and members had embraced their military potential in order to fight the daimyo Oda Nobunaga in his push for hegemony. In order to accomplish his goal, Nobunaga needed to force religious organizations to surrender their economic and political power, and this the sect resisted. They succeeded in holding off defeat longer than many of Honganji's daimyo allies did.

How and why did the sect's strength and military readiness increase so much in that century? It happened through a combination of forces that included Honganji members' willingness to fight for their own reasons, and warriors' insistence that the Patriarch first suppress and later harness that willingness. Because of this pressure from above, successive Patriarchs improved the effectiveness of their tools for controlling the behavior of sectarians.

In the war against Nobunaga, the tools worked impressively, but no Patriarch gained absolute power over his followers, just as no daimyo did over his. The sect was no seamless monolith. Honganji members overall never became blind fanatics eager to follow the Patriarch without question, though many, no doubt, fought with the expectation of being reborn in the Pure Land should they fall in battle. To this end, they often carried slips of paper with "*Namu Amida butsu*" (Hail Amida Buddha) written on them, the phrase Honganji members chanted as their main religious practice. Even in the 1570s, however, Honganji members in some areas failed to support the Patriarch and instead sided with Nobunaga.[7] The key to understanding *ikkō ikki* is to recognize the diversity of both the sect members and their aims.

Until now, there has been no work published in English that focuses solely on *ikkō ikki* and examines the leagues and their activities on their own terms. An unpublished doctoral dissertation focuses on the *ikki* in Kaga as the largest and most successful of the *ikkō ikki*, and another discusses *ikkō ikki* as part of Honganji's political activities. One article devotes a few pages of an essay to *ikkō ikki* in the context of other *ikki* during the Muromachi era.[8] Several treat the development of the sect and its theology, especially the contributions of its founder Shinran, and the eighth Patriarch, Rennyo.[9] In terms of political history, two works on Oda Nobunaga necessarily describe his fight against Honganji at its most powerful.[10] All of these works are concerned with the *ikki* as the military arm of the Honganji sect and, because of their main concerns, view *ikkō ikki* from the top down.

By contrast, *War and Faith* treats the whole, broad phenomenon of *ikkō ikki* and seeks to understand it on its own terms. It addresses the *ikkō* leagues' relationship to the sect within the context of *sengoku* Japan, and focuses as much as possible on the Honganji sect's followers rather than on its leaders, even in matters of doctrine. Because a religion's lay members often entertain beliefs and interpretations contrary to the faith's official teachings, theologians' pronouncements are not taken as evidence of followers' own beliefs. Instead, evidence of members' actual beliefs has been sought to the limited extent possible.[11]

In the context of Japanese society, membership in the sect worked as a powerful glue that kept Honganji sectarians in extremely cohesive units, and helped these units transcend geographical regions. Combined with Honganji's hierarchical (not egalitarian) organization, their faith made them likely to respond to direction from priests and Patriarchs. Contemporary documents testify that by the 1570s, the sectarians attributed more power to the Patriarch than Honganji's teachings theoretically permitted.

According to Honganji doctrine, only Amida's power could cause someone to be reborn in the Pure Land; no human being had any such power. Nevertheless, many members, perhaps most, believed that the Patriarch could assure them a place in the Pure Land, or consign them to hell. Thus, many of his followers had powerful incentives to obey him—and equally strong disincentives to cross him. To sum up, for the regionally restricted *ikki* activities, religious cohesion contributed far more to making Honganji leagues successful than sectarian doctrine contributed to their initial formation. With the Patriarch-led wars, especially the one against Nobunaga, religious belief produced both league formation and tenacious fighting.

Although the story of *ikkō ikki* and the leagues' changing relationships with the Patriarch entails interactions between followers and leaders, and my concerns lie primarily with the followers, the Patriarchs loom over much of this volume. There are two reasons for this. One is the sources, the most detailed of which are the diaries of imperial aristocrats and non-Honganji priests, and Honganji sectarian histories and memoirs. All tended to pay more attention to the actions of those at the top of the sect than to those at the bottom. Courtier diaries generally discussed *ikkō ikki* when a) they affected the courtiers' income, or b) the events involved prominent warriors. Of course, neither case resulted in telling the story from a league's perspective. Most sectarian texts relate to histories of temples or to doctrine, so they generally discuss priests and Patriarchs, not members. Thus leaders dominate the sources, and the members' stories can be seen mostly from outside or tangentially.[12]

The other reason has to do with the choice of chronology as an organizing principle, and periodization. A discussion of process, such as the one by which Honganji members and warriors helped forge the military power of the mid- to late sixteenth-century Patriarch, depends on the reader having a clear narrative grasp of the important events. The diversity and temporal overlaps of *ikkō ikki* episodes, however, render a simple yet meaningful periodization of those episodes impossible. Therefore, chapter breaks occur during relative lulls in the action, and often coincide with the accession of a new Patriarch.

Terminology

Terminology as applied to samurai is problematic. Terms used in primary sources usually differ according to the author's status or preference. Historians use a variety of terms, and not all agree on their definitions. Some are universally accepted and understood: shogun, *shugo,* daimyo. Others, like *kokujin* and *zaichi ryōshu* (provincial person and local landlord, respectively) can refer to an array of samurai from the *shugo-dai* (assistant *shugo*) and castellan level down to small landholders with jurisdiction over a single village, since all held land and lived in the provinces. Either term can be used to refer to either extreme, or to the entire group, depending on the historian's focus and the region under discussion. As a result, this terminology can easily confuse the reader; indeed, it can hardly fail to do so. It is well, then, to clarify the terms employed here.

The highest-level warrior was, of course, the shogun. Below him were the *shugo* and daimyo, also high-level. The next most powerful are those referred to in this study as *kokujin,* the warriors who filled the ranks of *shugo-dai,* their competitors, and castellans. In the interest of clarity, I have restricted the use of this term to these relatively powerful men.

A *kokujin*'s top retainers served as generals and advisors, much as the *kokujin* often did for their own lords. Members of collateral branches of these families, and men of similar standing, came next. Both together, in my terminology, constituted the mid-level warriors.

Lower-level samurai consisted of warriors who had jurisdiction over no more than a village or two, and were only one step above the village elite, namely village headmen and *jizamurai,* those who spent part of their time on cultivation and part of it in warfare. Higher ranks of samurai did not usually see *jizamurai* as "real" samurai; at best, they were "small samurai," who went unnamed in war tales, or *hyakushō,* which in that era meant taxpayers.

The terminology applied to religious organizations is even more problematic. In most cases, I use the word sect to describe the group led by the Honganji temple. When comparing it to other religious groups, I may also use school, branch, or faction to denote institutions. In this book, none of these words carries the specialized meanings often assigned to them in religious studies, especially those of the European religious traditions.

Although temples are buildings, and therefore inanimate, for convenience their names are used both abstractly, referring to the sect's leaders, and concretely, referring to its physical facilities. Thus "Honganji" could teach, make policy, and wage wars, as well as be built, attacked, and burned down.

ONE
Honganji and Its World

According to a European visitor writing in 1561, Honganji followers looked on Kennyo (1543–92), the eleventh Patriarch of Honganji temple, with

> such . . . veneration . . that even a glimpse of him moves them to tears as they beg him to absolve them from their sins. They give this *bonze* [priest] so much money in alms that he controls a large part of the country's wealth. Every year a great festival is held in his honour, and so many people wait at the gate of the temple to enter that many die in the stampede which results when they open the gates. Such people, however, are considered very lucky to have died in this way, and some at their own request are dropped into the crowd around the gates and are thus killed.[1]

Even allowing for misinterpretation and exaggeration—the visitor was Gaspar Vilela, a Jesuit missionary and therefore hardly a disinterested observer—the description is striking. Here, one feels, was Honganji at the peak of its economic and military power.

Although the sect had reached this pinnacle by the second half of the sixteenth century, its origins were humble. Like the other True Pure Land sects that it would later outshine, the Honganji sect began with a priest named Shinran, who lived from 1173 to 1262. More literally, the Honganji temple began as a chapel at his gravesite. The sect's increasing might developed over more than two centuries, at first largely through the proselytizing and organizational efforts of its leaders. After 1465, members themselves also fueled the growth in the sect's power, especially through their collective activities as *ikkō ikki*.

According to tradition, Honganji's founder Shinran was the child of a middle-level imperial aristocrat. He entered the great Tendai complex of Enryakuji in 1181 or 1182 at the age of 9, taking the tonsure at the sub-temple Shōren'in on the eastern outskirts of Kyoto.[2] He later studied under another priest at Enryakuji, Hōnen (1133–1212), who founded the Pure Land sect (Jōdoshū) by focusing his teachings on the worship of Amida, already a feature of Tendai practice though only one of many. According to Amidist teachings, the Buddha Amida promised to save all sentient beings, and his worshippers hoped to be reborn in his Pure Land, where they would achieve enlightenment effortlessly.

Amida's promise took on additional importance after the middle of the eleventh century, when Buddhist priests calculated that the world had entered a historical phase called *mappō* (lit., the decline of the Buddhist law). Buddhism taught that history occurs in cycles called kalpa. Each kalpa begins with the birth of a new Buddha, which commences a phase in which Buddhist law flourishes, a kind of golden age. After the Buddha's death, a new phase of the reflected law begins, during which it is still possible, but difficult, for people to follow the Buddha's teachings and achieve enlightenment. After that phase comes *mappō,* the end of the law, which is characterized by disorder and natural disasters: famine, earthquakes, floods, wars, and so on. During *mappō,* human abilities degenerate such that no one can achieve enlightenment through his own efforts. Partly as a response to *mappō,* some priests sought other ways to approach religion and found Amida to provide hope.

Hōnen taught that through worshipping only Amida, people could find salvation, that is, rebirth in Amida's Pure Land. This goal could be achieved by chanting the *nenbutsu,* the phrase "*Namu Amida butsu*" ("Hail Amida Buddha"), "wholeheartedly while walking, while standing still, while sitting, and while lying down."[3] Hōnen attracted many disciples, of whom Shinran was only one, and the Pure Land movement diversified along several paths, as these disciples brought their own perspectives and experiences to bear on such issues as the true meaning of the *nenbutsu* and what makes it effective.

Shinran's teachings came to differ from those of Hōnen in two ways that were to become central to the Honganji sect's doctrinal and institutional development. First, he identified faith (*shinjin*, lit., the believing heart) in Amida and in Amida's "other power" (*tariki*), as the important components of obtaining salvation. Shinran taught members to chant the *nenbutsu* as the central practice of worship, but he cautioned against believing that the chanting resulted in heavenly rebirth. Rather, members chanted the *nenbutsu* out of the gratitude called forth by Amida's grace, and therefore even the chanting was a result of Amida's power; in other words, of Amida.[4] The only way to enter Amida's paradise was to rely entirely on *his* power.

Second, unlike Hōnen, Shinran believed there was no need to follow the ascetic traditions of clerical life, such as maintaining celibacy. Instead, he encouraged his followers to marry, as he did himself. His descendants, who created Honganji temple and the sect named after it, later based their legitimacy simply on being direct descendants of the founder. Although the leadership of smaller Honganji sect temples sometimes adopted boys or men to take over the temple when the head died, this did not occur at Honganji itself.[5] The position of Patriarch, leader of Honganji, was passed on hereditarily through Shinran's biological descendants, or at least those believed to be his biological descendants. The Patriarch's lineage formed the basis for the way the Honganji sect differentiated itself from the numerous other groups that claimed Shinran as their founder.[6] Shinran's other followers valued a teaching lineage—direct, face-to-face transmission of the teachings—over the biological or blood lineage.

Like some other religious figures of his time,[7] Shinran denied that he was a teacher with disciples, instead claiming that he had no followers, only companions on the same path in search of enlightenment. His denial did not stop his companions from styling themselves disciples and claiming him as their teacher, and later as the founder of their schools of Buddhism. Shinran's greatest success was in the Kantō region of eastern Honshu, where he attracted a large following of the local elite: lower-ranking warriors and village leaders.[8] By the middle of the thirteenth century, most of his followers were concentrated in the Kantō. Sectarian identities formed later, but these early congregations, founded by Shinran's students, provided one basis for later sectarian institutional development.

After Shinran's death in 1262, his daughter Kakushin (1224–83) honored his memory by building the Ōtani memorial chapel near the Shōren'in temple in Kyoto where her father had first taken religious orders. She took care of the site until her death 21 years later. In her will, she left the memorial chapel to Shinran's followers in the Kantō, with the understanding that the property's caretakers would always be chosen from her (and therefore Shinran's) descendants. After all, who should tend his grave if not his own descendants?

The arrangement amounted to multiple ownership and, therefore, proved troublesome. Since the grave and chapel belonged collectively to Shinran's congregations in the Kantō, and the right to oversee the property belonged to Kakushin's descendants, the relationship between the congregations and the caretaker was ambiguous. Who had the right to designate the caretaker's heir? If one thinks of the post as a hereditary privilege, it could be decided by the caretaker and his family. The Kantō congregations saw it differently, as a position they had authority to assign, especially when two different men claimed the post.

Kakushin's son Kakue (1239–1307) became caretaker with no difficulty, and in 1302, late in his life, he chose his son Kakunyo (1270–1351) as heir. Another of Kakushin's children, however, Kakue's half-brother Yuizen (1266–unknown), contested the succession. Yuizen took over the chapel by force in 1306, the year before Kakue died, and requested that the site's owners in the Kantō confirm his position. Instead, they removed him from the chapel. They also, however, refused to confirm Kakunyo and put the memorial chapel in the care of a man named Shimotsuma Shōzen, one of the family's retainers.[9]

Kakunyo, however, insisted on the validity of his claim and traveled throughout the Kantō, visiting priests and congregations, and building support for his appointment. He finally succeeded in 1310, when the congregations agreed that Kakunyo should be appointed caretaker. Before taking up his position, however, they insisted that he sign a pledge not to treat the gravesite as his own personal property. The agreement thus addressed the tension arising from the ambiguous ownership by reaffirming the primacy of the Kantō congregations' rights.[10]

By appointing a Shimotsuma as caretaker in the interim, the Kantō congregations perhaps narrowly avoided violating Kakushin's stipulation because the grave was still tended by a member of the household. It is possible that they did not want to alienate Shinran's descendants' household from the post altogether. Honganji's own insistence on its leader's biological descent from Shinran dated from a later time, so social identity with the household may have been paramount at the beginning of the fourteenth century. At any rate, it seems clear that they wanted Kakunyo to understand that the caretaker appointment was still in their hands.

Although Kakunyo complied, evidently he was not satisfied with the arrangement. From the first, the Ōtani chapel had attracted pilgrims visiting Shinran's grave. As more and more people made the trip to Ōtani, Kakunyo evidently began to think that such an important pilgrimage site deserved a temple, not just a memorial chapel, and he set about founding one: Honganji.

Not surprisingly, historians have speculated about his motives for raising the chapel's status. *Ikkō ikki* scholar Inoue Toshio believed that nothing less would satisfy Kakunyo's "aristocratic mentality" or his sense that Shinran's descendants should have the greater say in decisions regarding the grave.[11] He may have acted because he desired a wider range of religious activity than that available to the caretaker, as the official Honganji history tells it,[12] or simply out of personal ambition. Presumably the lion's share of the income from pilgrims went to the Kantō congregations, and Kakunyo may have wanted to control it himself. Probably his concerns encompassed all of these factors, and in spite of the pledge exacted from him by the Kantō congregations, Kakunyo's efforts succeeded quickly. A priest named Hōchi from the Kantō granted the chapel temple status in 1312, only two years after Kakunyo had been installed as caretaker. The first decisive steps toward the emergence of a distinct sect, then, were taken by Shinran's own family, that is, his daughter Kakushin and great-grandson Kakunyo.

Hōchi conferred the name Senjuji, or "Temple of the Exclusive Practice," referring to the *nenbutsu,* on the new temple. The powerful Tendai monastery on Mt. Hiei, Enryakuji, however, objected to this name, claiming that it referred to heretical teachings, that is, the idea that Amida provided the *only* path to enlightenment. By the fall of 1312, Kakunyo relinquished the Senjuji name before settling on Honganji (lit., "Temple of the Original Vow") sometime before 1321.[13]

The growth from gravesite chapel to great power was gradual. Before the 1400s, several teaching lineages that went back to Shinran's own disciples existed, and their practices diverged in a number of ways. Eventually, these would take on sectarian identities, but throughout the fourteenth century they existed as loosely defined teaching lines, and priests often shifted from one teaching line to another as they learned from different masters. Most teaching lines lacked an authoritative leader, though all traced their doctrines to Shinran. Starting in the fifteenth century, these lines began to differentiate themselves from each other, each developing its own doctrine and ritual practices. Ultimately, specific temples emerged as main temples or leaders for their sects.[14]

As has been noted, Honganji Patriarchs ultimately built their legitimacy on their claim as Shinran's direct descendants, but they first chose to create a theological link to Shinran and his teachings. They had more trouble than other True Pure Land temples in establishing a face-to-face transmission lineage because the Honganji Patriarchal line descended from Shinran's daughter, and evidently that disqualified her as a conduit for the teachings.

Kakunyo dealt with this challenge by tracing his link to Shinran's direct teachings through his father's cousin, Nyoshin (1235–1300), also a descendant of Shinran who had lived with and been taught by him.[15] Kakunyo studied personally with Nyoshin, and the connection was made. For this reason, the sect designates Nyoshin as the second head of Honganji, though he was never responsible for the chapel and died before the temple was founded. The character for "nyo" in his religious name has been and still is used by all the Patriarchs who followed.

Honganji's leaders came to rely on a more charismatic concept of legitimacy, claiming that only the Patriarchs could interpret Shinran's teachings accurately because, among the True Pure Land sects, they alone shared his blood. By the mid-fifteenth century, the eighth Honganji Patriarch, Rennyo (1415–99), insisted that other True Pure Land schools, which boasted intellectual lineages back to Shinran's earliest disciples, had already distorted his teachings. Shinran had explicitly denied having or even wanting disciples or followers, and, therefore, no one had the right to identify himself as one.[16] Shinran's descendants, Rennyo argued, were uniquely fitted to transmit his teachings without distortion or heresy simply because they were *descendants* and not disciples. Thus, although Honganji followers continued to revere Nyoshin as the second Patriarch, thereby preserving a legitimacy derived from the unbroken line of direct transmission, by the mid-fifteenth century, claims based on Shinran's supposed unbroken blood line had become paramount.[17]

After Kakunyo founded the temple, it fell to other Patriarchs to enhance Honganji's standing and increase its direct following. The patriarchal nature of Honganji's leadership afforded the sect one tool that was unavailable to other Buddhist schools: marriage politics. The Patriarchs and priests could not fail to use it.

In pre-modern Japan, the family was a political unit, and kinship, whether biological, marital, or through adoption, was also a political tie. When a woman and man married, the union involved much more than the two principals, unless they were of such lowly status that there were few economic, political, or social assets involved. Most often, marriages consummated strategic or economic alliances meant to benefit both families in some way. For wealthier families, the option of polygamy increased the number of potentially advantageous marriage ties.[18] Because of the political nature of family and kinship, a Patriarch's or priest's marriage necessarily involved practical considerations, not only on their part but also on the part of their future in-laws.

Among samurai, the alliance could secure the promise of military cooperation. Marriages sometimes connected a military or religious family with an imperial courtier's, which conferred some status and provided an entrée, however narrow, to the court. The usefulness of the connection hinged on the aristocrat's proximity to the emperor and on which courtier faction he supported. For the courtier, the kinship tie to the samurai could bring financial assistance—and possibly physical protection.

There were other ways, in addition to marriage, of establishing kinship between two families; one was adoption, which could be combined with a marriage alliance to good effect. A family with only daughters could adopt a male heir, who would usually marry one of the daughters. Sometimes a childless family adopted a daughter and then an heir to marry her, or they adopted a male heir and then arranged a marriage between him and the daughter of a third family. In the latter two instances, the original family became connected with both of the other families, not just one. Honganji's Patriarchal family made good use of adoptive relationships, though it could not adopt a Patriarchal heir because of the issue of legitimacy based on the blood lineage. The main family's collateral branches, however, did sometimes make use of the double adoption and marriage tactic.

Another form of adoption involved a looser relationship than one in which the adoptee became a full member of a family. A person of higher status might sponsor a youth's coming-of-age ceremony, making and paying for the arrangements for the rite, and in genealogies, the youth was listed as adopted by the sponsor. In this case, the adoption was a bit like acquiring a godparent. The adopter possessed greater status than the adoptee, and through his sponsorship conferred some of his prestige on the young man, who in turn owed loyalty of some kind to his patron. In warrior families, a samurai often took part of his superior's given name to form his new adult name, signaling his affiliation with the superior.

The Patriarch's heir was chosen in much the same way other families, warrior and courtier, chose their heirs. Normal practice, but not law, made the first-born son heir, but the decision was not the family head's alone. In warrior families, the decision took into account the wishes of the highest level of retainers, the equivalent of which, in Honganji's case, would have been the Patriarch's closest relatives. In all cases, the head's current or principal wife had a strong hand in selecting the heir, and often used her leverage to benefit one of her own sons, first-born or not. When she succeeded, it had to do with her personal power, which might depend on that of her natal family.

In examining connections between families of different status—courtier, samurai, clerical—it is well to remember that *sengoku* society was fluid, especially as it related to actual power. Status derived from such markers as titles and ranks conferred by the imperial court or shogunate, and was not necessarily a mark of power or wealth. Instead, it might reflect his strength, especially when a samurai accumulated territories and armies, and so petitioned the court for higher rank. The same samurai, however, might lose his power despite his court ranking or hold power without requesting rank.

Among courtiers, higher status generally had nothing to do with wealth and often failed to reflect influence either. Even aristocrats of the highest rank, for instance the head of a *sekkanke* family, the exclusive providers of men eligible to assume the exalted post of imperial regent, might be out of the court's favor and therefore unimportant. By the same token, a courtier could become more powerful, or less so, in the event of changes in dominance among imperial factions, where influence could depend on individual relationships between aristocrats and, say, the emperor or his possible heirs. Marriage with a courtier family might still add prestige to a religious family, even though it did not necessarily give the latter any practical power. Indeed, precisely what kind of power or influence the court held is a matter of debate within the scholarly community,[19] and so the benefits conferred by relationships with courtiers are not often clear, though people evidently perceived benefits. Family relationships, then, helped the pre-modern family protect and advance its interests, however unreliably.

One can see from its genealogical record how the Patriarch's family arranged marriages and adoptions to enable them to marry into families of high court rank, and eventually into a daimyo family—technically of lower social rank than the courtiers, but usually with greater political and economic strength. Family and marriage connections also helped the Honganji sect spread in its earlier days.[20]

In the late fourteenth century, the fifth Patriarch, Shakunyo (1350–93), and his three sons brought the sect's teachings to the Hokuriku area, especially the provinces of Echizen, Kaga, and Etchū. Two of the sons settled there and formed ties with local priests and institutions while leading the temples they or their father had founded. Honganji adherents from the Hokuriku would become Honganji's strongest and most committed followers.

The middle son presided over an especially active temple called Chōshōji in Echizen. He later founded a collateral temple in Kaga, Honrenji, taking up permanent residence in the latter, reportedly because of marital problems.[21] By the sixteenth century, Chōshōji and its branches had gained significant power in both Echizen and Kaga, in large part because of their founders' relationship to the Patriarch. Chōshōji's priests and followers would play a leading role in a number of *ikkō ikki* conflicts.

Shakunyo's sons and their descendants followed careers that helped anchor the sect in the Hokuriku, though they did not all pursue careers as Honganji sect priests. At least one of Shakunyo's grandsons became a samurai, a vassal of the *shugo* of Echizen, Shiba Yoshikado, and died in battle in 1475. Others joined different temples or sects, such as the popular Amidist sect Jishū or Heisenji, a Tendai sect temple closely affiliated with the Hakusan shrine, a major pilgrimage center in Kaga and therefore another local center of power.[22] These choices contributed to integrating the Honganji temples into the region.

Evidently, even in the fifteenth century, sectarian identity was still relatively unimportant to Honganji, which allowed family members to join different religious groups. The tendency toward an exclusive relationship with the sect had begun, however; in all, more than half of Shakunyo's grandchildren and great-grandchildren married or pursued careers within the Honganji sect. Their numbers represent a significant increase over the rate at which previous generations worked within the sect. By the sixteenth century, close relatives of the Patriarchs and their siblings devoted themselves solely to the sect, an indication both of the sect's spread—more followers meant more temples and more priests—and of its growing institutionalization.[23]

The followers that Honganji priests and Patriarchs attracted to the sect came primarily from families of lower status. An increase in trade and commercialization brought ordinary people into contact with religious organizations that offered them more support than the older Buddhist schools, which had joined the court and shogunate as centers of power. Amidism opened a way into Buddhism for less privileged members of society, especially because they needed less time or money to perform the rituals that Amidist sects required. The most important ritual consisted of chanting the *nenbutsu*, which could be done anywhere at any time.

Additionally, Pure Land and True Pure Land sects offered salvation to those whose daily lives prevented them from observing standard Buddhist prohibitions, like the one against taking life. This had posed a problem not only for warriors, but also for farmers, fishermen, and woodcutters, who killed animals and insects, sometimes inadvertently. Shinran's teachings even allowed for a normal sexual life. Although *mappō* supposedly made it impossible for human beings to achieve enlightenment, Hōnen's and Shinran's teachings paradoxically opened the door for ever greater numbers of people to hope for salvation.

In spite of the common impression that Shinran's and Honganji's followers were mostly peasants, their earlier adherents were mostly lower-level warriors, artisans, and merchants. It is now thought that most of Shinran's followers in the Kantō were not simple farmers but warriors, albeit non-elite ones (e.g., not *shugo* or *shugo-dai*).[24] Outside the Kantō, core members of True Pure Land Buddhism were merchants, artisans, and workers, especially those in the timber, woodworking, mining, metal casting, and shipping industries, scholars believe.[25]

Evidence supporting these conclusions is extensive, though circumstantial. Many of the oldest congregations were located in areas associated with mining, timber, and other trades not tied to agriculture.[26] Early Honganji sect temples were often found along rivers, especially in delta regions, suggesting involvement with the transport trade and traveling merchants.[27] Miners, woodcutters, metal casters, and others also needed access to shipping routes, or their trades would be useless. Further, True Pure Land temples often enshrined images of Prince Shōtoku, a figure especially venerated by artisans, which might be the case in congregations that included many such workers.

Some direct evidence supports the circumstantial indications. According to a work written in 1540,[28] Honpukuji, an old Honganji sect temple in southern Ōmi Province, was created by businessmen. A former shrine priest turned dyer first built a *dōjō* devoted to True Pure Land worship.[29] His son turned the *dōjō* into a Zen chapel, only to have his own son, Jirōsaburō, return it to a place to worship True Pure Land Buddhism. In 1413, along with a metal-grinder and a malt dealer, Jirōsaburō made a pilgrimage to Kyoto and visited both Honganji and Bukkōji. Three years later, on another pilgrimage with the malt-dealer, he met the sixth Honganji Patriarch, Gyōnyo, beginning a long and fruitful association with him and his successors.[30]

This background indicates that, at least in southern Ōmi, the Honganji sect found an early audience among men in non-farming professions. Not only was the founder of the *dōjō* a dyer, but the two men who went on pilgrimage to Bukkōji and Honganji were also an artisan and a merchant. Honpukuji and its precursor *dōjō* were located in a fishing village on the eastern shore of Lake Biwa, and the other Honganji congregations that began in that region in the early fifteenth century were also in fishing or commercial towns, not in areas associated with farming.

The importance of non-cultivators in Honpukuji's congregation appears in other stories as well. According to the same history cited above, in 1469 a sacred image stored temporarily at Honpukuji had to be transferred to a safer location. Members loaded it onto the Honpukuji priest's boat and smuggled it out of town, bypassing seven tax barriers on the way. Avoiding the barriers required boating skill and knowledge of the lake, as well as practice in evading the authorities. The boat obviously was in the hands of professionals, possibly men with experience in smuggling as well as in shipping or fishing.[31]

Furthermore, Honpukuji's list of hosts for monthly meetings included oil sellers, coopers, and a palanquin maker.[32] It is no surprise that residents of a fishing village and port pursued occupations related to those industries (e.g., selling oil and making barrels), but the evidence lends more force to the supposition that Honganji members in similar villages were drawn from the same population.

The overall status composition of Honganji's membership began to change in the late fifteenth century as its teachings spread into the countryside and attracted a following among lower-level warriors and village leaders. Most of the warriors held lands and enjoyed a limited power of their own, factors that would also shape the history of Honganji and its changing place in the world. Nevertheless, the towns continued to be of great importance to the sect, including a new kind of town, the *jinaichō* (lit., town within a temple).

Jinaichō were commercial towns sponsored by Honganji temples and located along shipping and transportation routes. Their locations made them attractive to merchants and artisans, and the towns quickly became economic centers for nearby communities as well. *Jinaichō* temple towns followed a grid pattern, differentiating them from another kind of temple town, the *monzenmachi* (lit., town in front of a [temple] gate). *Monzenmachi* lined the streets leading to a temple or the paths along which religious festival processions moved. They evolved from the demands of pilgrims and festival spectators; by contrast, the *jinaichō* were constructed specifically to attract merchants.

Outside authorities usually treated the *jinaichō* like the temples themselves, awarding them exemptions from taxes and rents as well as the right to bar entry to warrior officials. That meant that residents of the town paid dues and owed services to the temple, instead of to warriors. Construction related to festivals and religious services might be supplied by carpenters, for example, and all the townspeople might contribute funds and labor for construction and repairs at the temple itself.[33]

Physically, moats and earthen embankments surrounded *jinaichō*, serving both as fortifications for self-defense and as town borders. In some cases, the fortifications were extensive and formidable, though in others the latter function dominated, serving more to mark the town's borders rather than to protect the residents from outside attack. Finally, the temple served as the town's administrative and ritual center. Still, one ought not to assume that all *jinaichō* residents consequently were or had to be Honganji sect members. Evidently non-adherents also lived and worked in the towns, though sect members outnumbered them.[34]

The privilege to bar entry to warrior officials, called *shugo funyū*, might, but did not necessarily, include the power to withdraw parcels of land from warrior jurisdiction of any kind. The province's military governor granted this privilege, or some degree of it, to institutions such as temples. The privileges could be as broad as permitting no warrior to enter the land specified, or as narrow as providing exemption only from certain kinds of taxes. Because of these exemptions, the physical demarcation of the town's borders mattered a good deal; those towns with extensive *funyū* rights could serve as sanctuaries for anyone fleeing warriors. They might even protect non-combatants during wartime.

For *jinaichō*, the *shugo funyū* rights reinforced other tax exemptions, since no official could even enter the town to collect the funds. In most cases, the temple also investigated and punished criminal activity within the town. Furthermore, the right to bar warriors still applied in the event of war. The towns, then, became safe havens for non-combatants. If a samurai expected war to draw near, he might entrust his relatives to a temple town for safety.[35]

Temples took their *shugo funyū* rights very seriously. On one occasion, a daimyo's vassal went to Osaka, Honganji's location, to present a gift to the Patriarch. Rather than allow an exception and permit the vassal to enter the town, the temple instead sent a delegation to meet the warrior at the edge of town and collect his gift there.[36]

Initially, most temple towns received their exemptions from warrior authorities, but once the custom was established, other towns apparently claimed them unilaterally. Predictably, the latter method often led to trouble. In the Hokuriku, a Honganji priest complained that his colleagues encouraged the creation of new temples and temple towns, thereby creating friction with the civil authorities because the residents refused to submit levies to warriors. The friction reached the point, according to this priest, that some temple towns were destroyed.[37] In other words, some towns had claimed the privilege without authorization. Naturally, the samurai who would have collected the levies did not recognize the privilege, since they had not granted it in the first place. Although there was a logic to the temples' practice of collecting taxes and keeping them, they still disregarded warrior authority when doing so, behavior that could only invite disaster.

By the end of the sixteenth century, dues sent to Honganji temple from the temple towns amounted to the lion's share of Honganji's income. The towns' significance in the history of *ikkō ikki* goes even further, however. Several *ikkō ikki* conflicts arose directly over issues of taxation and criminal jurisdiction in Honganji sect temples and *jinaichō*. As daimyo began to assert more control over their territory, they often summarily repudiated the towns' exemptions. Such an action was behind the Mikawa *ikkō ikki,* a rebellion against Tokugawa Ieyasu (1542–1616) in 1563. Furthermore, most of the temple towns in the capital region provided crucial military—in addition to financial—support to Honganji during its contest with Nobunaga, which itself was sparked by Nobunaga's demands infringing on Osaka's rights. Although the prevailing image of *ikkō ikki* puts rural villagers at center stage, the merchants and artisans of the Honganji sect's temple towns belong there as well.

As the Honganji sect grew, slowly at first, then more rapidily, so did the need for organization. The sect's structure took the form of a pyramid (see Fig. 1). At the top was Honganji temple, under the Patriarch. At the second level came temples that had received their names and ritual objects from the Patriarch, and who also sent donations back to Honganji. Those temples in turn gave names and ritual objects to temples associated

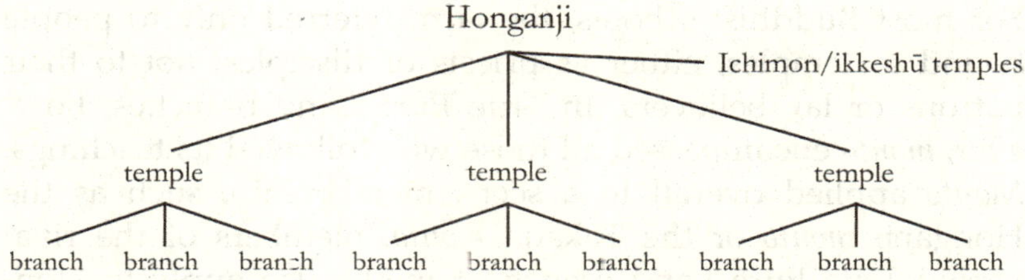

Fig. 1 Structure of the Honganji sect

with them, which sent donations back. Some temples also had branch *dōjō*, chapels overseen by "long-haired" priests, that is, men who led a group of people in Amida worship but who had not taken the tonsure.[38] A *dōjō* could be anything from a room in one man's house to a small building he may have built in his compound, and it received only ritual objects from its associated temple, not a special temple name. Each of the temples and their branches, including the chapels, had congregations: groups of sect members who worshipped there and made donations.

The size of a congregation varied. A branch temple or chapel might have only two or three worshippers in their congregation, while others might accommodate more than one hundred. None kept records of the congregation members, by name, number, or otherwise, though temples did keep track of their branches. More branches made a temple more important because its influence extended farther and, no doubt, also because it garnered greater revenues. One temple in the province of Mikawa counted more than one hundred branches by 1484, not only in Mikawa but also in neighboring Owari and, further still, in Ise.[39] Many of its branches were simple *dōjō*, and the total number of people associated with the temple could have been as small as one thousand or as large as ten thousand. Nonetheless, indisputably the temple had a region-wide following, not one confined to its own province.

Honganji members overall were referred to as *monto*, from *mon* for gate, by extension a temple, and *to* for group or people, therefore members or adherents of a religious group. For most Buddhist schools, the term referred only to people bound to temples, either as priests or disciples, not to their patrons or lay believers. In True Pure Land branches, however, *monto* encompassed all those who followed its teachings. *Monto* applied overall to a sect's membership, such as the Honganji *monto* or the Takada *monto,* members of the rival Senjuji True Pure Land branch. It might also apply to Honganji adherents from a specific area, such as the Ōmi *monto,* the believers who lived in that province.

Readers who are familiar with Honganji history often associate a congregation with groups known as *kō*. The word *kō* refers to a religious meeting in which doctrine is expounded. In Honganji tradition, the word *kō* was used in the phrase *hōonkō,* (lit., meetings to express gratitude [to Shinran]). These meetings commemorated Shinran's life and teachings. Beginning in the late sixteenth or seventeenth century, the word applied to tightly knit groups of Honganji members who met at least once a month to worship, and probably to gossip and exchange news.[40] They also served as systems for social and even financial support for the adherents, and a form of *kō* still operates today.

Some groups of people called *kō* also existed in the fifteenth century, as did small monthly meetings of local believers. Some historians equate the two and view them as the forerunners of the modern-day *kō*. If so, this would have made the *kō* the smallest administrative unit of the Honganji institution, the unit by which individual members were organized and that formed the "financial and military basis of the *ikkō ikki.*"[41] At least one scholar has argued that the eighth Patriarch, Rennyo, used the *kō* to organize Honganji followers under his direct control, bypassing local priests and thus setting the stage for *ikkō ikki.*[42]

More recent research has revealed that the *kō* and the small monthly meetings were disparate groups. I would argue then that *kō* could not have been the fundamental unit of the sect, nor the basis for *ikkō* leagues. No Patriarch could have used them to bypass priests and effectively create two pyramids, one that gave him authority over priests and the other authority over followers. Monthly meetings did not fill those roles either. Without a small *kō* unit, then, the Honganji institutional structure that pulled together the members must have been the temple or *dōjō*.

Fifteenth-century *kō* encompassed people drawn from geographical areas as large as several villages or even a whole county (*gun*). The word rarely referred to any group that could have been as small as the congregation of one temple or *dōjō*. Some consisted of priests, not lay members. Although some sent gifts to the Patriarch,[43] the *kō* did not serve as the sect's financial base. Donations from the members given through the temples did.

Some smaller *kō* did exist by the middle of the sixteenth century, especially in urban areas where they also played an economic role. *Kō* in Osaka supplied goods and services to the main temple, which was located there at the time, and were about the same size as later *kō*. Nevertheless, goods and services from outside Osaka were sent by groups with different names, not by *kō*, with one exception.[44] Honganji did acknowledge dues from some *kō* that were sent specifically for Honganji's *hōonkō* service.[45] It seems, then, that small *kō* were rare, or perhaps connected to temple towns at that time; but they were not ubiquitous Honganji groups nor the temple's main source of income.

Kō were not military groups either, even in the late sixteenth century. When Honganji fought against Oda Nobunaga during the 1570s, the Patriarch mobilized his followers for war, yet he sent very few letters transmitting instructions to *kō*. In the main collection of his letters, *Kennyo shōnin bun'an*, out of the 42 missives in which he exhorted members to fight against Nobunaga, only two were addressed to *kō*: the nineteenth-day *kō* of Hakui *gun* and the twentieth-day *kō* of Kashima *gun*, both of Noto Province. Others were addressed to either larger or smaller groups, for example, all the followers and all the priests of Kii Province, or to the "three districts" (*gō*) of Kii.[46] Furthermore, since the letter identified the two *kō* on the *gun* level, they must have been organized at that level, not in villages.

Small groups of people did meet to worship and socialize, to be sure, but the meetings appear to have been associated with temples or *dōjō*. At Honpukuji, a Honganji sect temple in Ōmi Province, each meeting was led by a different man,[47] some with religious names and some without. Conceivably the meetings were held in each man's home, but even if they were, Honpukuji's priest is the one who kept track of them. The official Honganji sect institution still consisted primarily of temples or *dōjō*, and members organized around them.

Honganji's World: Other Temples

Before the fifteenth century, three things interfered with the spread of Honganji's teaching. One was its dependence on the ability and inclinations of individual Patriarchs to do the traveling and preaching necessary to win followers. A second was the competition it faced from other Amidist teachings and their more concrete practices. Both of these difficulties would be overcome by the activities of a remarkably gifted and energetic Patriarch who preached in the vernacular instead of classical Chinese, and found means to convey his simple explanations to the broadest possible range of people.

The third obstacle was posed by the older temples, such as Enryakuji in Kyoto and Kōfukuji in Nara, which viewed all the Amidist sects with suspicion. Although Hōnen, the founder of Pure Land Buddhism, and his disciple Shinran both began their religious careers at the Tendai monastery of Enryakuji, they ultimately found that temple inhospitable, even hostile, to their teachings.

Enryakuji characterized Hōnen and his followers as practitioners of the exclusive *nenbutsu*, "exclusive" being a derogatory term referring to relying not on a variety of religious practices but solely on Amida worship for salvation. The dismissal of all other non-Amidist practices implied that they were pointless, and even worse, it contradicted orthodox Buddhist teachings, which held that there were many paths to enlightenment. Thus, to the older schools the exclusive *nenbutsu* was more than misguided: it was heresy. At least, they had the basis for heresy charges, should they ever wish to bring them, which seemed to be whenever their own economic or political power was threatened by the new groups.

The first direct opposition to the Pure Land teaching came from Tendai monks at Enryakuji, who were initially satisfied after Hōnen instituted rules to minimize friction between his followers and others. Kōfukuji added its voice to the criticism of Hōnen's teachings, and in 1207, some of his followers were executed by the imperial court. He and many of his followers, including Shinran, were exiled from the capital.

Historians disagree on the meaning of this suppression and its harshness. Some see the severity of punishment as a sign of how much the old schools felt threatened by the new teachings. Others point out that the men who were executed had spent the evening in quarters occupied by the retired emperor's ladies, which may have posed a threat to the perceived chastity of the retired emperor's consorts, but not necessarily to the teachings.[48] If heresy were the main concern, one might expect Hōnen to have been executed, since he was the man primarily responsible for teaching the exclusive *nenbutsu*. Yet Hōnen's life was spared. In any event, the prosecution, so to speak, argued successfully that the *nenbutsu* teachings led to reprehensible behavior. Thus began a long but intermittent history of the suppression of Amidist sects, including Honganji.

The rejection of the older sects' rituals and the spread of the *nenbutsu* did threaten temples such as Enryakuji and Kōfukuji. The more the Amidist schools attracted patrons and practitioners, the less the older temples received support, economic and otherwise, as they lost supporters to the simpler practices. As more people adopted the *nenbutsu*, the older schools lost both members and patrons, making it harder for them to maintain their income, let alone thrive.

The imperial court also had an interest in helping the established schools. Ever since the court first adopted the religion centuries earlier, the worship of Buddhism and support of its temples were seen as vital to the protection of the state. Therefore, when the established schools pointed out that by undermining the temples, heresies would also undermine the state, the court obligingly backed the suppression of the new sects.

Nevertheless, the periods of widespread suppression, and the punishments levied, were limited. Compared to either religious persecution in Europe at the same time, or the persecution of Christians in Japan under the Tokugawa, the assault on Amidism was mild. Partly this was because Hōnen and Shinran addressed some of the fears of the authorities by issuing rules of conduct intended to minimize socially disruptive behavior. They prohibited followers from criticizing other schools of Buddhism, for example, a rule that would reduce friction with their rivals and also affirmed the validity of other Buddhist approaches to enlightenment. In other words, Honganji responded directly to the charge of promoting the exclusive *nenbutsu*. In spite of Hōnen's and Shinran's efforts, however, the old temples continued to fight Amidist teachings with charges of heresy, even though Honganji's priests refuted the charges repeatedly.

Aside from the attempted suppression by the older Buddhist schools, Honganji faced the pressure of competition from other True Pure Land groups. At first the Honganji sect attracted fewer adherents than other Amidist sects, probably because its doctrine was difficult to understand. Honganji's teachings relied solely on the abstract concepts of faith and *tariki*, when other sects offered the same salvation through more tangible means. For example, the Bukkōji sect, which enjoyed the greatest early success, enrolled followers' names or likenesses in salvation registers. These functioned as a "karmic link to the Pure Land of the one Buddha. . . . Hence, to have one's name entered into the register is to assume a karmic link to the Pure Land," leading to rebirth there after death in this world, according to one fourteenth-century salvation register.[49] Nearly two centuries later, a Honganji sect priest bemoaned the effectiveness of these practices, writing that Bukkōji, "using the registers and picture lineages, assembled multitudes of people, and drew everyone's attention."[50]

The picture lineages and salvation registers seem to have been an especially potent attraction. In both, people saw their names or likenesses physically linked with famous priests, which must have been comforting. The Amidist Jishū priests distributed amulets, which also gave people something concrete to hold, in this case literally, in addition to listing them in its death register. Many people apparently found these practices easy to understand and were able to feel confident they would be reborn in the Pure Land because, after all, the karmic link was there for all to see.

If one followed Honganji, though, one needed not only faith, but also the complete absence of any reliance even on one's own will to believe; real faith required an acceptance of total helplessness. The Honganji faith guaranteed salvation to those with true faith, but it lacked ways to prove a given individual had achieved the right kind of faith. Accepting the sect's teaching was relatively easy, but how could people be certain that their faith was untainted by any sense that they themselves produced it?[51] As we know, many people from all kinds of True Pure Land sects went to Honganji to honor Shinran. Few embraced Honganji's teachings until much later.

In spite of Bukkōji's popularity, people still lacked the sense of belonging to a religious community, a congregation of believers. Before the middle of the fifteenth century, few Amidist sects were strongly defined, and Amidist beliefs in general had spread widely. The history of one temple in Etchū, Zuisenji, illustrates how fluid temples' religious affiliations might be. According to tradition, Zuisenji was founded by Shakunyo in 1390 with the support of a local man of property, Keizen. After Keizen's death, it is said, his daughter looked after the temple, though one account claims that members of the Shimotsuma family, Honganji's servants and officials, oversaw it.[52] The Honganji priest Nyojō (1412–60), brother of the seventh Patriarch, later took it over briefly before moving on to found a new temple, Honsenji, in the neighboring province of Kaga. His adopted sons then officiated at Zuisenji for a while, and finally, sometime after Nyojō's death in 1460, his wife arranged for her nephew to become Zuisenji's main priest.[53] Thus, according to the traditional narrative, Zuisenji was affiliated with Honganji, and Honganji alone, continuously since its founding.

Zuisenji's early history and affiliation look more complicated when one abandons that particular narrative and turns to other forms of the historical record. Shakunyo may not have founded the temple.[54] Even if Shakunyo did found Zuisenji, apparently no one from Honganji exercised authority over it for the next 70 years, until Nyojō's nephew-in-law was installed as head priest there. In the interim, Keizen's daughter did look after it for a time, but she was a nun of the Jishū. As for Nyojō's tenure as priest at Zuisenji, some scholars believe that Nyojō left and founded Honsenji simply because he was not, in fact, welcomed and installed as head priest at the former temple.[55]

The fluidity of these early affiliations, as demonstrated most vividly by the tenure of Keizen's daughter, the Jishū nun, strongly suggests that Zuisenji was a pan-Amidist temple much like Zenkōji in Shinano Province, which was also devoted to Amida worship but avoided exclusive sectarian affiliations.[56] Furthermore, the Honganji sect was only differentiated from other sects after the middle of the fifteenth century, when Zuisenji became absorbed into the newly defined Honganji organization.

Until the middle of the fifteenth century, then, Honganji enjoyed only limited success. The spread of Amidism in Japan, however, contributed to the base on which the Honganji sect later built with great success.

Honganji's Secular World

True Pure Land Buddhism was one of the so-called new Kamakura Buddhist sects, identified as such because the founders lived during the period that the Kamakura shogunate dominated Japan's government. For most of Honganji's history up to 1600, however, the Muromachi shogunate (1338–1573) governed Japan through its *shugo*, provincial military governors. The shogunate presided over a country at war, as its founding in 1338 began a civil war that the third shogun settled in 1392. The next 50 years were relatively peaceful, but in 1441, one of the *shugo* assassinated the sixth shogun, Ashikaga Yoshinori, and started the unraveling of the Muromachi government.

No shogun after Yoshinori wielded real power.[57] By 1460, a number of *shugo* houses were in disarray, embroiled in succession disputes that arose partly from the shogun's weakness. Technically, only the shogun had the power to make a *shugo* appointment, and earlier shoguns had been able to decide between rival claimants and make their choices stick. By 1460, this was no longer the case. The seventh shogun took office at the age of eight and died two years later. His successor, his younger brother, also became shogun when he was eight, so the real power fell on the deputy shogun, a post that rotated between men from five different families. Because the post carried more power than ever before, factional tensions among and within these families intensified, and some joined the *shugo* houses rent by succession disputes.

The eighth shogun designated his younger brother as heir until 1465, when his own son was born. The appearance of a new heir set the stage for a succession dispute that provided an excuse for the shogun's most powerful supporters, the Yamana and Hosokawa families, to fight over control of the government. In 1467, the first year of Ōnin, war broke out in Kyoto. Over the next ten years, the war destroyed more than two-thirds of the city of Kyoto and spread into the countryside. The shogunate continued to exercise some control over the region surrounding the capital for several more decades, although the shogun himself lost even more power. In 1493, the deputy shogun Hosokawa Masamoto (1466–1507) forced the sitting shogun, Ashikaga Yoshitane (1466–1523), to abdicate and installed his own candidate. Masamoto's act was unprecedented, but most subsequent shogunal successions followed the pattern he established.

As the shogunate lost the power to influence events in most of Japan, the *sengoku* daimyo emerged, a new kind of leader who typically redrew the entire structure of government and landholding in the territory he was able to control. In the earlier years of the Muromachi shogunate, provincial power came from above, with a *shugo* appointment from the shogun. In *sengoku*, however, power came from the bottom up, and military prowess alone guaranteed a daimyo's position. The daimyo faced threats from neighbors with territorial ambitions, and often from his own retainers or family members eager to take his place. Warfare, though not constant, was endemic and liable to break out at any time. This was the context in which the Honganji sect grew, and the members formed *ikkō ikki* to pursue political aims.

The disorder of the times contributed to making the *ikkō* leagues the strongest of their kind, and provided many of the battles in which they engaged, making *ikkō ikki* very much a phenomenon of *sengoku*. Nevertheless, *ikkō ikki* fit within a long tradition of other *ikki*, and the *ikkō* leagues' success depended on this history as well. For most people familiar with Japanese history, the term *ikki* evokes the peasant protests of the Tokugawa period (1600–1868), but the Muromachi-period *ikki* were more diverse both in membership and activities.

Ikki were groups of people bound together by ritual for a specific purpose. Although some *ikki* had long-term aims, in most cases, once the purpose had been achieved, the *ikki* dissolved. The process began when a group assembled to discuss possible responses to problems or concerns outside the patterns of everyday life, such as a major crop failure or a looming battle. The discussion concluded when the majority of attendees agreed on a course of action. The group then created a document, a kind of contract in which the attendees vowed to follow the joint decision. The document usually invited the punishment of the gods and Buddhas to fall on anyone who failed to pursue the action. All the attendees signed it, then burned the document and mixed its ashes with water, which all of them drank in turn. The group was bound by the vow, the shared experience of the ritual, and the shared ingestion of the document, which made the same document physically a part of their bodies. The assembly was typically held at a shrine or temple, so that the gods or Buddhas could witness the deliberations and the vows. As part of the ceremony, some kind of metal, like a bell or even a sword, was struck, probably to alert the god, and the *ikki* formation was complete.

It is worth remembering that at the time people saw the world as filled with spirits of all kinds, with potentially benign or malign intent. A god's or Buddha's punishment could involve war or natural disasters, sudden accidental death, or a fatal illness that ravaged an entire family or village. They could cause a field to flood, a crop to fail, food to rot, children to die. Gods were everywhere, and although they weren't all-powerful, they could easily make one's life or death miserable. The *ikki* vow, then, was potent and meaningful.

An *ikki* could be created out of a group that met regularly for mundane purposes, like the council of a village, and formed to deal with out-of-the-ordinary situations. All *ikki* members shared a common status, but the reader must keep in mind that status in Muromachi Japan was complicated and contextual; one person could hold different statuses, depending on the circumstances. The members of Enryakuji's population came from different backgrounds and lived with hierarchical distinctions in their community, from the abbot of the monastery to the warrior monks who followed his orders. Yet all were members of the temple community and as such could participate in deliberations on issues that affected the entire temple complex. Within a village, there would be distinctions between elders, cultivators, and small landholders, all of whom shared tax- and rent-payer status. Some warriors also had that status, as did members of other villages. This multiplicity of statuses, then, allowed *ikki* to transcend some status markings while respecting others.[58]

The contextuality of statuses is especially important to bear in mind with regard to *ikkō ikki*. Scholars have suggested that the Honganji sect's egalitarian theology permitted villagers and local warriors to transcend the status barriers between them in order to form *ikki*.[59] More likely, in this case the shared religious identity (status), rather than any specific ideology or doctrine, overrode the political or economic status distinctions that applied in other kinds of relationships, that is, tax collector/taxpayer or authority figure/subordinate. If the complex-wide meetings of Enryakuji overrode the distinctions between priests of aristocratic origin and warrior monks, then Honganji sect membership could override the much narrower gap between villagers and local warriors.

For Muromachi-era *ikki*, the historian Minegishi Sumio offers the helpful distinction between warrior *ikki* and village *ikki*.[60] The two shared the ritual formation and the status solidarity, but often differed in aims. Warrior *ikki* generally played a military role or a political/administrative one. Village *ikki* tended to form over economic concerns.

Warriors formed the groups first identified as *ikki*. The war tale *Taiheiki*, dating from the fourteenth century and the first text to employ the word *ikki* to designate a group of this kind, mentions groups of warriors with names like the "white banner *ikki*" or the "red banner *ikki*." These *ikki* dated from the 1330s, arising in the wars that led to the creation of the Muromachi shogunate. Some of these organizations, at one time thought to be temporary battlefield alliances, have subsequently turned out to have existed over a period of as many as 80 years.[61] They seem to have been regional alliances among warriors who were not vassals of the *shugo* who governed their province, though they organized in order to support him when he went into battle. Historians call these *kokujin ikki*, referring to warriors with local powers and responsibilities.

At first glance, one might think that *ikki*, with their lateral (as opposed to vertical) properties and lack of a leader, undercut the warrior hierarchy. Vassalage, after all, was a personal relationship between master and subordinate, and *ikki* precluded this kind of connection. Yet, the fourteenth-century warrior *ikki* fit within the hierarchy, enabling a *shugo* to call on military support that otherwise might not be available to him. This point bears keeping in mind with regard to *ikkō ikki* as well, since they often formed in order to provide military reinforcements to high-ranking warriors.

Regional *ikki* also addressed themselves to their own needs even when they had formed initially to assist a *shugo*. In Bingo Province in 1336, for instance, 67 signatories to a contract formed a group called the *kakutagai ikki*. Their contract included several articles intended to regulate the internal relations of the *ikki*, in addition to the clauses promising military support to the *shugo* family. They protected the continuity of a warrior's family line when he died in battle or from illness, leaving an underage child as his heir. In such a case, they agreed to support the child and provide for his education, and also to oppose any move to confiscate the late member's lands on the grounds of the heir's young age. Another clause stated that if fighting broke out between two *ikki* members, the rest of the *ikki* was to intervene, stop the fighting, and mediate the dispute. If that proved impossible, they promised to side with the member they determined to be in the right. The contract also forbade gambling, extreme drunkenness, and verbal fighting. Anyone who engaged in these activities, and did not respond to corrective measures, was to be expelled from the *ikki*.[62] These clauses testify to the long-term nature of this *ikki*, a league whose concerns surpassed those of a temporary battlefield alliance. The *ikki* provided a forum for inter-warrior disputes and protection against unreasonable attack, supplying the guarantees that an overlord might give and without handing others an excuse to interfere in a warrior's control over his own area.

A similar warrior *ikki* is called the *ichizoku*, or extended-family, *ikki*,[63] in which cadet branches of a military family pledged their support to the main branch. One might think that kinship itself bound family members to act together, but that was not necessarily the case. Members of an *ichizoku ikki* vowed to consult all family heads before deciding on a course of military action. The *ichizoku ikki* was similar to a *kokujin ikki*, with the difference that kinship provided the organizational framework instead of region and shared warrior status. Not all extended-family members bore the same family name, so another possible advantage for the *ichizoku ikki* was to remind everyone that they did share kinship.[64]

In the fifteenth century, then, warrior *ikki* were alliances defined by region and sometimes by kinship. They either bound the members to one particular *shugo* or to act together once the *ikki* chose sides in a given conflict. In effect, they became local administrative units as well as military units and might become long-term arrangements. *Ikki* allowed warriors to maintain an area's stability without becoming part of a warrior band, at least for a time. These *ikki* were not uncommon.[65]

Village *ikki* comprised three main types, most of which formed to win economic relief from the authorities: the *shō* (estate) *ikki,* the *tokusei* (virtuous government, i.e., debt or special tax cancellation) *ikki,* and the *do* (or *tsuchi,* soil) *ikki*. The *shō ikki,* as its name implies, involved cultivators who worked the same estate and who made their appeals to the estate owner. Usually, *shōen* residents complained of mistreatment by estate officials or asked for rent relief because of crop damage or failure. They generally formed an *ikki* when other, less drastic appeals had failed. The ritual often preceded a mass exodus of cultivators from the village, which was legal only if they had paid their rents and taxes before absconding.[66]

Tokusei ikki marked a new economic stage for villagers with the expansion of a market economy and an increase in monetization. Tax burdens increased partly because aristocrats, temples, and the shogunate augmented their income by erecting tax barriers along the route used to ship goods to markets in the capital. Furthermore, cultivators and local warriors sometimes pawned goods or mortgaged their land, often to obtain seed rice for plantings. If the harvest from the planting failed or produced low yields, the growers could not always repay their debts. As cultivators fell into ever-greater debt, they forfeited land and became tenants only to mortgage other land to survive. Their demands for debt relief included the return of lands they had lost to the moneylenders. The shogunate had sometimes offered debt-cancellation edicts to help its warriors, who also fell into debt, and residents of the rural areas began to organize *ikki* to demand these edicts for themselves.

In a *shō ikki,* the members appealed to the owner of an estate, and the size or range of the estate—estate lands were not usually contiguous and could be scattered throughout a region—often dictated the size of the *ikki. Tokusei ikki* took their appeals to the shogun, whose authority transcended local borders; the area from which *tokusei ikki* drew their participants could encompass as much as several provinces. The number of participants also grew because the debtor population included warriors, cultivators, and others.

Tokusei ikki marched on and in Kyoto, the seat of the shogunate. Often these demonstrations turned into riots, as *ikki* members attacked pawnbrokers and moneylenders, usually warehouse owners and sake brewers. Sometimes they attacked tax barriers along the road. They liberated pawned goods, looted the rest, and burned ledgers that recorded the lending agreements. They set fires at temples—which also lent money—and battled shogunate forces trying to restore order. Over time, the word *ikki* took on the additional meaning of "riot" because of this kind of violence.

The first massive *tokusei ikki* to attack the capital occurred in the eleventh month of 1428, after local uprisings in Ōmi and Yamashiro. This *ikki* drew debtors from throughout central Honshu, from Lake Biwa to the eastern edges of the Inland Sea, including the provinces of Ōmi, Yamashiro, Yamato, Kii, Izumi, and Kawachi. They continued through the fifteenth century, but at the beginning of the sixteenth century *tokusei ikki* began to taper off as the shogunate exercised less and less power.[67]

Many *tokusei ikki* were also called *do ikki* because they consisted of people of "the earth" (*do* or *tsuchi*), that is, people who lived in the countryside. Diarists and others at the time used the term *do ikki* broadly to designate any group of rural commoners who formed a group around one purpose. These commoners may or may not have all signed a formal pledge, but they did share a goal. For example, in 1501 a powerful warrior near Kyoto recruited villagers as reinforcements, promising tax reductions as payment for their services. When they agreed to follow him, an aristocratic diarist described the warrior's forces as including "a *do ikki* from the neighboring villages and others, several thousand people."[68] Here, the diarist applied the phrase *do ikki* to a group of villagers who fought on behalf of a local warrior. *Do ikki*, then, functions almost as a generic term for villagers who shared a goal and engaged in non-everyday behavior in order to obtain it. Sources often also referred to *ikkō ikki* as *do ikki* of the *ikkō* sect, so the phrase alone tells us little about any particular event.

Finally, there was one more important kind of *ikki*: the *kuni* or *sōkoku* (provincial) *ikki*, which brought together warrior and village *ikki* by joining warriors and village heads in a coalition.[69] *Kuni ikki* were similar to *kokujin ikki* as they formed when warriors found it necessary to work together without an overlord. They included village heads because their aim was to rule over whole counties, even provinces, and govern them in place of a *shugo*.

An early relatively stable and famous *kuni ikki* formed in Yamashiro in 1485 to drive out two warring factions whose battles ravaged the province.[70] The Yamashiro *kuni ikki* included warriors between the ages of 15 and 60, as well as villagers from throughout the province. Together they succeeded in expelling the warriors and their armies by the eleventh day of the twelfth month of 1485.[71] For the next eight years, the *ikki* took over the administration of the southern part of the province, partly by returning all estates to the direct management of the owners. The *ikki* also banned new tax barriers. The Yamashiro *kuni ikki* ruled until it was destroyed in 1493 by warriors who wanted control of the province.[72]

The Yamashiro *ikki*'s combination of *kokujin ikki* and *do ikki* dovetailed but did not merge into one working body. The group that ruled Yamashiro, though ostensibly consisting of all adult warriors, in practice had 36 warrior members. They communicated their directions to village councils, who carried out much of the day-to-day governing. Historians usually attribute the Yamashiro *ikki*'s end in 1493 to the unwieldiness of the organization, which made it incapable of mounting a strong defense when they were attacked.[73]

The history of *ikkō ikki* must be seen within the context of these other *ikki* as well as those of religion and politics, as both warrior *ikki* and village *ikki* contributed aspects of their organizations to the *ikkō* leagues. *Ikkō ikki* did not arise simply from the ideology and organization of their religion, although those factors also played a large role in how the *ikki* functioned and which activities the leagues pursued. *Ikkō ikki* shared just enough with each other to give them a label of their own, but some shared more characteristics with previous leagues than they did with each other.

Authority in Japan was diffuse throughout the Muromachi period, shared among the imperial court, the shogunate, its *shugo*, temples, estate owners, layers of warrior authority within the provinces, village councils, and *ikki*. As a new religious entity and a growing power, Honganji Patriarchs fought to establish the sect as one to be reckoned with. Although they pursued a number of ways to accomplish that aim, *ikkō ikki* proved to be both the most useful, and the most dangerous, feature of the sect's growing visibility and power.

TWO

Rennyo and the First Ikkō Ikki, *1457–1475*

The rise of *ikkō ikki* and the work of Rennyo (1415–99), Honganji's eighth Patriarch, are inseparable, although not in the sense that Rennyo supported the *ikki*. On the contrary, he kept his distance from the leagues to the best of his ability, denying any connection with or responsibility for them. Rather, the sectarian developments for which Rennyo is best known—the dissemination of Honganji teachings through letters written in the vernacular, and the concomitant increase in the number of Honganji followers—helped to create the conditions that allowed the *ikkō ikki* phenomenon to become so important in the century following his death.

Rennyo's interpretation of True Pure Land teachings, as distilled into his popular letters, has so influenced Honganji doctrine that he has been called the second founder of the sect.[1] For inspiration and understanding, people still buy and read a collection of 88 of his letters. The ideology that drove *ikkō* leagues and their actions also originated in part from Rennyo's letters, though his teachings were interpreted in ways he almost certainly never meant them to be.

The late fifteenth-century Honganji members took up arms for a variety of motives: to protect the main temple, in self-defense, to ally themselves with one military commander, and to rebel against another. Not surprisingly, these motives changed as a result of developments within the Honganji sect as a whole. As the sect's followers increased in number, the leagues strengthened. And as Rennyo's teachings identified the sect ever more clearly in opposition to other Amidist sects, the groupings became more cohesive, transcending larger boundaries.

Overall, the years between 1457 and 1488 saw the emergence of a clearly defined Honganji sect institution, with the basic units of its structure established. They also saw the creation of a teaching canon designed to reach ordinary people, including the illiterate. Finally, they saw the emergence and strengthening of the *ikkō ikki* phenomenon, which started with the formation of a small band of Honganji followers in Ōmi Province and eventually resulted in leagues that united members of an entire region.

The Honganji sect's rapid growth in the fifteenth century, after 250 years of attracting relatively few supporters, was not unique, though it was impressive. At the same time, its True Pure Land rival, the Takada sect, also experienced a high rate of growth. This increase in membership and the formalization of sectarian structures grew, perhaps in part, out of the increasing political disorder associated with the Ōnin War and its aftermath. The Muromachi shogunate was left greatly weakened, creating fierce competition among warriors for territorial dominance throughout the country. Under these disorderly and dangerous circumstances, one can easily imagine people being drawn to a different kind of organization, one that offered more hope of stability.

Honganji's spread and institutionalization under Rennyo occurred largely because he identified other Amidist sects' beliefs as heresies, and people accepted his assessment. Why? Perhaps the legitimacy conferred on Rennyo by the combination of a teaching lineage and genealogical history that stretched back to Shinran helped people to accept his strict sect definitions. Further, Rennyo spoke to the people directly through letters that were no doubt read aloud; few other religious leaders of the time reached so many with such immediacy.[2] Rennyo attacked other Amidist groups at their foundations, stripping them of their legitimacy with a religious authority that would have been hard for local priests or preachers to combat. Thus, those who did accept Rennyo's teachings were less likely to pursue other Amidist practices at the same time or to abandon Honganji for another group.

Older Buddhist sects like Tendai also felt threatened, economically and otherwise, by the rapidly growing Honganji sect and periodically attacked its teachings as heretical. To survive this kind of opposition, successive Patriarchs attracted relatively important backers who could help shield their sect. One way the family did this was through the manipulation of family relationships, especially through marriage and adoption, just as other families of the time did.[3]

Rennyo

The eighth Patriarch, Rennyo, was born in 1415, grandson to the then-current Patriarch of Honganji. The child's father, Zonnyo (1396–1457), would become the seventh Patriarch, and his mother, of unknown ancestry, had been in service to Zonnyo's mother.[4] When Rennyo was six, his father had the opportunity to marry a woman known to us only as Nyoen,[5] who came from a warrior house, the Ebina, which served the Muromachi shogunate. However, one condition of that marriage was that Zonnyo send Rennyo's mother away, so he did.

What specific benefit Honganji received by the connection to the Ebina is unclear, but it appears that the marriage elevated Zonnyo's social status to some degree. Nyoen's family was in a position to set conditions on her marriage, and Zonnyo acceded to them, suggesting that the marital alliance meant more to him and his institution than it did to her family. This marriage produced four daughters and two more sons, the older son being born in 1433, when Zonnyo was 38 years old and Rennyo already 19.

Zonnyo always treated Rennyo as his successor, in spite of his mother's low status. Specifically, he arranged for Rennyo to be adopted by the head of the Hino family[6] and to study at Shōren'in, where Rennyo took the tonsure at the age of 16 (before his younger half-brother was born).[7] Both steps were preliminary to assuming the post of Patriarch, as they emphasized the heir's connection to Shinran, himself a member of the Hino family who had taken the tonsure at Shōren'in.[8]

Rennyo's education and training were designed to prepare him for Honganji leadership. In a kind of apprenticeship, he copied doctrinal works and assisted his father in temple business. Zonnyo sometimes gave his son's copies to subordinate temples as sacred objects as a focus for worship and to affirm their relationship with Honganji, implying again that Rennyo would succeed him.[9]

Like other Patriarchs-to-be, Rennyo underwent additional religious training at Kōfukuji, in his case under the supervision of the Daijōin head priest Kyōkaku, whose mother reportedly had come from the Honganji Patriarch's family.[10] The young man prepared further by accompanying his father on trips undertaken to spread Honganji's teachings, and he went alone on pilgrimages to sites in the east that were associated with Shinran and his followers.[11] All these aspects of Rennyo's education pointed to him as Zonnyo's recognized successor.

Even the birth of Rennyo's half-brother did not, apparently, change his status. Zonnyo took no steps toward preparing another of his sons to follow him, even as they grew up. When Zonnyo died in 1457, however, Rennyo's stepmother wanted her eldest son to become Patriarch, and she arranged for him, then age 25, to be placed at Shōren'in, preparatory to succeeding his father. Rennyo contested the change and with the help of his uncle Nyojō found supporters, primarily in the Hokuriku region. The leaders of the Hokuriku temples managed to override Nyoen's plans, making Rennyo the eighth Patriarch.[12] Her eldest son ended his days as the priest of a small temple in Kaga.

Nyoen's case seems to be analogous to similar situations in warrior families. A widow temporarily exercised power right after her husband's death, especially if no heir had been designated, and she worked with his retainers to select one. In Nyoen's case, it appears that she tried to override her husband's choice of heir, but she must have had some support from other family members in order to do so. Otherwise, Nyojō would not have had to go personally as far as the Hokuriku to find backers for Rennyo's claim.

Rennyo, then, owed his appointment to priests from the Hokuriku region, and he relied on them to ensure the stability of his reign. It should be no surprise, then, that Rennyo provided his own children as much independence and power within the sect as he could. He would have wanted to spare them the insecurity of tenure that he had suffered.

By the time Rennyo took office in 1457, he was 43 years old and had already fathered seven children—three daughters and four sons. His first wife (of five) had died in 1455, and he married her sister sometime within the following two years.[13] Their first child was born in 1458.[14] The father of these women, Ise Sadafusa, came from a collateral branch of the prominent Ise family and served the shogunate as a minor official.[15] These marriages then suggest that the Honganji Patriarch shared approximately the same status as a lower-level shogunate official.

At that time, Rennyo and his family were relatively poor. Again following custom, he sent several of his older children to other temples for boarding, probably in order to reduce his own household's living expenses. He did, however, have some high connections.

Actual power moved from family to family with great fluidity in the late fifteenth century and even more so in the sixteenth, so it was hard to tell which ties would ultimately prove useful. Rennyo and his successors nonetheless continued to maintain kinship relations (literal and fictive) with courtiers and warriors, and at times their connections provided crucial support.

That Rennyo enjoyed so many ties to courtiers and warrior officials is noteworthy. If his in-laws at this time were only minor officials, they were officials nonetheless and related to men of high rank. His adoptive father—that is, the sponsor at his coming-of-age ceremony—was the head of the Hino family, arguably the most important family of courtiers at the time. The Uramatsu Hino line provided wives to the Ashikaga shogunal house, and Rennyo arranged for his eldest son Junnyo, born in 1442, to be adopted by the head of this line, Hino Katsumitsu.[16] Katsumitsu's sister was one of the most famous shogunal wives in Japanese history, Hino Tomiko, who married the eighth shogun Yoshimasa and wielded extensive power as his widow.

The Patriarchal family also had other important connections. The priest Kyōkaku, who identified his mother as related to an unspecified Honganji Patriarch, came from the Kujō family of courtiers, who served as regents (*kanpaku*) to the emperor and were therefore at the top rank of courtier families.[17] Shōren'in, where all the Patriarchs took the tonsure, was closely associated with both the Hino family and the main Ashikaga house. Like the Honganji Patriarchs, Ashikaga Yoshinori, for example, took the tonsure at Shōren'in in 1418, ten years before his return to lay life as the sixth shogun.[18] It is unlikely that future Patriarchs became acquainted with future shoguns (or even shoguns' cousins) while studying at Shōren'in; nevertheless, the family of Honganji Patriarchs had close ties to Shōren'in, which in turn had close ties to people in the seats of power, and these ties surely proved useful to the Honganji house.

The willingness of temples affiliated with other sects to take in Rennyo's older children testifies to the rather loose sectarian identity of the time and also to mutually beneficial relationships with Honganji. Rennyo's aunt joined the Chinzai branch of Pure Land Buddhism, and other temples of that branch took in two of his sons and a daughter as boarders. Also, Nanzenji, one of the major Zen temples of Kyoto sponsored by the shogunate, took in another son.[19]

Both the Hino and Ise families were patrons of the Chinzai branch, and this connection may account for how easily these temples welcomed Rennyo's family members. The success he and his father had in placing so many Honganji children in important temples testifies to their family's status, just as the necessity of sending children out testifies to their poverty. Later in Rennyo's life, as the sect began to prosper, he would send his children to highly ranked Honganji-affiliated temples instead of to temples of other sects, reflecting both the Honganji sect's improved fortunes and its growing institutionalization.[20]

The First Ikkō *Leagues*

In his first few years as Patriarch, Rennyo concentrated his preaching in southern Ōmi Province, just east of Kyoto. Out of twenty-eight sacred objects that he dedicated to branch temples between 1457 and 1464, only three went outside Ōmi: one to Mikawa, one to Owari, and one to Izumi. Six of the remaining twenty-five went to Shiga County on the western shore of Lake Biwa—fully five of those going to the same *dōjō*—and the other nineteen went to communities on the eastern shore of the lake.[21] Rennyo's contacts in areas to the southeast, especially Mikawa, reflected close relationships despite the distance between the capital and the temples, but his activities in Ōmi produced the most dramatic immediate results. They were not, however, desirable ones: the powerful Tendai monastery Enryakuji, sitting atop Mt. Hiei, which stood between Lake Biwa and the capital, felt economically threatened by Rennyo's successes in what it regarded as its back yard and took steps to end them.

Enryakuji's first major reaction to Honganji's spread in Ōmi came on the eighth day of the first month of 1465, in the form of a letter from members of Saitōin, one of Enryakuji's subsidiary temples. The letter to Honganji accused its leaders of, among other things, "spreading the exclusive *nenbutsu*, slandering the three treasures [of Buddhism] . . . establishing a new religious school [without proper authorization] . . . burning Buddhist statues and sutras, denigrating the gods" and otherwise demonstrating themselves to be "enemies of the Buddha and enemies of the gods." The letter insisted that "for the sake of Buddhism, for the sake of the state, [Honganji] must not go unrebuked," and ordered Honganji to cease its objectionable activities immediately.[22] It was an ominous start to the new year.

Clearly, Enryakuji's leaders considered themselves authorized to punish Honganji's errant clerics, and Rennyo, correctly interpreting this letter as the prelude to a physical attack on the temple, called for help from his supporters nearby. About a dozen men arrived from Katata, Ōmi, to defend the temple, but apparently there was no sense of urgency. When Enryakuji's forces arrived a few days later, they found the gates unbarred and the few guards asleep.[23] Even if the guards had been awake, though, Honganji's defenders, numbering fewer than twenty men, would have been overwhelmed as Enryakuji had recruited local warriors in addition to their usual forces, bringing the total number of attackers to about 150 men.[24]

Rennyo and his young son Jitsunyo fled the assault, finding shelter in a non-affiliated temple nearby. They also managed to save the temple's most important icon, a carved image of Shinran. When word of the attack reached Honpukuji, one of the oldest Honganji sect temples, in Katata, its priest Hōjū gathered a force of about eighty men who belatedly raced to Honganji's defense.[25] The Katata forces managed to regain possession of the temple itself, but they failed to prevent Enryakuji and its allies from sacking the temple and making off with sutras, Buddhist images, and other valuable and sacred objects.[26]

After the destruction of the Ōtani Honganji, some priests suggested that they demonstrate their orthodoxy to Tendai representatives. They took the attack's pretext at face value and reasoned that once Enryakuji realized that their teachings were acceptable, it would leave them alone. Others, however, successfully argued that Enryakuji cared more about its income than doctrinal purity, and that a cash payment would be more welcome to the Tendai monastery than an invitation to a religious debate would.[27] Accordingly, payment was arranged with the help of Shōren'in, a logical intermediary because it was friendly to Honganji, even though it was a subsidiary of Enryakuji. The incident seemed to be settled.[28]

Unfortunately for Honganji, however, just over two months later, Enryakuji decided to launch a second attack. A letter sent on 3/20 to Gion shrine, an Enryakuji affiliate, advised shrine officials of the decision and requested help from the shrine's lower-level functionaries, who often assisted the temple in demonstrations of force.[29] The following day, these forces destroyed what remained of Honganji, and on the twenty-fourth, they expanded their attack to include targets in Ōmi. The beleaguered sect drew on the little warrior support it had; the shogunate issued a letter to Enryakuji, ordering it to desist immediately.[30] Enryakuji also failed to obtain the cooperation of the Ise family, which was prominent in Ōmi and, it will be remembered, included Rennyo's in-laws.[31] Despite the shogunal support for Honganji, however, Enryakuji ceased its attacks only when its demands—again related to heresy—were met.

Enryakuji repeated its attacks on towns in Ōmi several times throughout the summer, fall, and into the following year.[32] Each time, Honganji followers put up spirited resistance, gathering in a castle at Kanegamori on the east side of Lake Biwa and fortifying Honpukuji on the west side of the lake. After the hostilities had continued for several months, Rennyo insisted that his followers stop fighting and urged them to find other ways of settling the problem with Enryakuji. They finally agreed, vacating their fortresses and arranging yet another cash payment to Enryakuji.[33]

At some point during these tumultuous months—the date itself is obscure—Honganji also accepted nominal status as a subordinate of Saitōin, the division of Enryakuji that had instigated the attacks. That gesture mollified its enemy on two counts: financial and administrative. Honganji continued to pay dues to Enryakuji as a branch temple for some time thereafter, perhaps until into the 1540s.[34]

Enryakuji continued to insist on regulating the kinds of objects worshipped in Honganji temples and *dōjō*. For example, it banned the use or distribution of a ten-character invocation Rennyo had used because the invocation included the term "unhindered light," a term the Tendai temple seems to have identified with Honganji's claim to independence, which it denied.[35] Enryakuji confiscated the ten-character scrolls but finally granted the Ōmi temples permission to continue using the ten-character invocations—after they offered cash for the privilege.[36] However, Rennyo ceased making them at about this time, turning instead to a six-character form that avoided the wording Enryakuji disliked.

At the same time that these events took place, tensions within the shogunate had increased to a breaking point.[37] Shortly after the outbreak of the Ōnin War, in 1468, Enryakuji once again attacked the towns of Kanegamori and Katata. This time the charges were not even nominally religious in nature; instead they accused the residents of piracy on the lake and failure to provide lumber for the rebuilding of the shogun's palace in Kyoto. These allegations had no clear connection to Honganji or its members *per se*. Nevertheless, the defense was mounted primarily by Honganji's followers, and it was led again by priests from the branch temples at Katata and Kanegamori. This effort again ended in defeat, leaving much of Katata and its neighboring town, Ima-Katata, in ashes. The resolution came only in the following year, when the Ōmi residents once again sent money to Enryakuji.[38]

The role of Honganji adherents in the resistance of Katata and Kanegamori in 1468 indicates that the sectarians were prominent among those who would take up arms in defense of the town under any kind of attack, not just to defend Honganji or its branch temples. In other words, their actions make sense within the context of a warrior *ikki*, perhaps the fishing-village equivalent of an *ikki* of *jizamurai*. Their ability to handle weapons that required some training supports this interpretation, and the point merits bearing in mind while looking at *ikkō ikki* actions elsewhere.

The first two attacks by Enryakuji on Honganji, however, are more clearly related to the Honganji sect. Who better to aid Honganji and its branch temples than Honganji members? The groups of people who met at the temples and *dōjō* could have formed a basis for the *ikki* by responding to the need for fighters. Priests led the forces. In this case, warrior, villager, townsman, or other status had little relevance—what mattered was sect membership. After the battles ceased, the *ikki* members returned to their everyday lives.

In these fights at Honganji and in Ōmi, which can be seen as the first episodes of *ikkō ikki*, Enryakuji evidently regarded Honganji as a renegade temple that belonged under Enryakuji's jurisdiction. Enryakuji treated its concerns as an internal matter; for instance, it did not petition the court to suppress the sect but rather concentrated on applying pressure directly on Honganji, forcing it to accept regulation. Yet, control over Honganji appears to have been less important to the Tendai monastery than money, which it had been steadily losing in Ōmi, where some of its branch temples reaffiliated with Honganji.

Although Enryakuji repeatedly justified its attacks with charges of heresy, and on the surface a few of its actions bear that out—notably the "unhindered light" scrolls—matters were resolved primarily by cash payments.[39] As we have seen, Honganji branch temples were even permitted to use the ten-character "unhindered light" invocation, provided that money changed hands. The pattern of settlements supports the convictions of those pragmatic Honganji priests in 1465, who argued that Enryakuji was more concerned with money than alleged heresy. Indeed, most historians accept that interpretation.

To some, the *ikkō ikki* of 1465 and 1468 may appear to have joined uprisings against Enryakuji's authority. Arguably, Enryakuji had some jurisdiction over religious matters in general and Honganji in particular. Similarly, it had extensive land holdings in Ōmi, which may have given it the right to enforce the collection of taxes for the shogun's palace and to combat piracy on the lake. Therefore, resistance to Enryakuji's attacks might possibly be construed as resistance to its authority. Yet, in 1465, the shogunate and Ise family supported Honganji against the Tendai monastery, and, given the outcomes, in all cases Enryakuji's actions appear to have been more about extracting payments than about heresy or matters of law. Authority itself was fragmented in the Muromachi period, even before the Ōnin War, and in this context, an uprising against one authority could even mean complying with another. In general, conceptualizing *ikkō ikki* and their struggles as uprisings obscures more than it explains, as these cases have demonstrated.

Of all the *ikkō* leagues' struggles, these battles with Enryakuji most closely approached the familiar model of religious warfare: two religious groups fighting with each other ostensibly over doctrinal matters, but with strong underpinnings of economic friction. This was not to be the standard model for the conflicts of *ikkō ikki*, however. Although contending sides might divide along religious lines in outbreaks during the next century, Honganji would not again fight another religious group as its main opponent, with religious issues the main reason for the battle. In the future, Honganji's primary opponents would be warriors, albeit warriors who sometimes allied themselves with other religious sects.

Honganji, then, lost its first battles, resulting in the destruction of the temple facilities. In spite of the willingness of sectarians to come to Honganji's defense, there were too few of them to succeed. In the 1470s, however, their numbers would grow dramatically, resulting in much larger forces when they were needed.

Yoshizaki

Rennyo spent most of the six years from 1465 to 1471 in Ōmi, with occasional trips elsewhere, notably to the provinces of Settsu and Mikawa. He moved from town to town, preaching and conducting services, enjoying extended and repeated stays in both Katata and Kanegamori. No move was made to rebuild Honganji at Ōtani or anywhere else during this time, though in Ōtsu a new hall was built to house Shinran's sacred image, and Rennyo's oldest son Junnyo (1442–83) was put in charge of it.[40] Once, the Honpukuji priest Hōjū suggested to Rennyo that he settle permanently in Katata. Given the harassment of Enryakuji over the years, though, it is small wonder that Rennyo replied by pointing toward Enryakuji saying simply, "That is [so] close."[41]

In the end, Rennyo relocated to a town called Yoshizaki, on the border between the provinces of Echizen and Kaga, more than 150 miles away from Katata (and Enryakuji). Yoshizaki was the base for his most successful proselytizing, and his stay there allowed his teachings to spread throughout the Hokuriku.

A number of factors probably influenced Rennyo's decision to move to the Hokuriku region and to Yoshizaki specifically. For one, the worship of Amida was already widespread in the Hokuriku, as well as in the nearby provinces of Shinano and Hida, suggesting that Rennyo's preaching might be welcomed in the area.

For another, men of his father's and grandfather's generations had already founded temples there: Hongakuji and Chōshōji in Echizen; Honrenji, Honsenji, and Kōgyōji in Kaga; and Shōkōji in Etchū. Shōkōji and Honsenji were founded by Rennyo's uncle Nyojō, whose assistance had enabled Rennyo to become Patriarch less than fifteen years previously. Some temples already connected to other Amidist traditions, like Senkōji, Kōtokuji, and Guganji, all in Kaga, had been persuaded by Rennyo's father to affiliate with Honganji. They did not, however, all maintain close Honganji sect ties continuously between their initial connections with the sect and 1471 when Rennyo arrived, a time when religious affiliations were relatively fluid anyway. Nevertheless, their priests were familiar with Honganji teachings, and the seeds for future growth that earlier generations had sown were ready to sprout.

Yoshizaki offered other attractions. It was distant from the capitals of both Kaga and Echizen, and at first consideration might seem as isolated as it is today. Nonetheless, the site actually offered fairly ready access to the capital and elsewhere, ensuring a flow of communications, supplies, and, as it turned out, pilgrims. If the proximity of the trade routes suggests that Yoshizaki would have been an attractive target for bandits or others, it benefited from being easily fortified: Rennyo's temple sat on top of a hill on the coast, surrounded on three sides by water, strategically a very defensible site. Rennyo may have hoped to remain apart from the power struggles erupting around the countryside, but his experiences with Enryakuji taught him to be prepared. Later events would prove his caution justified, as the townspeople had to build even stronger defenses because of roving bands of warriors who attacked sites along the border.[42]

Finally, Rennyo already had numerous connections to Yoshizaki and its immediate surroundings. Hongakuji, an Echizen temple that had been formally affiliated with the Honganji sect for at least twenty years,[43] administered part of the estate in which Yoshizaki was located.[44] The estate itself was owned by the Daijōin sub-temple of Kōfukuji, formerly headed by none other than Rennyo's relative Kyōkaku. Although Kyōkaku had retired in 1438, he and Rennyo remained close until the former's death in 1473. Rennyo probably had dealings with the new Daijōin abbot, Jinson, through Kyōkaku.[45] In addition, at that time Rennyo had a cordial relationship with the new ruler of Echizen, Asakura Toshikage (1428–81), so any or all of these men may have helped Rennyo establish himself in Yoshizaki.[46]

The Hokuriku region, then, looked like a hospitable and relatively safe choice. Kyoto continued to be dangerous, as the Ōnin War still raged there. Even if Enryakuji had posed no threat to Rennyo in Ōmi, life there would still have been disrupted by conflicts related to the shogunal power struggle. Rennyo also had precedent for waiting out a war by escaping to a distant refuge: his grandfather Gyōnyo had done so before him, staying at Zuisenji in the 1430s to avoid the dangers of war and famine.[47]

Struggles for power did rage within Echizen and Kaga in 1471—Asakura Toshikage, one of the first of a new kind of military commander, the *sengoku* daimyo, came to power by force shortly before Rennyo moved to his province.[48] In Kaga, warriors continued to fight for control of the province for years after Rennyo arrived. Nevertheless, as we have noted, Yoshizaki lay far from the centers of power in either province, and it seemed unlikely to be severely disrupted by those conflicts.[49] Rennyo stayed there for four years, attracting hundreds of pilgrims and recruiting new members. Those years also saw the beginnings of the sect members' momentous involvement in the politics of Kaga and its region.

While at Yoshizaki, Rennyo perfected what would become the sect's most important preaching tool, even after his death: his pastoral letters, or *ofumi*, which fostered the swift growth of the sect's membership. The *ofumi*, written in vernacular Japanese rather than the classical Chinese normally used for religious texts, explained the sect's tenets simply, using words easily understood by the relatively uneducated. They were almost certainly intended to be read aloud.[50] Rennyo had addressed the first of these letters, written in 1461, to Dōsai,[51] a priest from Kanegamori who later proved to be a staunch ally, but he seems to have recognized the form's utility in proselytizing only later after arriving at Yoshizaki.

There are so many extant copies of these letters—evidence of their popularity—that it is impossible to determine how many of them Rennyo actually wrote. The contents of many varied little, as Rennyo frequently repeated the same wording when he discussed matters of doctrine. These letters were in turn often copied by members, introducing the opportunity for errors each time. As a result, scholars find it difficult to decide if two letters with only minor differences should be counted as separate original letters, that is, written by Rennyo, or one original with flawed copies.[52]

The most complete scholarly compilation of Rennyo's *ofumi* includes more than two hundred different letters,[53] written over a span of 37 years. Rennyo wrote one-third them while at Yoshizaki, and 59 were written in the years 1473 and 1474 alone. The only comparable cluster came in 1498, the year before Rennyo died, when he wrote 38 letters.[54] Eventually, under his son's supervision, a compilation of 80 letters emerged as a canon that followers copied for religious instruction.[55] These letters are still popular, and, in keeping with Rennyo's intent to make them accessible to as many people as possible, can be bought in a paperback edition at most Japanese bookstores today.

Several *ofumi* deal with the question of what Rennyo saw as mistaken teachings, which he both defined and corrected. He wrote most of these, too, at Yoshizaki, suggesting that Rennyo attracted people familiar with, or belonging to, other Amidist sects, not those wholly new to Amida worship.[56] Clearly, Rennyo used the *ofumi* as his main tools to define Honganji orthodoxy, and the beliefs he called mistaken can be identified with the teachings of other Pure Land sects like the Jishū and the rival True Pure Land Takada sect. The membership of other Amidist groups declined as the Honganji sect grew, further evidence suggesting that Rennyo drew people who already believed in or knew about Amidism.[57]

Residents of the region responded enthusiastically to Rennyo's presence. Within two years, Yoshizaki grew into a busy town that one source described as "no different from the capital [Kyoto] or Kamakura."[58] This description is doubtless an exaggeration (unless the comparison is to post-Ōnin War Kyoto, a city in ruins), but nevertheless Yoshizaki certainly became a magnet for believers as well as a thriving commercial center. It was the direct precursor of later *jinaichō*, which were planned cities, whereas Yoshizaki appears to have been a spontaneous creation.

In a letter dated in the eighth month of 1473, Rennyo described Yoshizaki as a town of one or two hundred buildings in addition to his temple. Many of these buildings were inns lining the main street, which ran the length of the town between its northern and southern gates. The town's physical size suggests how many visitors it drew more clearly than it indicates the permanent population. Rennyo's letter went on to say that Yoshizaki attracted people from Kaga, Echizen, and Etchū, "religious and lay, men and women [numbering] several thousands or tens of thousands."[59]

Rennyo had envisioned Yoshizaki as a religious center, accommodating anyone engaged in the pursuit of true faith or in the expression of gratitude for having found it. To his dismay, he discovered that the large number of worshippers created a demand for goods and services that attracted people with profit, not Amida, on their minds. In another letter written in the ninth month of 1473, a month or so after the one quoted above, Rennyo complained of too many people coming to Yoshizaki for non-religious reasons and prohibited the coming and going of those who were "not interested in affirming their *nenbutsu* faith and achieving rebirth in paradise."[60] This would not be the last time Rennyo lay down a rule he was unable to enforce.

Who flocked to Yoshizaki? Much time, effort, and ink has been expended on scholarly theories about the social origins of Honganji members at this time without the emergence of a consensus answer, let alone a definitive one. The people who came to Yoshizaki did so because they could; either they had the time and wealth to make the trip, and to make the visit worthwhile by staying for a time, or they plied their trade on the road, peddling, shipping, or accompanying merchandise en route. Some may have been farmers who went to Yoshizaki during the winter and some the village leaders whom Rennyo targeted as the most effective voices for bringing his message to the largest number of people. The visitors and residents must have included the merchants, artisans, and shippers who had already found a place within the Honganji fold in other regions. No doubt all of these groups were represented at Yoshizaki and in the growing membership of the Honganji sect, but the evidence is too thin to show in what numbers, or even in what proportions, any of these groups came.

Nevertheless, in spite of the incomplete historical record, several points can be made about Honganji's members at that time. Non-agricultural workers continued to play an important role in Honganji's success. During Rennyo's tenure, new temples still tended to be founded in places associated with the timber and mining industries, as well as along major trade routes. Some temples, like Shōrenji in Hida Province, attracted members with skills in building and maintaining roads.[61] Members in Kaga built temples in mountainous regions, again, areas associated with industries like timber and mining. Although common sense may suggest otherwise because of the difficulty of the terrain, many important trade routes did run through the mountains, if only for access to those industries' products.[62] Many temples were also founded in ports in provinces such as Owari and Harima, as well as in the Hokuriku, showing the continuing association of Honganji with merchants and shippers.[63]

Important as these groups continued to be, word of Honganji's teachings did reach farming villages, where they also found a receptive audience, at least among the village elite. In Kaga, converts included warriors and *jizamurai*.[64] Rennyo's own travels would have helped reach farmers, but as there was considerable interaction between villages and local commercial centers, especially through *jizamurai* who used the markets, the teachings could eventually spread from the towns into the villages even without his trips.[65]

We have little more evidence for the number of Honganji members or for the sect's trajectory of growth than we do for the members' origins. Temples in Japan at this time kept no records analogous to parish registers in which births or christenings, marriages, and deaths were entered, and from which congregation size can be extrapolated. Many temples kept lists of branch temples, *dōjō*, and local congregations (*monto*) but included no information that suggests how many people formed the congregations or gathered in the temples or *dōjō*. In addition, few of these records date from the fifteenth century, and none mentions when the congregations, temples, or *dōjō* were formed. Thus, from one early example, we know that in 1484 the Mikawa temple Jōgūji listed 105 branches, but not when any of them were founded, much less whether all together they served three hundred or ten thousand followers.[66]

Many *dōjō* that thrived and subsequently became temples compiled their own histories in later years and modern historians have mined such records for information. Unfortunately, most of these histories were written centuries after the foundation of their temples, and incorporated unsubstantiated legends, especially concerning who founded them, how, and when. Thus, they are unreliable. Even if we take the alleged founding dates to be accurate, we still cannot extrapolate the total number of temples and *dōjō* active at that time. After all, it is unlikely that all *dōjō* eventually became temples; some must have failed, changed to other sectarian affiliations, or been absorbed into other congregations. Some that did become temples must also have disappeared over the centuries.

The most reliable evidence of the growth of the sect—the dedications on objects given to temples or *dōjō* certifying their affiliation with Honganji—tended to emerge after the growth itself took place. The greatest number of these objects came not from Rennyo but from his successor Jitsunyo (1458–1525), making their provenance unclear. Circumstantial evidence, such as the frequency of reports about the *ikkōshū* in other sources, the need for rules of conduct for members, and the fights that involved Honganji members in Kaga Province, indicates that membership grew primarily under Rennyo. In other words, members were recruited first, and the institutions that served them only emerged after the membership began to increase.[67]

According to Rennyo's son Jitsugo (1492–1584), in 1473, two years after Rennyo had arrived in Yoshizaki, he decided to visit the Kantō region, much like earlier pilgrimages he had made. Apparently, he only got as far as Etchū. After reaching Zuisenji temple there, so many people gathered to see him, it is said, that every day some were crushed to death in the crowds. After a short time, Rennyo abandoned his plans to go east and snuck out of Zuisenji in the middle of the night to return to Yoshizaki.[68] If so many people gathered to see Rennyo in Etchū that he decided against continuing his journey further, his fame must have spread beyond the towns and well into the countryside, though one must not assume that everyone who came to see him was already a sect member.[69] Indeed, a skeptic might suggest that Rennyo met with a hostile crowd, not a welcoming one. Either way, he had succeeded in spreading his teachings widely enough to reach a multitude of people and had become a major religious figure.

As head of the family, Rennyo was responsible for finding appropriate occupations and positions for his numerous sons. He began to do so even before he had become Patriarch himself by founding new temples on their behalf and installing them as the head priests.

The first of these new temples may have been Shōkōji, founded in a town called Hasadani in Kaga and headed by Rennyo's third son Renkō (1450–1531). One temple record claims that Rennyo founded the temple as early as 1451, though others credit Renkō. The difference is probably a matter of terminology and interpretation, meaning that Rennyo created the temple but that Renkō served as its first titular head, which he could do even as an infant.

The placement of Rennyo's sons Renjō (1446–71) and Rengo (1468–1543) illustrate both how important family politics were at the time and how intertwined they could become, not just for Honganji but also for other families. Renjō had been sent to head both Honsenji and Zuisenji temples and was succeeded after his death by his brother Rengo. As we know, Rennyo did not found these temples; Zuisenji had been founded a few generations earlier, and Rennyo's uncle Nyojō founded Honsenji. In the Honganji sect, temple headships were passed on hereditarily, like Patriarch posts, with the important exception that temple heads could adopt heirs. Installing Renjō, and later Rengo, in Honsenji nevertheless took some maneuvering.

Nyojō had no son to whom he could bequeath Honsenji, but he did have a daughter. Following a common practice of the time, Nyojō adopted Renjō, who married the daughter, Rennyo's cousin. The couple in their turn adopted Rengo, Renjō's half-brother, who married their daughter.[70] This solved four problems, two in each generation: finding heirs for Honsenji in spite of the head priest producing only daughters and finding places for two of Rennyo's sons. This was still a significant investment of Honganji resources in both the temple and the region, reflecting the sect's local success and the region's importance to Rennyo.

As affiliations in the Honganji and other sects became more clearly defined and binding, the membership also grew. Evidently, Rennyo saw the need for special temples to mediate between Honganji and its local branches. He did not add a layer to the existing pyramid, making its branches report to regional temples which then reported to Honganji. Instead, he created temples to *represent* Honganji locally and act in the Patriarch's stead.

The new temples' leaders needed to be close to the Patriarch so as to confer the same kind of legitimacy that Honganji claimed; they had to be descended from Shinran. Rennyo decided to call on his sons for this purpose and continued to create temples for more and more of them. These temples are usually called *ikkeshū*, literally one-house or one-family temples, referring to their heads belonging to the Patriarch's family.

Rennyo's work in the Hokuriku, then, was threefold: 1) defining the beliefs of the sect, thereby differentiating it from other Pure Land and True Pure Land faiths; 2) attracting new members; and 3) creating a structure intended to reinforce his teachings. In spite of his efforts to maintain orthodoxy among the members, it is unlikely that all who joined the sect understood its teachings as Rennyo intended, since his concept of faith was abstruse. Furthermore, information was often spread by word of mouth, and even though people in societies dependent on the spoken word often remember much longer and more difficult messages than most people today can, the meaning could easily have changed in transmission anyway. In addition to the problems that accompany the oral transmission of difficult concepts was the question of interpretation, which no doubt changed from person to person.

Some interpretations could lead to trouble. There are reports of *ikkō* sectarians attacking other temples and shrines or refusing to pay taxes. Such reports attributed this behavior to the sectarians' ostensible belief that they need no longer fear the threats of divine punishment on which the authorities had relied to insure compliance. Thus, observers suggested, the members thought that they could get away with anything because they expected to go to the Pure Land when they died. Others seemed to think that Honganji adherents expected Amida to protect them in this world, even from other gods and Buddhas, if they had faith in him. As outsiders saw it, then, the *ikkō* sect undermined society because of the single reliance on Amida that the word *ikkō* implies.

Rennyo tried to distance himself and his followers both from these attacks and from the label of *ikkō* sect, admonishing members in his *ofumi* that Honganji was not the *ikkō* sect. Instead, they should refer to themselves as members of the True Pure Land sect, following Shinran's practice.[71]

This point was essential at the time because there was another distinct sect that went by the name of *ikkō*. It was derived from a Pure Land faction and also taught followers to denigrate the gods and so on. A number of this *ikkō* sect's members were absorbed into the Honganji sect,[72] though they did not necessarily understand some of the differences between the teachings, in spite of Rennyo's repeated clarifications. Eventually, the real *ikkō* sect declined and disappeared, and its members probably gravitated to other Amidist groups. The Honganji sect ultimately became widely identified as the *ikkō* sect, and Rennyo proved helpless to stop the process.

Justifiably or not, Honganji sect members became known for being disruptive and a threat to society. To protect the sect against the danger of suppression, Rennyo drew on one of the traditional powers of a religious leader: to set rules of behavior for the community of followers, as Shinran had also once done. In a letter addressed to members and dated the ninth month of 1473, he set down a few preliminary rules for his followers.[73] Two months later, he issued a formal set of eleven rules that members were all supposed to follow; these rules and their practical implications were crucial to the future of the sect. The text ran as follows:[74]

1. Do not belittle the various gods, Buddhas, or bodhisattvas.
2. Do not slander any of the other religious teachings or sects.
3. Do not criticize other sects on the basis of our sect's practices.
4. Even though there are no taboos taught in Buddhist law, strictly observe the taboos publicly and with other sects.
5. It is not right to praise the Buddhist law in ways not transmitted in our sect.
6. As *nenbutsu* believers, obey the military governors and land stewards of the province and do not denigrate them.
7. It is not right for those who are ignorant to speak freely and admiringly of the teachings of our sect, relying on their own ideas, in front of members of other sects.
8. It is not right for those who are not yet settled in their faith to speak admiringly of the teachings of faith, based on what they have heard.
9. Do not eat fish or birds at *nenbutsu* meetings.
10. Since in *sake*, one loses the ability to think deeply and distinguish right from wrong, do not drink on days when there are *nenbutsu* meetings.
11. Among *nenbutsu* believers, all gambling must stop.

Rennyo concludes by saying that "anyone who disobeys the eleven articles [above] will be expelled from [our] group."[75]

There are many ways to approach the meaning of the rules. On the surface, they speak directly to the relations between Honganji's adherents and society at large. While he charged believers not to "praise the Buddhist law [in ways] not transmitted in our sect" (item five)—in other words, to adhere to orthodoxy and not to participate in other kinds of Buddhist rituals and services—Rennyo also insisted that Honganji members nonetheless respect the beliefs of other sects. They should do so by refraining from public criticism of them (items one, two, and three) and to join in observing customs not required by Honganji doctrine (item four). The rule against eating fish or birds at meetings (item nine) also suggests concern for the opinion of the community, which would have seen such behavior as a shocking disregard of Buddhist custom and law at a religious service.

Rennyo wanted to be sure that nobody falsely claimed to be preaching Honganji doctrine, so he wrote rules forbidding discussion of doctrine by "those who are ignorant" or "not yet settled in their faith" (items seven and eight). These rules served the dual purpose of protecting his newly formed orthodoxy and avoiding the public criticism that even the inadvertent preaching of heresy would invite. Furthermore, they indicate that some people were unclear on Honganji's teachings as Rennyo interpreted them.

Finally, the article insisting that followers "obey the military governors and land stewards" (item six) has been widely cited to support the idea that Honganji doctrines undermined the authority of these men, as if only Honganji sect believers ever disregarded their orders or tried to avoid taxation. Part of the reasoning behind such an interpretation is the idea that Rennyo would not have to prohibit something that Honganji members did not do.

Another explanation for item six is that Rennyo held his followers to a high standard of cooperation, telling them that in their capacity as *nenbutsu* believers, they were obliged to obey the authorities.[76] He may have hoped in that way to avoid the kind of suppression that new forms of Buddhism often faced, or even that such cooperation would attract warrior patronage. Thus, most of the eleven articles aim to protect the sect from criticism and reprisals from other groups, even to the extent of, in effect, forbidding Honganji sect followers from engaging in religious debates (item three), an activity popular among a number of other religious groups.[77] If all Honganji adherents had maintained these standards, the sect would have been a model of civil and religious decorum that few, if any, contemporary Buddhist schools could have rivaled.

One of Rennyo's letters, dated 1474/3/7 stated as much by equating following the sect's rules with avoiding public attention. He criticized members who sought to promote the sect by publicizing its teachings, behavior he termed outrageous, implying that shunning the spotlight, rather than seeking publicity, was the best way to help the sect.[78] Nevertheless, since Rennyo never sought to protect his institution by compromising it, there is more to the rules than this surface reading suggests. At their core is the whole contentious issue of faith, what it means, how it manifests itself, and, most especially, who defines it.

Specifically, item six, which begins by saying "as *nenbutsu* [believers], obey the military governors," can be read as encompassing a deeper meaning about faith. If Rennyo had left off the phrase "as *nenbutsu* believers," the rule would still stand. He included it, however, and so linked the behavior with the followers' identities as believers. Obeying the authorities became a matter or a demonstration of faith. Items seven and eight, which forbid "those who are ignorant" or "not yet settled in their faith" to expound on doctrine can also be read as cautioning against arrogance, which is also incompatible with faith.

In a letter written in 1475, Rennyo evoked Shinran as the author of the rules. He thereby gave them even greater legitimacy and elevated them to "articles of faith."[79] Failure to follow the rules became a transgression against Shinran's teachings, and therefore a failure of faith.

The specifics of Honganji's belief and the kind of authority Rennyo wielded mean that the rules can, then, also be read as a picture of how he understood faith to manifest itself in behavior. The punishment for breaking the rules was expulsion from the sect, not a fine or corporal punishment of some kind. Religious leaders of other Buddhist groups also issued rules guiding the behavior of the priests or nuns in their communities, and expulsion was a common punishment for breaking those rules. In the Honganji sect, however, expulsion came to take on a greater meaning for members. Rennyo had emphasized Honganji's exclusivity when he pointedly identified other sects' teachings with heresy, and his followers understood the implications.

For members of most other Buddhist sects, expulsion from a community still left one the option of joining another. Since standard Buddhist teaching held that there are many different paths to enlightenment, no one leaving a particular community needed to feel that his hopes for enlightenment or salvation were irrevocably dashed. There was always another path to follow.

The Honganji faith, by contrast, along with a few others, including the Nichiren or Lotus Sect, held to the belief that their way was the only possible way under the current circumstances. For Honganji, *mappō*, the age of the law's decline, left people no other choice but to rely on Amida's power for salvation because they had no way to reach enlightenment through their own efforts. Thus, expulsion from the Honganji sect's community of believers deprived one of any hope for an auspicious rebirth, and the expelled members were destined for a hell, or so the followers understood.

Looking at the rules from this perspective, we can say that, to Rennyo, those who had faith could quietly rely on rebirth in the Pure Land after death and should naturally live their lives simply without needing to criticize other teachings. They would recognize that Amida's vow and the promise of enlightenment took effect *after* death, even though the irrevocable settling of the matter occurred in this life, unlike some factions that believed the settling of rebirth made one a Buddha in this life.[80] Consequently, believers would behave appropriately in this life, obeying the authorities, observing customs, and avoiding trouble with other religious groups. Those without genuinely settled faith were also welcome in the sect, provided that they did not create trouble for their co-religionists by talking about beliefs they could not fully understand until they gained true faith.

Items one, two, and six—on not belittling or slandering other deities and sects, and on obeying the civil authorities—have particularly clear links to beliefs rejected by Rennyo's doctrine but accepted by some of the members, it would appear. Rennyo revisited these issues and their relationship to true faith more explicitly in a letter dated 1474/2/17, in which he admonished his readers not to "ignore the military governors and the land stewards, saying that you have achieved faith, but all the more fulfill your duties completely. Also, do not treat the various gods, Buddhas, and Bodhisattvas lightly" as they are all encompassed in Amida and in the *nenbutsu*.[81] To Rennyo, achieving faith did not mean feeling free to do anything one wanted, whether out of a sense of superiority or out of confidence that no punishment could really be harmful. If anything, it meant recognizing ever more clearly that one should fulfill all the obligations of one's position in life and that, therefore, disobeying the governors and land stewards would clearly demonstrate a lack of faith, not its presence.

Similarly, believing that Amida's mercy absolved one of the need to respect other deities, presumably because they were either inferior or simply ineffective, and that Amida would protect his worshippers, also betrayed a fundamental misunderstanding incompatible with real faith. One with true faith would understand that all deities are contained within Amida; denigrating the other deities necessarily meant denigrating Amida. Conversely, if one chanted the *nenbutsu* in praise of Amida, by extension one praised all the other deities at the same time. Breaking the rules demonstrated heresy, then, and not faith, justifying expulsion from the sect as an appropriate punishment.[82]

Although Rennyo repeatedly admonished his followers to obey the authorities and not to belittle or slander other deities, it is safe to assume that some members did anyway and that some references to disruptive *ikkō* sect members meant Honganji sectarians. At least some Honganji adherents still refused to forward rents or taxes of one kind or another, though for this the heresies might have been beside the point. Some also attacked temples and shrines, acts that fell under the category of slander at the time. Since it would be a mistake to equate Rennyo's entire concept of faith with the picture drawn by the rules, so would it be a mistake to equate all members' perception of the teachings and behavior toward other institutions and their representatives with Rennyo's. The evident differences between Honganji's or Rennyo's teachings and the members' beliefs would play a large role in some of the *ikki* and their actions.

On one level, Rennyo's rules regulated behavior in a community and punished disobedience with expulsion from the community. If the rules applied to Yoshizaki, a community defined by geography, they could have had nothing to do with faith *per se.* The community, however, was not geographical but spiritual and without physical boundaries. Disobeying rules put one outside the sect.

What, exactly, did that mean? In theory, at least to someone with a modern perspective, one could place one's faith in Amida by oneself. If individual faith is the core requirement for an auspicious rebirth, then one need not be a member of a defined group in order to achieve it. *Tariki* faith cannot be taught because learning empowers one, and the whole point of *tariki* is that it is beyond any individual's control. It lies in Amida's hands, not in the believer's and not in a priest's. Arguably, expulsion from the sect might be conducive to true faith in that it could make one realize even more deeply that he or she has no possible way to reach salvation except by putting the whole process in Amida's hands.

If Honganji members at the time saw the issue this way, the threat of expulsion from the sect would have become meaningless. To some extent, so would membership in the sect because salvation rested with Amida and in the believer's relationship with Amida. Smaller communities of believers, which already existed at temples and *dōjō,* could be formed without the need for a rigidly structured hierarchical organization. In Europe's Christian context, similar beliefs emphasizing the centrality of an individual's relationship with God led to the Reformation, which rejected the authority of the Pope.

Yet Honganji retained its Pope, and the threat of expulsion retained its terrors. This makes sense only if Rennyo's rules defined matters of faith, and expulsion denied an individual's ability to have faith. Otherwise, the central relationship for a believer was the one between him or her and the Honganji sect—just as for a fifteenth- or sixteenth-century Roman Catholic, whose primary relationship was between him or her and the church.

When viewed within the terms of the European Reformation, then, Honganji was a contradiction. The Roman Catholic church taught lay members that if they belonged to the church and participated in its sacraments, they could be saved. The priests had the ability to mediate between the member and God, as could saints, and could forgive members' sins on God's behalf. By contrast, Honganji explicitly denied the priest's or Patriarch's ability to mediate between the believer and Amida or to grant salvation to people. They merely shared Shinran's teachings and helpfully pointed out heretical (i.e., competing) interpretations of his works. Yet, to preserve Honganji's authority and institution, consciously or not, its leaders needed to make sure that expulsion had serious consequences.

To sum up, behind Rennyo's rules of behavior we can glimpse a more fundamental struggle between the institutional need to control the members' disruptive behavior and the difficulty of doing so in an institution based on a concept of faith experienced by individuals. Rennyo resolved this conflict by devising a set of rules that carefully defined true faith by how it manifested itself outwardly, such that people who disobeyed the rules thereby showed their own *lack* of faith. He still expected members who had not yet attained true faith, but who aspired to it, to observe the same set of rules, even though those rules were grounded in his definition of faith. Rennyo's attempts to regulate his members' behavior failed to keep good relations between sect members and other religious and political authorities, but it did set a precedent for future Honganji Patriarchs to define certain kinds of behavior as demonstrating faith or, by extension, a decided lack of it. In this way, Honganji was not nearly as radical a faith religion as Methodism, and it had a rationale to retain its Patriarch and hierarchy.

Disorder

Meanwhile, the reconfiguration of political power that began in the 1460s continued unabated, and Honganji members were soon to be heavily involved. In Echizen, once held by the Shiba family, a *shugo* house that was experiencing difficulties even before the Ōnin War broke out, the struggle for control pitted two deputy-governor houses against each other: the Asakura and the Kai. Asakura Toshikage, previously allied with one faction in the Ōnin War, the western army, changed sides and joined the eastern army in the second month of 1471[83] in exchange for an official appointment to the post of *shugo* of Echizen, somewhat in advance of his taking actual control of the whole province. (Alliances in the Ōnin War and afterward were fluid and, predictably, were normally concluded with an eye to individual advantage rather than to supposed loyalties.) Toshikage completed his conquest of Echizen on 1472/8/6 by defeating his Kai opponents decisively on the battlefield. The surviving Kai and their local allies fled Echizen to find refuge in some of the neighboring provinces, especially in Kaga.[84]

Until 1473, the Honganji sect and its local branches stayed out of the conflict. Although some Honganji members, as well as leaders and priests, did have ties to one side or the other, individual members who were samurai or *jizamurai* no doubt fought in those capacities, but not as a group organized or led by Honganji sectarians or priests. The reigning Patriarch's close family had the most ties with warriors in the eastern army, but it also enjoyed cordial relations with some of the western army allies. Toshikage himself was reputedly a friend of Rennyo's.

Nevertheless, some Honganji temples in Echizen had historic ties with Toshikage's opponents. For example, in the middle of the fifteenth century, the temple Shōgoji, which had begun as an Amidist temple held by the Kai family, was absorbed into the Honganji sect network created by Kōgyōji temple. Shōgoji's formal affiliation took place when a priest from Kōgyōji married the daughter of the sitting priest of Shōgoji, a member of the Kai family who then retired in favor of his new son-in-law. Thus, the head priests of Shōgoji remained members of the Kai family, and the marriage brought Kōgyōji into the Kai sphere as well.[85] Furthermore, the new Shōgoji priest's uncle was a retainer in the Shiba forces formerly in control of Echizen and would die in 1475 at a battle between the Kai, allied at that time with the Shiba, and Asakura Toshikage.[86]

Armies in Kaga, too, fought for supremacy, and there the political situation was even more complicated than in Echizen. Kaga had been divided into two parts, northern and southern, each with its own *shugo*. Both were members of the Togashi family. In 1459, the northern part of Kaga was removed from Togashi hands and awarded instead to a warrior named Akamatsu Masanori, but the Togashi, represented after 1454 by Masachika (1455?–88), retained control of the southern part. When the Ōnin War broke out, both Masachika and Masanori joined the eastern faction, though Masanori soon abandoned his interests in Kaga in favor of those in his home province of Harima, approximately 250 miles to the southwest. Masachika's younger brother Kōchiyo, seeing opportunity in Masanori's flight, allied with the western faction and took over northern Kaga. Masachika contested Kōchiyo's claim, trying to gain control of the whole province, so they fought during the late 1460s and into the 1470s. The Togashi retainer band split into two factions, each supporting one of the two brothers.[87]

As long as the Kai, Shiba, and Asakura were fighting over Echizen, the struggle in Kaga involved primarily the two Togashi factions. After Asakura Toshikage defeated the Kai army and secured Echizen in the eighth month of 1472, however, the contingent that had fled to Kaga threw in its lot with Kōchiyo, who also supported the western army. Together, they were able to drive Masachika out of Kaga just short of one year later, early in the seventh month of 1473. He, in turn, fled to his eastern-army ally, Asakura Toshikage, in Echizen.[88]

Masachika's opponent Kōchiyo enjoyed the support of the Takada sect in addition to that of the exiled Kai forces and some Togashi retainers. The Takada and Honganji sects were rivals, at times bitter ones, perhaps partly because the two shared a similar doctrine, and so they competed for members within the same pool of potential adherents. The Honganji sect's claim that only Shinran's direct descendants were capable of understanding and passing down his teachings no doubt contributed to the friction between Honganji and the Takada branch, not to mention other True Pure Land sects. The claim implied, of course, that the Takada sect's teachings were invalid, though no Honganji representative said so outright.

Because of the Takada-Kai-Kōchiyo alliance and its success in Kaga, the Honganji community on the border at Yoshizaki was threatened directly for the first time since Rennyo had arrived. Within a few days of driving Masachika out of Kaga, around the tenth day of the seventh month of 1473, the Kai forces invaded Echizen, intending to reassert their claim to it. A month later, on 8/8, they engaged the Asakura army near Hosorogi-gō, where Yoshizaki was located. The Kai forces won the battle—the Asakura reportedly suffered some 70 killed and 800 wounded—but instead of pressing their advantage, they withdrew into Kaga.[89] Three weeks later, on 10/1, the Kai returned, burning territory in estates very close to Yoshizaki.[90] One of Rennyo's letters, dated two days after that raid, mentioned the danger of attacks by "*rōnin*" (i.e., the Kai exiles). Because of them, Rennyo wrote, the people at Yoshizaki had to spend all their time constructing fortifications.[91] Yoshizaki's location at the border of Kaga and Echizen, which had at one time seemed remote from the ongoing battles, rather suddenly found itself in the midst of fighting.

Masachika spent more than a year in Echizen, recruiting support for a new campaign to regain Kaga. During that year, he visited Yoshizaki[92] and there recruited a number of Honganji sect adherents to support his cause. When Masachika finally returned to fight his brother, Honganji sect members from both Echizen and Kaga would join him with apparent enthusiasm. In this case, then, the *ikkō ikki* formed in order to aid a *shugo* claimant, not for any kind of uprising.

The Honganji adherents may, however, have found even more reason to support Masachika because of the Takada sect's involvement with Masachika's brother.[93] Nearly a century later, one Honganji priest went as far as to blame the turmoil in Kaga on the sect's Takada rivals, claiming that "the Takada sect members joined with the warriors of Kaga, causing difficulties for Yoshizaki, and the province [Kaga] was plunged into disorder by their evil deeds."[94] However problematic this tale's explanation for the war in Kaga is, it nevertheless indicates that Honganji adherents may have been motivated as much by the presence of the Takada sect among Masachika's enemies, as they were by his own cause. Either way, the *ikkō ikki* formed to permit members to act as reinforcements in battle on behalf of a high-ranking warrior.

While Masachika looked for help in Echizen, Kai forces continued to harass Asakura Toshikage with border raids, although they often lost those skirmishes. After yet another unsuccessful raid in the intercalary fifth month of 1474, a representative for the Kai family went to Kyoto to consult with some of their allies. Many of them advised the Kai to keep fighting, and some offered help.[95] Following this trip, the dominant warlord of Mino Province, which had experienced difficulties because it bordered Echizen to the southeast, evidently decided that the fighting had gone on long enough. In the sixth month of 1474, the warlord forced Asakura Toshikage and the Kai exiles to accept a truce.[96] This deprived Kōchiyo of his strongest allies, creating an excellent opportunity for Masachika to regain his territory.

The push to retake Kaga began on the twenty-sixth day of the seventh month, when Masachika attacked his brother's forces at a place called Yamanouchi, in Kaga. Two and a half months later, on 10/14, Masachika's forces suffered heavy losses, so a few days later, around the sixteenth, he left Yamanouchi for Hakusan shrine in search of more allies. Not much more than a week later, on 10/24, Masachika's warriors, aided by Honganji sect adherents and shrine personnel from Hakusan, defeated the combined forces of two of Kōchiyo's top lieutenants, who reportedly killed themselves.[97] On the first day of the eleventh month, the Kōfukuji priest Jinson reported the defeat, ascribing the victory to the Honganji sect members and making no mention of Masachika: "The *ikkōshū* commoners [lit., *domin*, people of the soil] of Kaga, calling themselves the school of unhindered light, had a disagreement with the warriors, and all the warriors were expelled from the province. The deputy *shugo* sided with the warriors. The deputy *shugo* [named] Kosugi was killed, and about two thousand people of the *ikkōshū* were killed."[98]

Instead of a fight between warriors over control of a province, then, at least some outsiders saw the battle as one between warriors and non-warriors belonging to and organized by the Honganji sect. The large number of Honganji sect followers who fought may well have distracted witnesses from the warriors they had joined, and one need not accept Jinson's figures uncritically to infer the existence of so many Honganji members. People at the time generally exaggerated the numbers of those involved in battles, including the number of dead or wounded. Still, the figure of two thousand commoners dead is still higher than the mortality figures typically reported, indicating an unusually high number of nonelite fighters, far more than observers probably expected. Although later armies were quite large and drew heavily on commoners for foot soldiers, in 1474, big armies using commoners were relatively rare.

It must be noted, though, that Jinson was not alone in noticing the Honganji sect members and overlooking Masachika's soldiers, since at least some peasants also saw it as a religious war rather than a political one. In 1479, a warrior claiming ownership of some land that also was claimed by estate residents explained that the land was his as a reward for his efforts in a battle five years previously. The residents disagreed. They argued that since "the disturbance in this province was a war attacking the enemy of Buddhist law," that is, not another landed warrior, it was improper to reward battle service with a land claim. (Their appeal failed to propose an alternative, more fitting, reward.) Reportedly, the residents' assertion left the warrior speechless.[99] It is worth noting that none of the parties to this exchange were themselves Honganji adherents, as far as we know.[100] Nevertheless, both sects had been so involved in the battle that estate residents could cite their own fighting in stating their case.

Whether one credits the *ikkōshū* or Masachika for the victory, Kōchiyo suffered a catastrophic defeat, though he did not give up completely. Instead, he rallied his forces over the next few years, periodically attacking Masachika without noticeable success. Unfortunately for Masachika, his troubles would not be confined to Kōchiyo's persistence.

The assistance given Masachika, then, was the first Kaga *ikkō ikki* action, a struggle in which Honganji sect members participated specifically in their capacity as members. Their willingness to back the warrior may have resulted from the Takada sect presence in his enemy's army, to be sure. More importantly for us, though, is that they acted in support of a would-be *shugo,* they were successful, and they expected rewards.

Not long after Masachika's victory, friction mounted between him and his erstwhile allies, the Honganji sect members, and culminated the following year in a rebellion by the latter. Evidence from the period is scarce, so we can determine little beyond the fact that the rebellion took place and the Honganji sect members lost.

The most likely explanation for the rebellion is that Masachika and the Honganji sect members fought over rewards for their assistance. At least, pro-Honganji chronicles, written later, asserted that Masachika "forgot his obligations and gratitude" to the sectarians and turned against them.[101] Anti-Honganji chronicles claimed that the people of Kaga, "proud of Honganji's power, failed to send in the rents from the estates of temples and shrines" and condemned these actions as "outrageous, and unheard-of."[102] The two accounts, seemingly contradictory, might be reconcilable. As Honganji members well knew, when a warrior received villagers' help in battle, he commonly granted them a reduction in a tax called *hanzei*. Villagers came to expect the reduction and would demand it if the warrior failed to grant it. Sometimes their demands became violent, though they did not always win the debate.[103]

In Kaga, then, had Masachika indeed forgotten his "obligations," the Honganji sect members had precedent for action. Although rents were destined for temples and shrines, they usually passed through warriors' hands as well. Had Masachika failed to reward the Honganji sect members sufficiently, they might have protested by failing to cooperate with warriors and thereby withholding rents. Alternatively, the *ikki* members may have been warriors who later unilaterally claimed land as the reward Masachika had not granted. In either case, one would expect Honganji's supporters to charge Masachika with ingratitude, while their rivals charged the Honganji sect members with arrogance and greed.

Regardless of the motives ascribed to the actors, in 1475, Honganji members either formed *ikkō ikki* to protest Masachika's policies—an action typical of village *ikki*—or they did so in self-defense, as fighters. In any case, we first see unambiguously the kind of anti-authority *ikkō ikki* that defines the category for many of us: Honganji members defying a *shugo*.

The 1475 uprising may not have been entirely spontaneous, however. According to tradition, one of Rennyo's servants played a role in encouraging the members to fight against Masachika, making it seem as if Rennyo himself supported the rebellion.

As the story has it, with the dispute unresolved and tensions mounting, a delegation of non-warrior members and priests went to Rennyo at Yoshizaki for help, asking him to intervene with Masachika on their behalf. According to Honganji protocol, they were not entitled to meet the Patriarch face to face but instead had to discuss their business with Rennyo's secretary, Shimotsuma Rensō, also known as Aki no Rensō. For unknown reasons, the tale holds, Rensō seems to have felt strongly that the Honganji followers in Kaga should resist Masachika with force, although he knew that Rennyo felt otherwise.

When the delegates insisted on an audience with the Patriarch so they could hear his response for themselves, Rensō arranged for Rennyo to meet with the delegates. It turned out that the Patriarch only told them that Rensō had received his instructions, and they were to obey him. Rennyo then left the room. This encounter allowed the delegates to hear Rennyo's own voice tell them to follow Rensō, and it also followed Honganji's practice of maintaining Rennyo's position and dignity by preventing the members from speaking with or even addressing him.

Rennyo had given orders, the story claims, for Rensō to tell the Kaga members to submit to Masachika, but in fact he urged them to fight against the Kaga lord. His advice was disastrous. Masachika put down the revolt harshly, and many Honganji followers fled to Etchū, Kaga's neighbor to the east. Rennyo expelled Rensō from the sect when he discovered what advice the man had actually given.

Shortly after the debacle, Rennyo decided to leave Yoshizaki for good, departing with a small number of supporters under cover of darkness.[104] One can easily imagine the scene with Rennyo slipping out of his residence quietly and climbing into a small boat at the shore, perhaps by the light of flickering torches. Supposedly Rensō tried to accompany his master, only to be repudiated by him, and so he was left behind alone. Rensō tried to get reinstated, unsuccessfully, until he approached Rennyo in 1499, when the former Patriarch lay on his deathbed. Only then was he pardoned and allowed to be a sect member once again.[105] This, at least, is the story as told by Rennyo's tenth son, who was born more than fifteen years after Rensō's disgrace.

Some scholars believe that Rensō was made a scapegoat for what was, in fact, Rennyo's poor advice. Rennyo did decide to leave Yoshizaki for good shortly after the Kaga defeat, and his departure suggests the possibility that he intended to escape a deserved retribution. The evidence in favor of this interpretation is inconclusive, however. Knowing of Rensō's actions, Rennyo may also have feared being held responsible, albeit perhaps unjustly, and concluded that a change of residence was prudent. As it happens, Yoshizaki went unmolested, as did Honganji sect temples in Kaga, so if fear caused Rennyo to leave, it was apparently unfounded. The absence of a province-wide backlash against Honganji members and temples in Kaga also could mean that the problem concerned only Honganji members in a specific area.

True Pure Land historian Kinryū Shizuka advocates an entirely different, and intriguing, interpretation of the whole episode, arguing that the people involved in the dispute with Masachika were members of a different True Pure Land faction, the Sanmonto sect, and not Honganji adherents at all. He has found a document that describes a connection between the Honganji sect and "Ippen's *nenbutsu*," members of a different True Pure Land tradition. According to Shizuka's reconstruction, there was some kind of conflict between a faction of the Sanmonto followers and one of Masachika's retainers. The Sanmonto followers came to Rennyo to ask him to mediate and met with the results described above. After their defeat, they fled to Etchū until three years later, when they called more successfully on Rennyo's good offices, coming to an understanding with Masachika that allowed them to return to Kaga.[106]

Although Kinryū's theory is both interesting and plausible as far as it goes, it leaves several questions unanswered. If Sanmonto followers appealed to Rennyo as an intermediary, then Rennyo must have been on good terms with Togashi Masachika, as he might have been since Masachika came to power with the aid of Rennyo's followers. Yet, the sources we have identify the trouble within Kaga as caused by friction between Masachika and the people to whom he owed his success: Honganji members. If the Sanmonto, not Honganji adherents, helped Masachika gain victory, the remainder of the Kaga *ikkō ikki* story falls apart. Finally, if the troubles with the Sanmonto occurred in addition to the Honganji's friction, for another cause, why would they think Rennyo could help them? His own followers and Masachika had fallen out, so why expect him to have influence with Masachika? Answers must remain speculative.

Still, it must be said that evidence for any interpretation of what occurred in 1475 is scarce. Also, Honganji members were not the only group to be identified as the *ikkō* sect, so one ought not to equate them automatically with the groups mentioned in the documents. Although Kinryū's interpretation seems unlikely, it raises important issues.

The short-term repercussions of the 1475 incident were not great, but however minor, they contributed to the overall conditions that would give rise to further *ikkō ikki* activities. Masachika's victory weakened the sect in Kaga for a short while and increased the antagonism between him and sect members. Although the antagonism itself was relatively mild, as evidenced by Masachika's willingness to leave Honganji temples and priests alone, it existed nonetheless and would help to draw the lines of battle in a rebellion thirteen years later. Furthermore, together with the sect members' effectiveness in supporting Masachika in 1474, the next year's conflict enhanced the sect's image as a dangerous and disruptive religion, precisely the image Rennyo worked so hard to counter. Ten years after Enryakuji attacked Honganji, the fears of the elite were not allayed but rather played out. Conceivably Honganji's reputation attracted increasingly militant followers to the sect, but in any case, the reality looked ominously like the stereotype.

THREE

New Headquarters, New Ikki, *1475–1489*

The fourteen years Rennyo continued to serve as Patriarch before stepping down in 1489 saw a number of changes within the sect and in the Hokuriku that had important consequences for Honganji members and *sengoku* politics. Within the sect, Rennyo would rebuild Honganji temple on a grander scale, and the new compound reflected the sect's increased importance within Kyoto society as well as the greater wealth it reaped from its expanding membership. The new headquarters gave the Honganji sect and its followers a new and stable center, which no doubt contributed to the hardening of sectarian identity. By the time Rennyo retired, the identity had solidified.

The political situation in Kaga deteriorated in the 1470s and 1480s as Togashi Masachika failed to create a strong central government for the province, and Honganji members played a highly visible role in the events. In 1488, Masachika would be toppled by a coalition of his own retainers and humbler Honganji members, an event that shocked members of the shogunate and imperial court. By helping to overthrow Masachika, Honganji members confirmed warriors' and courtiers' impressions of them as militant, dangerous, and unpredictable. This image came to play a critical role in Honganji's political future.

For most of the two years following Rennyo's departure from Yoshizaki, he lived at Deguchi, in Kawachi province, writing letters and organizing followers primarily in the provinces of Kawachi, Settsu, and Izumi. Rennyo also conducted the services commemorating Shinran's death, the *hōonkō*, at Deguchi. Ordinarily, the *hōonkō* took place in the temple that enshrined Shinran's sacred image, which at the time was on the other side of Kyoto in Ōtsu, Ōmi Province. Since Rennyo decided not to go to Ōtsu for the services, one might suspect that he was considering making Deguchi his new headquarters, but in fact he did not want the image removed from Ōtsu. He probably had his own reasons for not traveling, perhaps hoping to find a site for a new Honganji closer to Kyoto.

While at Deguchi, Rennyo maintained close contact with other congregations and Honganji sect priests, too. For example, he wrote letters to his old friend Hōjū in Ōmi regularly, and the two often visited each other. Rennyo demonstrated the importance he gave their relationship one winter when Hōjū decided to pay his New Year's respects to his spiritual master in person. The elderly priest set out on foot from Katata to Rennyo's base, a distance of about thirty miles. Deep snow and his advanced age made traveling difficult, so he took shelter in a mountain village on the way. His companion went on ahead to tell Rennyo of Hōjū's approach, and out of concern for his friend's health, Rennyo sent a horse to fetch the priest from his cold mountain lodgings. When Hōjū finally arrived, Rennyo greeted him immediately, and they exchanged poems that Rennyo copied for Hōjū personally, a mark of high favor.[1] Rennyo understood how to keep old relationships strong, while cultivating new ones.

Within a few years after leaving Yoshizaki, Rennyo visited southern Ōmi and selected a site for the new Honganji main temple: the village of Yamashina just to the east of Kyoto, a few miles from the original site at Ōtani. One version of events claims that Rennyo first caught sight of the hamlet of Nomura in Yamashina while out riding with Dōsai, the priest from the Kanegamori *dōjō*. At once he dismounted, deciding then and there that he had found the ideal site for his new temple.[2] If that is what happened, then Rennyo was lucky. The land was held by a temple headed by Ashikaga Yoshimasa's son, and Rennyo had close ties to the Hino family, to which Yoshimasa's wife Hino Tomiko also belonged. She also visited the new Honganji shortly after Shinran's image was installed.[3] In view of this evidence, it seems likely that Rennyo's shogunal connections had more to do with the selection of the site than his first visual impression of it did.[4]

However Rennyo settled on the location, work on the temple began as early as the spring of 1478. Collecting donations from followers to pay for the work and building the Patriarch a place to live took first priority. Rennyo's letters describing the gradual construction of the Yamashina Honganji temple show him worried about his age, perhaps feeling that the work needed to be completed quickly. He reflected that he was 64 years old when he began work, already older than his father or grandfather had been when they died.[5] He need not have worried quite so much; he would live at least another twenty years.

Although the Patriarch's main lodgings were built first, the second project was more important: building a new Founders Hall to receive the image of Shinran that had been left in Ōtsu for so many years. When Rennyo asked his followers for contributions, members in southern Kawachi went to Yamato to get timber for more than 50 pillars, he noted, and work on the hall began in 1480. By 1480/8/28, the altar was being installed and prepared to receive the image. That night, Rennyo wrote, he could not sleep. He thought if he could complete a new Founders Hall during his lifetime, he could die "with an easy heart." Shinran's image was transferred to its new home on the eighteenth day of the eleventh month of 1480.[6]

Rennyo's plans for the temple were not yet complete. Next, he envisioned a large gate for the Founders Hall—his son

Jitsugo says this was a Chinese-style gate, so it was probably expensive[7]—and finally a main hall to hold an image of Amida. Work proceeded so smoothly that the image was installed in the new main hall by 1483/6/15, though the roof tiles were not yet in place. Rennyo sent to Kawachi for a tiler to do the job, which was finally completed, roof tiles and all, less than two months later, by 8/22.[8]

The buildings themselves were not large. The interiors of the Amida and Founder's halls were both square, measuring not quite eighteen feet wide and deep—hardly imposing dimensions, though the Amida Hall could boast a veranda that was just under six feet wide on the eastern side and about half that length on the remaining sides.[9] Within the temple precincts were gardens, even a bridge, that Rennyo planned as carefully as he did the buildings; but Chinese gate or no, the Yamashina Honganji did not set out to be overwhelming in its grandeur.

It did, however, set out to be secure. In addition to the religious facilities, the new Honganji boasted earthworks, moats, and other fortifications. The increase in membership and Rennyo's friendship with the shogun's in-laws were not enough to erase the memory of Enryakuji forces overrunning the Ōtani Honganji, and Rennyo was not a man to take chances.

Just as the Yamashina Honganji was being completed, Rennyo's oldest son Junnyo died at the age of 42. Junnyo had married twice and had three daughters with his wives but no sons. A son was adopted from a different True Pure Land branch that had come to be affiliated with Honganji doctrinally as well as by marriage; one of Rennyo's daughters had married the head priest, and Junnyo adopted one of their sons. It is said that this adopted son could not become Patriarch, precisely because he had been adopted and was not descended biologically from the male line; so, Junnyo's adopted son was installed at Kōzenji, in Deguchi.[10] Jitsunyo, Rennyo's first son by his second wife, was instead selected to succeed his father.[11]

The rejection of Junnyo's adopted son may have been part of shifts in Honganji family and marriage policies that reflected the tightening of sect affiliation and discipline as seen in Rennyo's rules. New *ikkeshū* temples, especially in the Hokuriku, gave power to the Patriarch's sons, in Rennyo's case, and siblings in the case of his successors. They had been formed with the object of strengthening Honganji oversight of priests, their orthodoxy and behavior, and that of Honganji *monto*.

The role of Honganji daughters in marriage politics also changed. In earlier days, the daughters of Honganji priests often married into households that could help advance the interests of the sect in the secular world. By the 1480s, they frequently married within the sect, often to close relatives who were themselves Honganji sect priests. Junnyo's first wife, as we have seen, was also his aunt, Rennyo's half-sister.

It has been argued that this policy of marrying relatives was intended to intensify the concentration of Shinran's "blood" in his descendants, an explanation that has been widely accepted.[12] The central problem of this argument is the weight given to matrilineal descent, that women's "blood" relationship to Shinran mattered as much as men's. Had that been the case, however, Junnyo's adopted son could have become Patriarch. As the offspring of Rennyo's daughter, he was as much Rennyo's grandson as Junnyo's own biological son would have been. Furthermore, Junnyo and his adopted son shared the same great-grandfather, Gyōnyo—Junnyo through the patrilineal line, the adopted son through the matrilineal one.[13] The adopted son, then, had at least as much of Shinran's "blood" as Junnyo did.

At this time, evidently, what mattered for the Patriarch was direct father-son transmission within one biological main line—a narrow definition of "bloodline"—more than any concentration of Shinran's "blood" by joining different lines, and this is where Junnyo's adopted son failed to qualify. Most likely, then, relatives intermarried not to concentrate "blood" but rather to maintain a tightly knit family circle.

Another possibility exists. Lineages of all kinds, be they "blood," patrilineal, matrilineal, or social, are flexible concepts. They can be manipulated in order to justify decisions made on different grounds entirely. After all, Honganji Patriarchs reckoned their descent through Shinran's *daughter,* Kakushin. It may be that concepts of lineage changed between the thirteenth and fifteenth centuries, such that matrilineal descent was no longer so important. It may also be, however, that Junnyo's adopted son was rejected for completely different reasons—perceived incompetence, political infighting, and so on—that were justified with patrilineal rhetoric.

Whatever the logic behind them, marriage alliances were important for the Honganji sect, much as they were for courtiers or warriors. Within the sect, marriages helped bind together important temples in scattered locations, as the original family ties had begun to weaken because of marriages contracted with other families. In these marriages, women were not mere objects, although they were often used either as symbols indicating the closeness of religious ties, or to give birth to offspring who embodied the alliance. At times, however, women from the Honganji Patriarch's house were married to priests in troubled temples, or even sent as guardians, to help enforce the "correct" teachings and return the temple and its followers to the orthodox fold. In other words, women played an active role in running the temple and preserving the teachings. The most famous example of this phenomenon concerns two generations of priests at the temple of Chōshōji, in Echizen.

Chōshōji was first headed by Rennyo's great-uncle, who later went on to found Honrenji in Kaga as well.[14] The great-uncle's grandson had charge of the temple when Rennyo was at Yoshizaki, and at one point, Rennyo visited Fujishima, where Chōshōji was located. According to one account, when he attended a service he found himself disappointed in the priest, concluding that the man was "not a vessel to which our followers ought to be entrusted." Rennyo removed the priest from office and in his place installed the man's nine-year-old son, with a reliable female relative from the Honrenji branch of the family to keep an eye on things.[15] This story was recorded almost a century later by a man who was no friend of Chōshōji, so we might question its reliability, but

Rennyo's own letters also testify to problems with the priest. Four letters dated in the ninth month of 1473 criticize the Chōshōji congregation and its leaders for heresy.[16] Apparently the problem—or at least the concern—continued because when the 9-year-old child was old enough to be married, his first wife was another relative of Rennyo, also imported from the Kaga temple Honrenji. After she died in 1497, he was married to one of Rennyo's youngest daughters.[17]

The policy of marrying daughters back into the sect seems to have begun with the Echizen and Kaga branches before the main branch took it up. Only three of Rennyo's fourteen daughters married outside the sect: one married the priest of another True Pure Land sect that was then absorbed into the Honganji sect,[18] and the other two contributed to Honganji's advancement by marrying courtiers.

The pursuit of marriage alliances and the associations they symbolized was to have important consequences in Honganji history. By 1530, the web of alliances would be extremely complex and ultimately important to Honganji policy in Kaga, contributing to what was, in essence, a civil war within the sect. For half a century, however, the policy worked well in binding the sect together.

Other Ikkō Ikki *in the Hokuriku*

While Rennyo was proselytizing from Deguchi and realizing his dream of rebuilding the Honganji temple at Yamashina, his followers in the Hokuriku were becoming increasingly active politically. Their strong sense of exclusive religious identity helped Honganji members act as a group, rather than through some other possible framework for uniting people across village boundaries. Religious services provided a gathering place and an opportunity for people from different towns, and possibly of different social levels, to discuss weather, taxes, and other everyday topics. Although other venues also offered this chance, when it came to taking direct action, the Honganji sect had two great advantages. One was that, by all indications, its members believed that they acted with Amida's support and that Amida's strength overshadowed that of other divine beings. The other was that people's shared religious identity made possible an *ikki* that transcended boundaries of political geography and social distinctions, that resulted in numerical strength and, most likely, in military prowess or experience.

As a result, Honganji members participated actively in the events of their day, and their activities were likely to be reported by others because they were highly visible. Etchū witnessed some battles with *ikkō ikki* as participants, as did Hida, although the details of the events are unclear. In Kaga, after helping Togashi Masachika gain power and then unsuccessfully rebelling against him, the Honganji sect followers and *ikki* did not melt away but rather, along with Honganji sect temples, began to help rule the province.

Although *ikkō ikki* activities were likely to be noted by others, usually in passing, primary sources for many of their actions are scarce. As a result, historians are left to sift through secondary sources, especially those of the genre known as war tales, fictionalized accounts of battles often written long after the participants had died. Because such tales were based on real events, they are often valuable, more so when there are other sources against which to check them. As fiction, though, much of the detail must be dismissed, especially that which relates to anecdotes about participants, however appealing the stories may be. Explanations or attributions of motives are always and everywhere suspect. A problem arises, then, when these war tales are the only remaining sources of information about a disturbance. One can often determine that something similar to what is described in the war tale happened, but the stories reliably provide only the barest outlines of events. The story of the Etchū *ikkō ikki* is one such example.

Our narrative comes from a work called *Tōsōki* (lit., "war chronicle"), which survives in three copies, none of which date from earlier than the second half of the eighteenth century.[19] According to *Tōsōki*, after the 1475 failed uprising against Togashi Masachika, a number of the defeated Honganji sect priests and adherents fled to neighboring Etchū and took up residence at or near Zuisenji temple. Some six years later, Masachika appealed to an Etchū warrior, Ishiguro Ukon Mitsuyoshi, to burn down the temple and kill the priests and refugees, for unknown reasons; perhaps Masachika feared the exiles would mount another uprising. Mitsuyoshi, eager to help out a neighbor (and no doubt to avoid an invasion), assembled a force including over two hundred men recruited from a nearby Tendai sect temple called Sōkaiji and attacked in the second month of 1481.

Zuisenji, having heard about the upcoming attack, made plans for defense and, in addition to their own forces, were helped by a group of Honganji sect members from a place called Yuwakudani, in Kaga. While Ishiguro Mitsuyoshi and his allies were busy with Zuisenji, the Yuwakudani contingent went behind his lines, first burning Sōkaiji and then attacking Mitsuyoshi's home base, Fukumitsu castle. In the end, Ishiguro recognized defeat, withdrew to another temple, and there committed ritual suicide. As a result, the war tale concludes, Zuisenji and another Honganji sect temple divided the *kuni*[20] between them and established their rule.[21]

Although some historians have accepted this narrative as factual, others have demonstrated that the story must be largely dismissed. Many of its details are patently false, and at least one real historical figure who is named as taking a conspicuous role in the action was not yet born. Nevertheless, no extant documents dated after 1481 mention the Ishiguro family of Fukumitsu castle or the Tendai temple Sōkaiji. This suggests that both places may well have been destroyed, whether in an *ikkō ikki* battle or otherwise. Furthermore, after 1481, Honganji branch temples moved more freely into areas in Etchū where they had not been before, perhaps because they were forbidden, another indication of an important shift in Etchū at about the time of the supposed battles.[22]

The most compelling evidence of some kind of league action in Etchū at this time comes from two documents about an estate in Etchū, which date from about the same time as the purported conflict. In the first and most important, a letter to the estate holder reports trouble with local people who, acting in concert with the *ikkōshū*, refused to send in their rents. When pressure was applied to make them pay up, a group planned a *do ikki*.[23] The letter unfortunately clarifies very little about the purported action. People on a number of estates in Etchū (and elsewhere) followed precisely the same pattern without the help of Honganji adherents,[24] so what difference the *ikkōshū* made remains speculative. The second document simply follows up the first, reporting the punishment of the peasant ringleaders.

These two letters are so far the only contemporary documents that shed any light on the *Tōsōki* story at all. As a result, one can say no more than that something occurred in Etchū around 1481 and that it probably involved the Honganji sect. Possibly as a result, the Ishiguro family of Fukumitsu castle and the Tendai temple of Sōkaiji were both destroyed.[25] If the war tale is to be believed, *ikkō ikki* still did not attack or intend to overthrow the existing government of Etchū but rather responded to an attack on one of their temples by hitting the enemy at home. Again, this looks more like a warrior *ikki* than an uprising. If the letters refer to the fighting on which the war tale was built, then it is not even clear that the Honganji sect had much to do with it. Rather, it sounds like the kind of trouble that estates throughout Japan experienced, with or without Honganji adherents.

There also appears to have been a conflict in Hida province, possibly in 1485, though again the sources are unreliable, and nothing but the mere outline is clear.[26] In this case, the local overlord, alarmed at what he saw as the increasing power of the Honganji branch temple Shōrenji, attacked it. At first the temple defended itself and forced the overlord into flight, but he regrouped and returned to the battle. Ultimately, Shōrenji lost; its head priest died in the battle, and his older brother disappeared. A servant fled into either Kaga or Echizen, taking the priest's child and the temple's treasures for safekeeping. Rennyo intervened to mediate between the overlord and Honganji followers in Hida, but the situation was not resolved until two years after his death, in 1501, when a descendant of the Shōrenji priest's family married a descendant of the overlord, signaling that a settlement had been made.[27]

As with the Etchū *ikkō ikki*, there are no supporting documents for this battle. Some time after 1501, there is some indication of a close relationship between the overlord's family and the Honganji sect, which corroborates the end of the story as the war tales have it.[28] However, even Rennyo's negotiations are only found in the tales, not in the contemporary record or in his son's copious biographical writings. Shōrenji certainly was destroyed at some point and re-established in Hida during Jitsunyo's tenure as Patriarch, though little more than that can be said with certainty.[29] Again, members appear to have formed *ikkō ikki* in order to defend their temple from attack, not as any attempt to do away with the warrior overlord. The bare outline of *ikkō ikki* fighting against overlords is accurate, but the overlords started the battles, not the *ikki*.

Although it is hard to draw conclusions based on the kind of evidence that exists for these conflicts, one point is worth making: Kaga was not the only province in which Honganji members found themselves in battle somehow. The temple in Hida lost, whereas the one in Etchū appears to have won, suggesting that the latter enjoyed a good deal of battle readiness and the help of some warriors or *jizamurai*. Both battles had long-term if mild repercussions. The more that Honganji members appeared to authorities in Kyoto to be politically and militarily active, the more pressure was put on Rennyo and his successors to restrain their followers' militancy, or to encourage it, depending on the circumstances.

Ikkō Ikki *as Administrative Units in Kaga, 1473–1488*

After the 1475 skirmish with Masachika, Honganji members did not simply fade out of the picture in Kaga. Rather, leagues comprising Honganji members remained active there, and Honganji temples also played a role in local administration. Because of this, some historians have declared that 1473 began more than a century of *ikki* rule in that province. This assessment, however, glosses over the rule of Togashi Masachika, who actually came to power in 1473, and his suppression of Honganji members a few years later.

Therefore, *ikki* rule did not start until after Masachika's death, if then, and yielded around 1530 to rule by Honganji itself, which effectively became the province's *shugo*. Nevertheless, *ikki* had a role in Masachika's polity, just not a dominant one. Honganji sect temples also exercised some authority in Masachika's Kaga, but overall, Honganji had little power over the *ikki*, or indeed over its own members generally, in the fifteenth century. It owed its later power to the actions of its followers and the resulting pressure from the civil authorities on Honganji to control them. This process began while Rennyo was at Yoshizaki—his eleven rules were a part of it—and it would continue, especially when Honganji members formed *ikki* in Kaga.

As supporting documents make clear, the leagues had no institutional role within the Honganji sect. They were not affiliated with specific temples,[30] had no religious oversight, and needed no authorization from any sectarian official to act. Nevertheless, since most or all of the *ikki* members were also Honganji adherents, presumably the sect's leaders had mechanisms to punish *ikki* for civil infractions as well as religious ones. On that basis, estate owners, the court, and the shogunate appealed to Honganji for assistance when they blamed *ikki* for their troubles.

Two *ikki*, one in Nomi-gun and the other in Enuma-gun, appear by name in documents prior to 1488. After that, there seem to have been four *ikki* in Kaga, one for each county: Kahoku-gun, Ishikawa-gun, Nomi-gun, and Enuma-gun, in order from north to south.[31] Although no extant documents mention county-wide *ikki* in other districts, they do occasionally mention the activities of smaller Honganji sect groups and temples during the 1480s. *Ikkō ikki* did not rule Kaga, but they were not absent from its politics.

In 1482, perhaps because of continuing disorder within the province, Enryakuji complained that, thanks to the Honganji sect, Kaga had become a "province without a master."[32] Kaga did have a master, though, in the person of the *shugo* Togashi Masachika, who continued trying to consolidate all power in Kaga. Honganji temples and members had some influence in Kaga, as Enryakuji averred, but they did not dominate the scene. Temples of other sects, warriors, and autonomous villages all had a hand in collecting and forwarding rents to estate owners in Kyoto and taxes to warriors, as well as in adjudicating disputes in their locales.

The estate (*shōen*), perhaps the best-documented type of land ownership in Kaga, provided the stage for much of the competition among these groups. Landholding in the form of estates was a complicated business, in part because it concerned rights to income from the land more than actual ownership of the land itself. Before addressing the question of responsibility for and power to administer territory, then, it may be helpful to review, in broad terms, the workings of a *shōen*.

A *shōen* encompassed several villages, or parts of villages, in a given area and usually belonged to a court aristocrat, temple, or shrine. Its internal administration consisted of a bewildering array of rights and responsibilities, from those held by cultivators at the bottom, to those of the owners at the top. By the late fifteenth century, in practical terms and in the simplest form, cultivators paid rents to the intendant (*daikan*), who worked on the village level. The *daikan* in turn sent these on—minus his own cut—to the administrator who held the appointment of *ryōke*. He in turn sent rents on to the owner. Any of these actors could withhold rents.

Most commonly, however, samurai filled the posts of *daikan* and *ryōke*, and, in addition to rents, they collected taxes for themselves, the *shugo*, and the shogunate, under whose jurisdiction they fell. So, when difficulties arose with the collection of the various levies, the shogunate mediated the conflicts between owner and samurai, even though the samurai worked on behalf of the estate owner. Owners who had not received their due appealed to the shogunate to have the income forwarded. Usually, the shogunate then issued orders to the offending warrior, to his superiors including the *shugo* (who sometimes *was* the offending warrior), and to the cultivators on the estates, should they need to direct their payments to a new warrior.

Owners could also request that the shogunate restore the estate to "direct control," which meant that they held the *ryōke* rights and could appoint *daikan* themselves. Alternatively, the shogunate might instruct the cultivators to send their payments directly to the owner. Direct control had its limits: the samurai who surrendered the *ryōke* rights could also sue the shogunate to have them returned, especially if his family had held *ryōke* rights to the same estate over several generations.

As the owners continued to lose income from their estates, they and the shogunate began to appeal to any other institution or group that the owners thought could help get it reinstated. The petitions that owners sent to the shogunate and others, and the orders subsequently issued by the shogunate, yield clear information about the patterns of and parties to the disputes.

The situation in Kaga differed from other places only in the extent to which the *ikki* and Honganji sect temples were involved, and even at that, many other provinces experienced parallel complications. Different regions had different configurations of power, and documents clearly show how fragmented rule was by the end of the fifteenth century.

A consistent aim of the *sengoku* daimyo who asserted power at this time and later was to assume their own direct rule over as much territory as they could hold. They succeeded in part by sweeping away prior systems of landholding and claiming the right to dispose of their lands unilaterally. The histories of two estates, Kuratsuki-no-shō and Nukata-no-shō, and the Kaga holdings of Kenninji, an important Zen temple in Kyoto, demonstrate some of the challenges of maintaining order in the *shōen* and indicate why daimyo might wish to abolish the estates. They also uncover the diversity of *ikki* alliances and actions in Kaga.

In 1481 Kaga, *ikki* were in the mix of authorities, but there was no single province-level league and only two *gun*-level leagues, not four. Instead, multiple *ikki* of different sizes acted independently and with different aims. One *ikki* usurped the power and income of the estate owners, while another *ikki* elsewhere helped the shogunate get the rents to the owner. Surprisingly, at one point an *ikki* issued orders *to* a Honganji sect temple, an incident that raises the question of who, exactly, formed the league.

Kuratsuki-no-shō

By 1476, an *ikki* had illegally claimed jurisdiction over land in Kuratsuki-no-shō, an estate that straddled the border between Ishikawa-gun and Kahoku-gun. The league's seizure of the land may have been a part of the previous year's rebellion against Masachika, and, in any case, they did not maintain it for long as the shogunate directed them to return the lands to the previous administrator, a warrior.[33] Apparently the *ikki* obliged, as this warrior and his family exercised authority in this area even under Honganji rule, until 1544.[34]

Given the scant evidence available, we know few specifics about the *ikki,* including who belonged to it.[35] Although *ikki* formed regularly at the time, even in regions with a weak Honganji presence, historians routinely designate *ikki* in Kaga as *ikkō ikki,* if only because of the Honganji sect's dominance. Any *ikki* formed of local people almost surely included Honganji members because they were so prevalent.

In this case, the timing suggests that Honganji members dominated or even monopolized the *ikki*. The seizure of control would have taken place in 1475 or 1476, just the time when some Honganji members might have unilaterally rewarded themselves for helping Togashi Masachika gain power. The document does not say if the *ikki* came from outside the village and seized the land, or if the *ikki* consisted of villagers pushing out the estate administrator. In any case, the *ikki*'s appropriation of land corresponds to the widespread perception of *ikkō ikki* in general: Honganji members chasing out samurai, seizing control, and refusing to pay rents and taxes.

Nearly ten years later in 1485, the shogunate appealed for help to a major Honganji sect temple that was located twenty miles to the south of the Kuratsuki-no-shō.[36] The warrior controlling the estate since 1476 had again been displaced, and the shogunate asked the temple to cooperate in dislodging the interloper: the *shugo*, Togashi Masachika. The letter calls on Shōkōji, an *ikkeshū* temple and thus an extension of Honganji, to act because the temple bore responsibilities for overseeing the area. Ironically, here the shogunate ordered a temple of the Honganji sect to fight against the province's *shugo*.

If the shogunate appealed to other authorities in Kaga, such as other temples or *shugo-dai*, copies of the letters seem not to have survived. Perhaps because the transgressor sat at the top of the provincial chain of warrior command, shogunate officials may have wanted to reach out to a different, non-warrior, authority that seemed able to provide fighters to enforce the shogunate's orders. It seems unlikely that Shōkōji was the only effective authority in Kaga at that time, though it may have been the most effective authority near Kuratsuki-no-shō, where the *shugo* was intent on bringing the area under his sole command. In any event, we know only that the Kyoto authorities believed that the temple had some military capacity that would enable it to help enforce the shogunate's orders.

The documents relating to Kuratsuki-no-shō appear to show that some Honganji adherents opposed the *shugo* and his retainers by taking their land and that Honganji temples, or at least Shōkōji, exercised some power that could also oppose the *shugo* yet obey the shogun. Documents from other holdings show more variations on the theme of interaction among competing authorities.

Nukata-no-shō

Nukata-no-shō, like Kuratsuki-no-shō, straddled a border between two Kaga *gun*, though in this case those were Enuma and Nomi. In 1463, the shogunate had awarded the aristocratic Nakanoin family direct control of its holdings in Nukata-no-shō.[37] According to official records, however, the family had difficulty maintaining its authority against the counter-claims of their former agents, the Asahi warrior family.

The Asahi family was not the Nakanoins' only problem either as the *shugo* also attempted to take over their lands in 1477. In this case, according to Nakanoin Michihide, "Honganji members [*monto*] acting as the *ikki* of the two counties, Nomi and Enuma,"[38] helped a representative of the *shugo* in his conquest. When the shogunate sought to assist the courtiers, it appealed to the greatest authority in the Honganji sect: Rennyo. Officials sent a letter informing him of the situation and telling him to make his followers desist by expelling the Kaga members from the sect.

The shogunate and Nakanoin Michihide seemed to share the perception that Honganji members answered to their temples. Alternatively, they might have hoped that the *ikki* members were not warriors bound to Masachika, but rather villagers outside the *shugo*'s direct chain of command. In that case, the Honganji members might be more loyal to their Patriarch than to their governor. Either way, their expectations were not borne out.

Rennyo replied that issuing such an order would be difficult since he was no longer in Kaga, implying that he had either little influence on, or little responsibility for, what happened there in his absence. Nevertheless, he offered to expel from the sect not all Kaga followers but only those members who sided with the *shugo*'s representative in taking over the estate. Rennyo's answer irked Michihide, who probably thought the Patriarch was disingenuous and simply refusing to exercise his authority.

In Rennyo's letter of reply to Michihide, he stated that not all Honganji members sided with the interloper, thereby separating the *ikki*, whatever its composition, from the Honganji sect as a whole, despite Michihide's impression. The offer to expel members who sided with the *shugo*, a move that Michihide found inadequate, was a major concession on Rennyo's part. At another time, he would equate expelling members with physically harming himself,[39] and there is good reason to suppose that followers would have taken the threat of expulsion very seriously as well.

Furthermore, Rennyo apparently had limited options for punishment. He could scold, threaten expulsion, or expel members. At no point does he seem to have considered fines or physical restraint as sanctions that he, as Patriarch, could impose on lay members. Patriarchs could punish priests, or their Shimotsuma retainers, in any of these ways, but although the line between priest and lay member was blurred, it seemed to come into focus with regard to punishment. For members, Rennyo could impose little but expulsion.

The short-term outcome of Rennyo's offer is unclear since no extant evidence follows up on that particular exchange. Two years later, Michihide went to Kaga himself to administer his holdings and stayed for two years, so at least we know that he held onto them.[40] Neither the leagues nor the governor's agent again appeared in letters disputing control over the estate, though the Asahi warrior family continued to press its suit for several more decades, albeit unsuccessfully.

In Nukata-no-shō, Honganji members helped the *shugo*, Togashi Masachika, to expand his territory and authority, in contrast to their opposition to him in Kuratsuki-no-shō, both in the 1470s and later. The shogunate's and Nakanoin Michihide's letters make the same assumptions about the powers and responsibility of Honganji sect temples with regard to their members. Rennyo flatly denied both, although he implied that the case might have been different were he still in Kaga. Again, the evidence is clear on the Kyoto peoples' expectations of the temples' power and less clear on the temples' real capabilities vis-à-vis *ikki*.

Kenninji's lands

Letters from a third set of holdings, those more scattered than the ones we have just discussed though all in one *gun*, Nomi, reflect a surprisingly different relationship among *ikki*, temples, and the shogunate. In 1487, villagers on the holdings of a subdivision of Kenninji, a shogunate-sponsored Zen temple in Kyoto, stopped sending in their various rents and dues. Kenninji appealed to several different authorities, including officials of the Kaga *shugo*, to order the villagers to pay what they owed.[41] The Kyoto temple received a reply to these orders from a group identified only as the *gunjū* (lit., within the county, a designation that referred to an *ikki* at the county level).[42] The *ikki*'s letter acknowledged receiving orders from the shogunate, Kenninji, and the governor, and offered to discuss the situation through a messenger.

Provincial officials did not leave matters up to the *gunjū*, however. Three weeks after the league's reply to Kenninji, two more letters went directly to the villagers responsible for the payments, one from the deputy governor and one from other provincial officials, once again ordering that the rents and dues be paid.[43] Nearly a month after that, the *gunjū* wrote to Shōkōji about the problem. Shōkōji was the same temple that the shogunate had turned to for help in Ishikawa-gun. The league passed on to the temple the shogun's order to collect the outstanding rents and dues.[44] The outcome of the order is unknown.

This *ikki*, then, was in a position to receive and obey orders from the shogunate and *shugo*, not to mention from estate holders. They made efforts to cooperate and even passed the shogunate's orders on to an important Honganji sect temple. Therein lies one of the seeming peculiarities of this case. If the *ikki* consisted of, or was dominated by, Honganji members, on what basis were they giving orders from the shogunate to Shōkōji, instead of the shogunate writing directly, as it had in Kuratsuki-no-shō? The *ikki* in this case must have been independent from the temples, and the way the various letters were addressed—from shogunate and shugo to *ikki*, from *ikki* to Kenninji and also to Shōkōji—strongly suggests that the shogunate recognized the *ikki*'s authority and possibly that the *ikki* derived its authority from the shogunate. In that capacity, as the shogunate's agent, an *ikki* might be justified in giving orders to a temple regardless of their members' religious bonds and relationships.

None of these incidents, or even the events in any one locale, represents a "typical" *ikki*, though one might say the complete set illustrates typical *ikkō ikki*. The typicality lies in the diversity of the *ikki*'s membership. Whatever the Kyoto authorities thought of them, Shōkōji's interactions show that the *ikki* were independent groups, not directly bound to the temples, though in some cases amenable to their guidance. The priests' moral authority over them was real but limited.

If any of an *ikki*'s actions seem inconsistent—their support of and resistance to Togashi Masachika, for example—their conduct was no more contradictory than Masachika's or that of other warriors at the time. Masachika and his officials supported the shogunate's efforts to collect funds for the estate owners in certain cases, but at other times, they tried to take estate lands for themselves. It makes more sense to think of the Kaga *ikkō ikki* as several *ikkō* leagues rather than as one large Kaga *ikki*. In spite of their common religion and, probably, similar socioeconomic composition, each *ikki* acted according to its members' own best interests, which could vary even within the same province.

To sum up, landholders of all kinds were losing control of their holdings and called for help from anyone who might be able to provide it. One Kyoto temple, unsure what to do in a situation involving its holdings in Kaga, wrote four appeals to collect evidence: one each to its warrior official, to Shōkōji, to the Enuma-gun *ikki*, and to the villagers on the estate.[45] These scattershot appeals indicate which persons or groups the temple thought *might* have been able to help. By the 1480s, those in this position included Honganji temples, but they also still included warriors and temples belonging to other sects. After 1473, Honganji temples, followers, and leagues contributed to Kaga rule, but they did not supersede all other administrators.

Masachika's Downfall

Togashi Masachika sought to enhance his control of Kaga by ignoring the prerogatives of estate owners and the shogunate, as we saw in Nukata-no-shō, for example. In 1477, the Kōfukuji priest Jinson lamented in his diary that, "The nearby provinces like Echizen, Kaga, Ōmi, Mino, Owari, Tōtōmi, Mikawa, Hida,

Noto, Yamato, and Kawachi neither obey the shogun's orders nor send in any of the rents. Aside from [troubles in] those [provinces], there is fighting in Kii, Settsu, Etchū, and Izumi, and so they also do not send in the rents." He noted further that even the provinces under the shogun's direct rule disobeyed his orders; elsewhere, in the rare cases when a governor tried to obey, his deputies and those under him would not. He ruefully concluded that, "the country of Japan completely fails to respond to orders."[46]

The situation did not improve soon either. Two years later, the courtier Konoe Masaie reported that his family's holdings "all [existed] in name and not in reality."[47] Togashi Masachika's incursions appear to have grown in number. Along with Nakanoin Michihide, who complained of the governor in 1477, other estate owners sought help in restraining Masachika's forays, including courtiers Sanjōnishi Sanetaka and Kanroji Chikanaga.[48] The problems with the governor continued and may have worsened; in 1480, the shogunate ordered the Kaga warrior Isshiki Masahiro to punish the governor's various incursions.[49] Again in 1486, the Kyoto Zen temple of Tenryūji complained that one of the governor's vassals had collected rents but had not sent them in.[50]

The evidence of sect-related incursions on estate owners' prerogatives is less clear. The *ikki* or sectarians sometimes interfered with estates much as the governor did, but sometimes they intervened to enforce the owners' rights. Disruptive Honganji sect members could include warriors, as was the case with Suzaki Keigaku, who would later fight conspicuously on the side of the *ikki*. He installed himself by force as a local manager (*daikan*) on an estate in 1485.[51] The owner of the estate complained, indicating that he did not think this would result in an improvement to his income, and no doubt it did not. In other cases, the disruptive members were of lower status.

In one interesting case, a temple in Kyoto complained about a group of ten Honganji sectarians who had failed to forward rents from one of its estates, despite a prior agreement to do so. This time, though, the ten members acted not on their own behalf but rather because they were suborned by yet another estate-holding temple, which had a rivalry with the one that owned the estate. The importance of the Honganji connection here is debatable.[52] Elsewhere *ikki* continued to help the owners, as in 1487, when the *ikki* of Nomi-gun helped to restore payments to Kenninji, as we have already seen.

The inroads Togashi Masachika and his vassals made on the estates, financially and administratively, are typical of how daimyo of the *sengoku* period established themselves and their domains. Their policies ultimately made vassals dependent on the daimyo for position and income, and effectively deprived estate owners of title to their lands. Masachika, however, was one potential daimyo who failed.

The remaking of a provincial administration was a difficult business, of course, and others besides Masachika failed to complete the process. Most scholars blame Masachika's downfall on the Honganji members and their leagues, arguing that the *ikki* were from the start heading toward a confrontation with him, one they believe he could never have won. Historians have ascribed the inevitable clash to various causes, ranging from the sect's ostensible religion-based egalitarianism to class conflict. At least one historian calls the Kaga *ikki* simply another warrior *ikki* with little to do with Honganji members at all. He sees the *ikki* as fundamentally decentralized at a time when the trend in government by warriors was to centralize.[53]

It *was* probably inevitable that Masachika would clash with the *ikki* because, like the warriors, they had interests to advance, and stood between the governor/daimyo and the villages. A daimyo could persuade warriors, *jizamurai*, and village leaders to leave the countryside and give up authority over land for a paid role in a different kind of military organization—a standing army based in a castle town. With separate warriors or villages, the daimyo's military resources could also convince these men that he could force them off their land, if he so wished.

Ikki, however, were different. An *ikki*, especially a *gun*-wide one, probably had a better chance of standing up to the daimyo than other warriors did. The members also had less reason to think that the risks accompanying dependence on the daimyo were worth taking. Together, they had power, and perhaps for that very reason, daimyo liked to break them up instead of trying to co-opt them. He would have no interest in harboring a group that might credibly challenge him.

Even if the daimyo could avoid a standoff with the *ikkō* leagues, his policies undermined the familiar order of society and the traditional privileges of warriors by creating a retainer band that was dependent on him, rather than on their own lands. These changes might not have resulted in an entirely new social order, but they certainly made a lot of warriors uneasy. As a result, they sometimes clung to the old privileges rather than accept a different life. Whichever group's interests dominated, if either did, many warriors and Honganji members shared a common objective: getting rid of Masachika.

In addition to the patchwork nature of local governance, Kaga's relations with other provinces in the late 1470s and 1480s reveal Masachika's weakness and fragmented authority. When the exiled Kai family, formerly of Echizen, renewed its fighting with its arch-rival Asakura Toshikage in 1479, the Kaga *shugo* could not prevent some groups from joining the Kai, in spite of Masachika's good relations with his neighbor.

The Kai made only modest headway for the first several years, and little changed in the two provinces' relationship. By 1484, though, a Kaga *ikki* had joined the Kai forces that were invading Echizen, which suggests a falling-out between the Echizen daimyo and his former Honganji allies, or some of them at least.[54] Until the mid-1480s, relations between Honganji and Toshikage had been good. Some Honganji sect temples, however, had traditionally close ties to the Kai, and they may have been involved in an attack on Echizen. In spite of the amicable relations between Asakura Toshikage and Togashi Masachika, the latter could not prevent the Kai exiles from using Kaga as their base. Nor could he stop the *ikki* from helping them.

Masachika, of course, was aware that his rule was not yet firm and, consequently, sought other means of garnering support from outside to help him consolidate both legitimacy (*de jure* authority) and effectiveness (*de facto* authority) in Kaga.[55] To gain legitimacy, he ingratiated himself with the Ashikaga shogunate, not realizing yet to what extent that institution was in decline. He arranged to be appointed *shugo* of the entire province of Kaga—his former title had given him authority over only half of it—and made a strong show of support for the shogun Ashikaga Yoshihisa (1465–89) in his expedition against Ōmi in 1487. Masachika's attempts to bolster his position in Kaga, however, would lead almost directly to his downfall.

On the twelfth day of the ninth month of 1487, Masachika answered Yoshihisa's call to join his campaign against the governor of Ōmi.[56] Few military leaders responded quickly, perhaps because they were guilty of the same kind of behavior Yoshihisa criticized and so were disinclined to punish the Ōmi governor. Masachika, however, did answer the call, and according to one report, he was the only daimyo who arrived in time to join Yoshihisa's procession leaving Kyoto.[57] (Some other daimyo joined the group later.) Several of Masachika's top vassals joined him, leaving Kaga in the hands of lesser warriors, a choice that was not the wisest but was perhaps unavoidable if he were to join the expedition.

In addition to removing his best generals from Kaga, Masachika had to increase the level of taxation to pay for his part in the campaign. From one estate alone, his representative demanded an extra payment of 200 *koku* of rice—approximately a thousand bushels—and the services of a hundred people (though he settled for a cash substitute for both levies: payment of 15 *kan* and 200 *mon*).[58] Between the increased taxation and decreased warrior presence in Kaga, not to mention the ambitions of the warriors who remained in the province, it should have been no surprise that trouble would break out while Masachika was away.

Details of the particular trouble remain unclear, mainly because of a lack of contemporary sources. We must rely, again, on a war tale, this one called *Kanchiron*. Doubtless the narrative is embellished, but most of the verifiable information is in accord with the extant evidence.[59] The war tale is the basis for the account that follows, unless otherwise indicated.

Whether because they were burdened with the extra taxation or emboldened by the diminished ranks of the samurai, or for some other reason, Honganji members organized themselves and refused to send in the rents and dues they owed. Their recalcitrance forced Masachika to abandon the shogun's expedition and return to Kaga from Ōmi at the end of 1487. Interestingly, the tale does not attribute the tax embargo to the general orneriness or arrogance of Honganji sect members. Rather, it tells us that the sectarians simply insisted they could not pay them. First, the extraordinary taxes levied in support of the Ōmi expedition had depleted their supplies. Second, they complained that the acting governor (a deputy) burned their homes, trampled their fields, and forced people to move away in order to make room for fortifications. And third, they concluded, no one had anything with which they could pay the rents.

Masachika refused to listen to their explanations, preferring to believe the rents had gone to support Honganji sect temples instead of to the appropriate recipients. The two parties refused to budge for several months with little progress toward a resolution on either side. In the fifth month, hearing that Masachika had asked for help from the daimyo of neighboring Echizen and Etchū provinces, the *ikki* leaders decided to launch an attack before Masachika's allies could arrive.[60]

If *Kanchiron* is accurate here and such an appeal had gone out, neither neighbor responded very quickly. Evidently, the *ikki* made its move close to 1488/5/26 because on that day a Kyoto priest recorded the following entry in his diary: "A *do ikki* rose up in Kaga, and the castle of Togashi no Suke [Masachika] is surrounded. Therefore, the shogun sent a messenger from Ōmi [where he was on campaign] to order Asakura to give support" to the besieged castle.[61] Asakura Toshikage did not, or could not, move quickly enough to help Masachika, however. His troops reportedly entered Kaga on 6/8 and encountered fierce opposition the following day, forcing them to withdraw.[62]

As for Masachika and the *ikki*, there was little fighting between them, even though the *ikki* forces had assembled and surrounded Masachika at Takao castle by the end of the fifth month. On the fifth day of the sixth month, one of Masachika's retainers rode out to address the *ikki*, criticizing them for their disloyalty and urging them to cease hostilities, to no avail. That same day, some five thousand horsemen from Etchū attacked the *ikki*, including in their number some of the warriors who had supported Kōchiyo and fought against Masachika, but who had decided to come to his aid this time. Unfortunately for the *shugo*, they were met by an equal force of anti-Masachika horsemen, and these warriors reportedly took the heads of three thousand Etchū men.

Returning our attention to the help from Echizen, even had Toshikage's forces persevered, it is unlikely they could have saved Masachika. On 7/6, two days after disaster befell the Etchū horsemen, some two thousand of Masachika's men rode out of the castle and attacked *ikki* forces at Nukata, but they were routed; only about three hundred of Masachika's forces survived. At that point, anticipating the worst, Masachika prepared to face defeat, arranging to send his wife and other non-combatants to safety.

The *ikki* side, tired from the fight at Nukata, put off the all-out attack for one day to give their men and horses a chance to rest. Early in the morning, between five and seven o'clock on the ninth day of the sixth month, the *ikki* army returned to the attack at Takao castle. Masachika's forces, overwhelmed, were wiped out. Masachika committed suicide along with the few vassals who had remained with him that long.[63]

Kanchiron's vivid account provides details that cannot be corroborated by other sources, but it is accurate in its broad outlines and often so where its details can be checked. The war tale's version of the cause—mistreatment of villagers and demands for excessive tribute—is not only plausible but also supported by evidence of Masachika's extra taxes. Its dates are usually correct as well, although some confusion remains about the date of Masachika's defeat.[64]

The war tale describes the *ikki* that defeated Masachika as a coalition of groups ranging from his highest retainers and *kokujin*, to priests and tanners. There is enough supporting evidence to accept *Kanchiron*'s description of the forces, though not in the numbers of combatants the war tale reports. At the top of the *ikki* coalition was Togashi Yasutaka, Masachika's uncle, who had once served as *shugo* of part of Kaga and now apparently wanted to do so again for the whole province. When the *ikki* was victorious, he was installed as his nephew's successor, serving as governor until his death.

In addition to Yasutaka and his retainers, members of local shrines, the priests from four Honganji temples, and warriors of various sorts rallied against Masachika. *Kanchiron* also mentions a samurai named Kasama Ietsugu leading a group of over seven thousand tanners and another, Yasuyoshi Ienaga, leading a group of over eight thousand *kawara-shū*.[65] Both the tanners and the *kawara-shū* may have been outcasts.

There is, however, some ambiguity about those labeled the *kawara-shū*. *Kawara* means riverbank, and the poverty-stricken people who lived there were commonly called *kawara-mono*. But Kawara is also a place name in Kaga and the base of a *kumi* organized at some point after Masachika's death.[66] Some historians see the *kawara-shū* as a precursor of the *kumi* by the same name, which would make them Honganji members.[67] In this case, however, some evidence indicates that the group designated as the *kawara-shū* might well have consisted of beggars and outcasts, the people of the riverbanks.

Nothing in the documents from which we know about the later *kawara kumi* suggests that it was nearly as large as the *kawara-shū* that joined the tanners and Honganji members in the fighting of 1488. Moreover, the *kawara-shū* was led by Yasuyoshi Ienaga and the *kumi* was identified with one Kawara Gen'emon. Since Yasuyoshi's informal name was Gen'emon-no-jō, this may have referred to him, though.

Furthermore, it is suggestive that *Kanchiron* lists the *kawara-shū* after the tanners' group of seven thousand rather than before, which would be odd if the *kawara-shū* consisted of people of higher status. So it seems most likely that these were people of low status. Why they joined the fight, however, is a different question and one even more difficult to pin down. There was nothing in Honganji practice that would have barred such people from joining the ranks of the believers. If many poor people or outcasts did join the sect, however, they left no traces other than their battlefield support, which could easily have been bought.

Completing the list of members of the 1488 *ikki* were Honganji adherents from the provinces of Etchū and Noto, who traveled to Kaga to fight alongside their co-religionists.[68] The rebellion against Masachika, then, was broad-based, suggesting that Masachika had alienated much of the population, including some of his own generals.

The scale of the rebellion is difficult to establish. It is impossible to determine how many people participated in the fighting. *Kanchiron*'s total for the *ikki* forces at the end of May was 135,000 men, 50,000 of them mounted.[69] This seems highly unlikely, and indeed war tales are notoriously unreliable when it comes to numbers because they were generally exaggerated for dramatic effect. Our Kyoto diarists are no more reliable, though, as they were too distant from the fighting to have any direct information; they simply repeated rumors. Diaries report figures of "several tens of thousands," up to 200,000,[70] and they often seem to have intended not to give accurate numbers but only to convey the idea that overwhelming numbers of people joined the uprising against Masachika.

More than anything, the figures indicate the participation of many people of relatively humble rank, rather than a battle waged only by samurai, which usually involved a comparatively small number of combatants. Those who commented on events, both at the time and later, saw Togashi Yasutaka as being installed by the *ikki* as its head—a strange perception given that an *ikki* has no head—rather than as the leader of the rebellion, which involved both *ikki* and non-*ikki* warriors. In a much-quoted phrase, one of Rennyo's sons would later write that Kaga had become "like a province held by commoners" because of the *ikki*'s success in installing Yasutaka as governor.[71] Rennyo's son evidently overlooked the *ikki*'s warrior allies. Few events underscored more clearly than this Kaga uprising one of the important lessons of the late fifteenth century: there was no longer any security for the position of warriors. Support from above, that is, the favor of the shogun, meant little or nothing because he could not help his appointees. Without the shogunate to help enforce their appointment, *shugo* became targets for ambitious underlings. Warrior organizations were being rebuilt from the bottom up.

The success of the *ikki* shocked elite society. The shogun, Ashikaga Yoshihisa, demanded that Rennyo expel from his sect all Honganji members who had joined the Kaga *ikki*. Although Rennyo had insisted for years that members obey the civil authorities and, therefore, should not have condoned the behavior of members who overthrew their duly appointed *shugo*, he hesitated to obey the shogun's command. "To expel our members in Kaga would be more painful than cutting my own body," he is reported to have said.[72]

Rennyo was spared this emotional pain, however, because of the friendship of Hosokawa Masamoto, one of the highest-ranking warriors in what remained of the Muromachi shogunate. With Masamoto's help, the shogunal punishment for the Honganji members in Kaga was reduced. Instead of expelling his followers, Rennyo was allowed to fulfill his duty by writing letters to the Kaga members that were harshly critical of their behavior, warning the sectarians that anyone who caused such trouble in the future would be expelled.[73] Perhaps even that message was painful for Rennyo to write or maybe he felt pressure to step down because of the *ikki* rebellion. In any event, Rennyo resigned his office the following year at the age of 75, and his son Jitsunyo became the Honganji Patriarch.

Rennyo, Sectarian Growth, and Religious Authority

By 1488, then, Honganji members and temples in the provinces were clearly playing significant roles in local politics. Only two of the *ikkō ikki*, in Kaga in 1475 and 1488, involved Honganji members in anything that can fairly be described as a rebellion. In the first, they seem to have withheld tribute from the *shugo* and estate owners and protested Togashi Masachika's efforts to force them to pay.

In the second, they and their allies overthrew Masachika after he had offended many levels of people: shogunal officials, estate owners, burdened villagers and *jizamurai*, even many of his own retainers. The last group, in fact, may well have been the moving force in the rebellion. Certainly, the *ikkō ikki* were only part of a larger coalition, and if they were the most numerous component, they did not take charge of the province once the dust had settled. Instead, they had a new *shugo*, Togashi Yasutaka, and the province was dominated by retainers of the Togashi.

In some other cases, *ikkō ikki* backed warriors trying to displace, and replace, *shugo*, but rather than being uprisings or rebellions, the *ikki* instead chose sides in ongoing struggles. They backed the winning side in Kaga when they helped Masachika gain power in 1473. Some *ikki* backed the losing side in Echizen, assisting the Kai family exiles in their futile struggle against Asakura Toshikage. Here, Honganji members seemed interested in changing the personnel at the top of the provincial government, not the system itself.

Scholars are still much in the dark about the *ikkō ikki* of Etchū and Hida. Nevertheless, there is no evidence that Etchū sectarians had rebellion on their mind or that anyone had set out to take over Hida. Even according to the war tales, which are anti-Honganji in tenor, in both provinces Honganji temples were attacked by warriors, not the other way around.

Thus, most *ikkō ikki* military actions up to 1488 occurred when members joined groups of samurai who were already engaged in operations defending Honganji sect temples under attack. The *ikkō ikki* administrative activities paralleled those of warriors, at times protecting estate owner's prerogatives to some degree and at others seizing their land.

In Kaga, the shogunate accepted and utilized the political role of the Nomi *gunjū,* which tried to help the Kyoto temple Kenninji continue to receive income from its estates. *Ikkō ikki* also cooperated with the *shugo,* as when the Nomi and Enuma *gunjū* helped his representative take over land held by the Nakanoin family. They did so in contravention of the shogunate's instructions, to be sure, but Masachika was their *shugo,* and they obeyed him. Although not all *ikki* actions endeared them to estate owners, they cannot be said to have resisted warrior authority, at least no more than any other warriors did.

So, we have seen *ikkō ikki* involved in a wide range of activities already. Most of the time, their activities differed little, if at all, from those of warriors, and they do not seem to have been out to create a new polity. At best, they brought a new dimension to the existing provincial structures, within which they functioned much more often than they did not.

Rennyo's contribution to the emergence of the Kaga leagues was limited. Arguably, without his preaching and *ofumi,* as well as the numerous other factors discussed previously, the sect's beliefs would not have spread so widely. Had there been significantly fewer members, the phenomenon of Honganji sect leagues could not have been widespread, and there would have been little advantage in seeking their aid, as Masachika had done. Rennyo's chief legacy to the *ikki* lay in his formulations of rules and punishments, which his successors found useful when they needed to draw on the *ikki*'s military power themselves.

As the Honganji sect expanded, Rennyo faced growing organizational and disciplinary problems, especially because some people interpreted Honganji's doctrine of faith and salvation as a challenge to the authority of other political and religious entities. As we have seen, Rennyo's primary response to this critique was to issue rules of behavior for sect members, rules that emphasized that faith in Amida was incompatible with socially disruptive behavior, or lack of respect for other gods or Buddhas.

In spite of Rennyo's efforts, Honganji followers continued to do what they had always done, even before they joined the sect: if they were cultivators, they resisted taxation they found excessive; if warriors, they supported other warriors in battle. What differentiated their actions as members of the Honganji sect from those made by non-members was that the sect provided its own organization. This Honganji organization provided a forum for cooperation that transcended village or even provincial boundaries. But other kinds of movements also transcended these limits; the large, non-sectarian *tokusei ikki* of the fifteenth century come immediately to mind. Few other movements, however, offered a framework as large or transcendent as the common religious bonds that overcame social boundaries as well as geographical ones. Warriors could find ready allies among their co-religionists. This does not mean that the religious bond rendered all members equal or that all conflicts of interest among members were overcome. It only means that those of different social statuses could join together when they had common or overlapping interests.

Rennyo's attitude toward his followers' political and military activities can best be described as ambivalent. He repeatedly exhorted them to obey the civil authorities and even threatened offenders with expulsion from the sect. Yet he did not follow through on these threats, even when Honganji sectarians in Kaga helped to oust the legitimate governor of their province. Furthermore, when he discussed religio-political matters in his letters, he told followers to hold secular law paramount, keep Buddhist law in their hearts, and follow customary law in their daily lives. These were important distinctions that nevertheless became problematic when a conflict between any two sets of laws arose. In later decades, Honganji leaders would call on followers to defend the Buddhist law—Honganji, its branches, members, and teachings—against secular law, when secular law or leaders threatened the sect's existence.

If Rennyo was reluctant to take it upon himself to regulate his followers' political actions, the ruling elite was eager to have him do so. The rules that Rennyo issued in 1473 can be seen as a reflection of that pressure, even if it was brought to bear indirectly through Rennyo's fears of retaliation against the faith in general for the misbehavior of a few. Ironically, the completely uncontroversial action of a religious leader creating rules for his community of believers would open the door to greater and more controversial power to be exercised by subsequent leaders over sect members.

One factor that differentiated Rennyo's rules from those of other religious leaders, and allowed the controversial later development of Patriarchal authority, was the nature of the sectarian community. His rules governed the behavior of believers living in ordinary, secular settings, not just those who lived in a religious community. Although his authority was ostensibly that of a teacher and moral exemplar, in formulating the rules, he proceeded to explain Shinran's concepts of faith as well as define the kinds of behavior that faith would produce. By threatening to expel members who did not follow the rules, he implicitly laid claim to the ability to recognize and certify a hopeless lack of faith. The hopelessness is only implied, but present nonetheless, because the rules make it clear that one need not have *attained* faith already to become a member of the sect, only to have the *desire* to attain faith. And the desire also would manifest itself in obedience to the rules. Rennyo's efforts to impose a kind of order on all members must have seemed far more helpful than dangerous to the authorities. It was only over time, with changing political situations and different religious leaders, that the potential for taking religious authority even farther would become manifest.

FOUR

Ikki *and a Patriarch's Orders, 1489–1525*

In Japan, the years between 1489 and 1525 were marked by turbulence and political intrigue, and Honganji and *ikkō ikki* had their own part in it. The power of the shogun continued to decline, especially after 1493 when the deputy shogun Hosokawa Masamoto deposed his superior, Ashikaga Yoshitane, and installed his own shogunal candidate, Yoshizumi (1480–1511). Masamoto's coup d'état was unprecedented at the time, but it became the standard pattern for succession in the Muromachi shogunate until its demise under Oda Nobunaga, in 1573.

Yoshitane resisted Masamoto's coup, of course, and tried to reverse it. For many years following the coup, several *shugo* supported him at one time or another, each probably hoping to be the power behind the next shogun, as Masamoto was with Yoshizumi. A serious challenge to Masamoto arose in 1506, thirteen years after he had exiled Yoshitane, when he found himself vulnerable because of a combination of ambitious vassals and succession problems. At that time, *ikkō ikki* broke out in nearly a dozen provinces throughout central Honshu, but they posed no problem to Masamoto because most of them pitted Honganji members against the deputy shogun's enemies.

Meanwhile, in Kaga the 1488 rebellion against Togashi Masachika had forestalled the emergence of a centralized provincial government with a clearly defined hierarchy of command, that is to say, a *sengoku* daimyo-style domain. Instead, Kaga continued to be ruled by a combination—the word coalition implies too much cooperation—of the new *shugo* Togashi Yasutaka, his nephew's former retainers, lesser warriors, *ikki* members, and Honganji temples. Although these groups cooperated in some ways, in others they appear to have functioned independently of each other. At times, the different groups within the province even maintained conflicting alliances, as we shall see.

Within the sect, the new Patriarch Jitsunyo consolidated the expansion and changes that his predecessor had brought about, especially supervising the editing of Rennyo's *ofumi* to produce a canonical text for the sect. Jitsunyo also strengthened the family council and collateral temples that Rennyo had created late in his life.

Jitsunyo's efforts, by concentrating on continuing and preserving Rennyo's contributions to doctrine and institutional structure, helped to give the ninth Patriarch a reputation for conservatism. According to one Honganji history, written about two hundred years later but based on earlier sources, Jitsunyo was so conservative that he would not change anything Rennyo had done, not even move a tree that Rennyo had planted.[1]

It seems all the more ironic, then, that Jitsunyo broke a major precedent by becoming the first Patriarch to order members into battle, thereby adding a basic new component to the relationship between sect leaders and followers. Previously, as we noted earlier, Rennyo had explicitly denied responsibility for *ikki* or their behavior, instead issuing rules for members that, if followed, would put a stop to the *ikki* disruptions. By contrast, Jitsunyo ended up asking members to form an *ikki* for explicitly military purposes and to attack a target he designated. That is, he added a major new element to the *ikki*-Honganji relationship, perhaps even creating a new kind of *ikkō ikki,* one that eventually enabled his great-grandson to lead the members much as a daimyo led his warriors.

If members had not cooperated, of course, the militarization of the Honganji sect could not have occurred. They did not cooperate blindly, however, nor did they necessarily follow the Patriarch's orders when those did not suit the members' interests. Subsequent Patriarchs dealt with that opposition by finding ways to ensure that the members identified their interests with the sect's, thus developing a formidable military potential.

Between 1489 and 1525, then, three basic trends affected the sect, the *monto,* and the *ikkō ikki.* One was the gradual strengthening of the Honganji sect institutionally, with a tightly linked hierarchy of collateral temples and a well-defined advisory council made up of priests closely related to the Patriarch. A second was more concerted involvement of *ikkō ikki* over a broader geographical range and in matters of national import. The third was increasing intertwinement of the *ikki* and Honganji's religious leaders. All of these trends would eventually come to affect events and governance in Kaga and elsewhere, but until the late 1520s, the province continued to be ruled in much the same fashion as before.

Post-Masachika Kaga

After Togashi Masachika's defeat and death in 1488, the advances he had made toward consolidating daimyo rule in Kaga were rolled back. The provincial government remained primarily in the hands of Masachika's retainers, for whom the new *shugo,* Togashi Yasutaka, was little more than a figurehead.[2]

In addition to the *shugo,* the former retainers and those they commanded, Honganji members and their *ikki* played a larger role than before. Owners of estates in other provinces increasingly directed their pleas for help to warriors who exercised power over ever larger areas, especially the new daimyo, whereas in Kaga they still sent letters to a multiplicity of political actors, indicating the lack of a strong or even emerging central authority.

Indeed, in other provinces strong warriors were the ones who most commonly obstructed the payments of rents.[3] In Kaga, too, before 1488 owners mostly complained of efforts by Masachika and his deputies to take over their lands. By contrast, after that date they complained of problems with lesser warriors. Honganji members and temples emerged as important actors only gradually over the twenty years or so that followed Masachika's defeat. Evidently not until the 1520s, near the end of Jitsunyo's tenure, did the shogunate turn directly to Honganji itself for help with Kaga. *Ikki*, though, remained active throughout.

Early reports of Masachika's overthrow had blamed Honganji members for the uprising, but within ten years, it was more widely acknowledged that the events involved a broader range of people. In the ninth month of 1496, for example, a Kōfukuji priest in Nara recorded that he had heard the Kaga *ikki* was "entirely the work of locals, also temples of various sects and warriors, too."[4] The reference to temples "of various sects" is tantalizing, especially because our scant evidence provides no clarification. Still, it suggests that sects besides Honganji were involved somehow and certainly indicates that a broad range of actors played roles in Kaga politics.

Many historians see Honganji *monto* behind every incident in which a Kaga village withheld payments of the various rents and taxes owed to distant claimants. They theorize that the *monto* felt free to do so because they would have feared no divine retribution for ignoring the pleas and threats of temples, shrines, and their allies, whether warrior or aristocrat. Of course, it may well be that Honganji believers did experience this lessening of fear and consequently tended to be less cowed by the traditional authorities. Yet the kinds of disruption experienced by owners of Kaga estates were about as common in places where the Honganji sect was much weaker. Clearly, not all recalcitrant villagers in Japan were Honganji members, and we have no reason to suppose that all recalcitrant villagers in Kaga were either. Besides, warriors also diverted rent and tax payments intended for others. So the prevalence of Honganji followers in Kaga did not necessarily lead to greater acts of disobedience to authority, though the lack of a strong *shugo* might have. Such a strong warrior leader might have done better at controlling both warriors and commoners in the province. Arguably, the *monto* presence actually served estate owners in a small way, by giving distant owners another institution—the Honganji sect—to which they could appeal in their ultimately doomed attempts to maintain a flow of income from their disappearing estates.

Fukuda-no-shō

Take the case of Kitano shrine's holdings in Fukuda-no-shō, which exemplifies the difficulties faced by estate owners in Kaga. On 1488/11/3, the shogunate awarded the shrine direct control of all its holdings in Kaga, a step that suggests Kitano had not been receiving the rents it expected. By the tenth month of 1489, however, a warrior named Shikichi Hikouemon-no-jō had taken over the shrine's holdings and kept the rents for himself, indicating the attempt at direct administration must have failed.[5]

The shrine tried to oust Hikouemon-no-jō with help from the shogunate, and when that proved insufficient, it asked the Honganji sect temple Shōkōji to add its influence to the effort. Shōkōji, too, proved unable to wrest the estate from the warrior, so the shrine turned back to the shogunate, again with dubious success. At one point, Kitano tried to overcome its difficulties by appointing Shikichi Hikouemon-no-jō its overseer on the estate (*daikan*), but it still did not receive the rents. In 1491, the shogunate again confirmed Kitano shrine's direct rule ordering the villagers to forward all rents to the shrine not the warrior, but this attempt, too, would fail.[6]

The reason for the shrine's appeal to the shogunate in 1489 is self-evident; less so is the legal capacity in which Shōkōji was to act. On what grounds did Kitano approach Shōkōji? None of the correspondence indicates that Honganji members played any part in Kitano's difficulties in Fukuda-no-shō, not even a lesser role as supporters of Hikouemon-no-jō. There is no indication that Hikouemon-no-jō himself was a Honganji member. Did the shrine want the temple to deploy some forces, possibly Honganji sectarians, to attack the usurper? Did it think that the temple could address the members who paid rents and order them to send the payments to Kitano instead of giving them to the warriors? Kitano's perception of Shōkōji's power is as vague as was the shogunate's in the case of Kuratsuki-no-shō, discussed in the previous chapter.

There are, nevertheless, two points to be noted here. One duplicates the point in the Kuratsuki-no-shō case: that Kyoto authorities believed, or perhaps only hoped, that Shōkōji would be willing and able to wield useful power. The second is that expectations of Shōkōji appear to have been the same as they had previously been under Masachika. The main change in the configuration of Kaga authority was the lack of a credible *shugo,* a significant change to be sure, but not one affecting the power structures of the *ikki* or Honganji sect temples.

Whatever the reasons for the appeal to Shōkōji, it yielded no visible result, as we have seen, and Kitano shrine continued to look for ways to secure its income. At some point between 1491 and 1505, the shogunate appointed a new shrine representative, Kanō Hikoshichirō, perhaps to replace Hikouemon-no-jō, but then removed him from office too because he failed to send the rents to the shrine. Once more, the shogunate awarded Kitano shrine direct control of its holdings. Hikoshichirō did not acquiesce to the change and plotted with some Honganji adherents to reassert his control of the area. In the fifth month of 1505, shogunate officials condemned the actions of Hikoshichirō and his Honganji supporters, and again ordered the villagers to send the rents directly to Kitano shrine. They were also instructed to punish anyone who sided with the warrior.[7]

In this case as well, we find Honganji members who were active but these engaged in activities different from what so many historians would expect. Instead of withholding rents and taxes for their own benefit, they were supporting a samurai who would most likely have collected even more in tribute than as a direct representative of the estate owner. For that reason, villagers tended to prefer direct rule. Therefore, it seems improbable that the Honganji followers were cultivators from Fukuda-no-shō, or at least from the portions of it held by Kitano shrine, since *monto* cultivators might not have benefited from the new circumstances.

Possibly Hikoshichirō shared Honganji sect beliefs, and the sect's members supported him for that reason. The documents do not identify Hikoshichirō as a Honganji member, however, and in the 1470s, his relatives had sided with Kōchiyo and the Takada sect followers against Masachika and the Honganji *monto*. Therefore, the Kanō as a whole seem not to have been sympathetic to Honganji, although it is always possible that Hikoshichirō belonged to a branch family with different religious affiliations.

It is a shame we know no more about the Honganji followers as that information might explain why they backed the warrior. For example, if these members depended on commerce for their livelihoods, Hikoshichirō may have offered to open markets or to protect the existing or newly forming temple towns, which encouraged trade. The most important aspect of the *monto*'s activities in this case is that Honganji members, or *ikki*, did not take control themselves, nor did they simply refuse to pay rents and taxes. In the early 1500s, evidently Kaga was still in the hands of quarreling warriors.

Four years after the incident with Kanō Hikoshichirō and the Honganji members, the Fukuda-no-shō holding was split between Kitano shrine and a member of the powerful Hatakeyama family, which also held rights within the estate. Both received payments from estate residents. Not much more than a year after that, however, in 1510, the shogunate once again returned all control to the shrine.[8]

During the twenty-one years between 1489 and 1510, then, the responsibility for collecting and forwarding rents on Kitano's lands in Fukuda-no-shō changed hands at least six times, not counting illegal seizures of authority. Similar frequent changes of rent collectors occurred elsewhere in Kaga, and sometimes the sectarians did play an important role in them.

Honganji members collected and submitted rents for one estate, Ōno-no-shō, as noted in the estate's records for 1493, for example.[9] Elsewhere, Kitano shrine appointed a Honganji sect temple—Kankiji—as its representative in another of its Kaga estates. In this area, there is no record of problems with the *monto* or *ikki*, so Kitano shrine's selection of Kankiji as manager seems unrelated to any specific local problems of members disrupting the collection of rents.[10] Rather, the appointment resembles the one enjoyed by Hongakuji in Echizen which dated from a time when there were relatively few Honganji followers in the region.

Through the 1490s, most estate owners' complaints focused on interloping warriors, not Honganji members. The instability of oversight thus resulted from the same difficulties between estate owners and warriors that were occurring everywhere in Japan at that time, although the lack of a strong *shugo* or daimyo in Kaga no doubt contributed to the problem. The documents do not support the contention that Honganji members, as *ikkō ikki,* dominated Kaga, locally or otherwise during this period. Undisciplined warriors did.

After about 1510, however, it became increasingly evident that the Honganji sect temples, members, and *ikki* were involved in ruling Kaga on a larger scale. A shogunal letter written in 1514 asked Shōkōji to help an estate representative trying to re-establish his control in a village in Kahoku-gun,[11] and one written in 1519 appealed to the *ikki* in Ishikawa-gun for help with rents.[12] In 1521, Kitano shrine wrote directly to the main temple, Honganji itself, for aid in collecting rents from *monto.*[13] The shogunate's 1514 letter to Shōkōji fits into the earlier pattern, but the later letters indicate changes in Honganji's and *ikki*'s power in Kaga.

It is important, though, not to equate *ikki* with Honganji members, any more than with villagers, as *ikki* may have included non-members even if the core participants were sectarians. Although documents from 1500 to 1525 mention Honganji and *ikki* more often than in previous ones, only in later years, especially after 1530, did the shogunate appeal frequently to specific *ikki* and to Honganji itself. During Jitsunyo's tenure, only the few documents discussed above involved them.

Although the shogunate and estate owners sometimes appealed to Honganji sect temples in Kaga for help, they still remained wary of the Honganji sectarians. The sectarians' militancy and potential military strength, demonstrated most strikingly in the overthrow of Togashi Masachika, continued to manifest themselves in ways that commanded the attention of possible enemies and allies alike. We have already seen the disturbances connected with the sect that occurred in the provinces of Etchū and Hida during the later years of Rennyo's tenure. Under Jitsunyo too, then, the province of Noto, to the northeast of Kaga, was threatened with an uprising for which Honganji members were blamed.

In 1490, several Honganji followers in Noto reportedly plotted to overthrow the governor there, "as [they had] in Kaga," but their plan was betrayed by one of the governor's retainers. The conspirators were arrested and put to death.[14] Then as now, rumors, accurate and inaccurate, spread rapidly. This particular report's validity cannot be ascertained because little documentation from *sengoku* Noto has survived, and none of it either proves or disproves the rumor. Nonetheless, people outside the province believed the report to be true, and so the Honganji sect's unsavory reputation grew.

Other events in the Hokuriku were no more reassuring to authorities in Kyoto. Kaga's governance was fragmented well into the 1520s, as were its military and political alliances, and the allies' activities. Two intertwined struggles in the 1490s involved Kaga fighters, both samurai and Honganji sect members, although Kaga itself was not the focus of either fight. The larger of the two struggles was related to fallout from Hosokawa Masamoto's coup d'état, when he ousted Ashikaga Yoshitane in favor of Yoshizumi in 1493. Seizing the occasion, the Kai family exiles tried once again to wrest power from the Asakura, who were supporting Yoshitane.

Meanwhile, the deposed shogun fled to Etchū, where governors from all the Hokuriku provinces, including Togashi

Yasutaka of Kaga, visited him on 1493/7/26.[15] Etchū would remain Yoshitane's base of operations for several years, as the former shogun gradually built a coalition of supporters. All the governors who visited Yoshitane thereby signaled their alliance with him and declared themselves to be Masamoto's opponents.

Yasutaka's decision to back Yoshitane, however, had little effect on other powerful forces in Kaga, since the *ikki,* Honganji members, and the *kokujin* who had overthrown Togashi Masachika acted independently, all pursuing their own policies. These divisions can be seen in the patterns that developed in the subsequent fighting, which stretched out for years.

In late 1494, nearly a year later, the Kai exiles again attacked Echizen in an attempt to dislodge their opponent, Asakura Sadakage. Fighters from Kaga, possibly Honganji members, augmented the exiles' numbers, despite the formal alliance between their governor, Yasutaka, and Sadakage.[16] Since Honganji members tended to act independently anyway, this choice may have had nothing to do with the larger struggle between Masamoto and Yoshitane, yet it might have. The Honganji members in Kaga at that time were working with Masamoto to the extent that when one of the Honganji sect lay leaders died suddenly, the news was reported directly to Masamoto and Yoshizumi.[17]

As late as 1496, the Kaga *gunjū ikki* consisted of *kokujin* and other warriors, along with Honganji members, but in spite of the unity implied by the word "*ikki,*" these groups failed to act in concert. As we noted earlier, the *Daijōin jisha zōjiki* reported on 1496/9/16 that the *ikki* included various temples and samurai. Its author further noted, "Lord Hosokawa ordered the *ikki* to support the shogun's entrance to the capital, but it is said that the *kokujin* refused to accept the order."[18] In other words, not only did the *ikki* contain non-Honganji warriors, but also identifiable components of the *ikki,* like the *kokujin,* sometimes acted on their own.

By 1496, then, the governor of Kaga supported Yoshitane and was, therefore, an ally of Asakura Sadakage. Yet many of the province's Honganji members backed Masamoto and Yoshizumi, and attacked Sadakage. Finally, a third group that included *kokujin* refused to side with Yoshizumi, although Masamoto evidently had reason to think they would have been willing to accept his orders. The governor, the Honganji members, and the *ikki* were all engaged, at least in part, in governing Kaga; they were not at war with each other, yet each juggled external alliances differently. This state of affairs could only exist in the absence of a strong provincial government, and it lasted until the late 1520s, a long time by *sengoku* standards.[19]

Political tensions in the Hokuriku and elsewhere remained high throughout the 1490s and into the early 1500s. The villagers' living conditions became ever more difficult in the early years of the sixteenth century, when the combination of unfavorable weather and warfare produced widespread crop failures and famine from 1503 until 1506. All of these factors must have contributed to the first truly widespread episode of fighting involving Honganji members, that of 1506.

Jitsunyo

Jitsunyo, Honganji's ninth Patriarch, strove to remain aloof from the *ikki*. Born in 1458, the first child of Rennyo and his second wife, Ren'yū, he was Rennyo's eighth child and fifth son. So, he was not at first expected to inherit sect leadership. In fact, his oldest half-brother, Junnyo, already 17 at the time of Jitsunyo's birth, was being groomed for the post. However, when Junnyo died in 1483 with no sons of his own,[20] 25-year-old Jitsunyo was named as successor in his stead and began his training.[21] In keeping with the tradition of having heirs adopted into the Hino family, Jitsunyo was adopted by Hino Katsumitsu, brother of the shogun's wife, Hino Tomiko, who also reportedly sponsored the future Patriarch at his coming-of-age ceremony.[22] Because of Honganji's practice of maintaining alliances with relatively elite families, Jitsunyo's contacts among the aristocracy and shogunate did not stop there, and in the 1470s, he married a woman from the aristocratic Takakura family, with whom he would have seven children.[23]

Jitsunyo has a reputation for being conservative, which may have been because he spent his first ten years as Patriarch under his father's domination. Even though Rennyo stepped down from office in 1489, he continued performing many important duties in the sect, such as distributing sacred objects, and his activities tapered off only gradually.[24] In addition, the retired Patriarch traveled throughout the Kinai preaching, and in 1496, he began building a temple in Settsu in an area that would become the city of Osaka.[25] That temple eventually would become the citadel known as the Ishiyama Honganji, the center of the sect's power from 1532 until 1580. In his retirement, then, Rennyo's energy and continuing involvement in sectarian matters made him remain, for many followers, the human representative of Honganji temple.

In the early months of 1499, Rennyo fell ill and moved from his new base in Osaka back to Yamashina. In his last days, he called together five of his sons—Jitsunyo, Renkō, Rensei, Renjun, and Rengo—and urged them to work together, supporting each other and making the Honganji sect prosper.[26] On the twenty-fifth day of the third month, surrounded by family, friends, and followers, Rennyo died. He left the Honganji institution greatly changed: bigger, wealthier, more secure, yet still with unmanageable followers. Jitsunyo's first ten years as Patriarch, then, can be seen as a period of transition from the father's rule to the son's, and one in which the activities of *ikkō ikki*, in Kaga or elsewhere, hardly affected the temple headquarters. At least, so it seemed.

Perhaps due in part to the way his father had diluted the power of the Patriarch through the creation of the advisory council, Jitsunyo's stewardship of Honganji changed little. At least, it changed little for six years or so, until Jitsunyo was pressured into using Honganji followers as an army.

The Ikkō Ikki *of 1506*

The year 1506 was a busy year for samurai all over Japan, and the amount of fighting, combined with famine and disease, made it an even busier one for the Buddhist priests who performed funerary rites. A listing of deaths recorded for that year in *Tōji kakochō,* a death register kept by Tōji temple in Kyoto, includes the following entries:

Tango Province, in battle between Isshiki and Takeda forces, several hundred people dead; Hōki Province, in battle, the governor and his son, 9 years old, as well as enemies and allies, several hundred people dead . . . Etchū Province, in battle [with] Jinbō and [those] below [him], enemies and allies, and also by drowning, several thousand people dead . . . Various provinces, here and there, dead from illness, the sword, starvation, various [causes], several thousand / tens of thousands of people as well as birds, beasts, fish, and insects.[27]

As might be expected from a list of deaths during *sengoku,* the register describes a grim world of warfare, disease, and famine. *Tōji kakochō* is also one of the few documents to provide a fleeting glimpse of the broad array of Honganji sect activities in the same year:

[1506] Kaga, Noto, Etchū, Mino, Owari, and others, various provinces, *ikkōshū* uprisings, several thousand people dead in battle . . .

[no date] Echizen, Mino and below, [several] provinces, the *ikkōshū* and others, several thousand people dead on both sides. . . .

[1506] In Yamato, Echizen, Etchū, Noto, Mino, Ōmi, Izu, Suruga, Yamashiro, Tango, and others, [in] various provinces, [by] the *ikkōshū* and others, [in] army rebellions, fights, and so on, several tens of thousands of people dead.[28]

Another death register kept by the same temple adds Kawachi, Echigo, and Mikawa to the list of provinces visited by *ikki* or other warfare during 1506.[29] Alhough the list is long—sixteen provinces, including all of the Hokuriku and much of the Kinai—it is far from exhaustive, at least as far as combat is concerned; regional conflicts erupted throughout Japan during this time, from Mutsu Province in the extreme north of Japan to Ōsumi at the southern end of Kyushu.[30]

Still, the number of provinces that these death registers identify as having experienced *ikkō ikki* uprisings is striking, even though the registers sometimes list the Honganji-related uprisings as only one possible source of fighting among many.

Combined with other sources, we have reports of *ikki* in as many as ten provinces: Settsu, Kawachi, Echizen, Kaga, Noto, Etchū, Echigo, Mino, Owari, and Mikawa. Although Honganji members from neighboring provinces in the Hokuriku had helped with the successful Kaga uprising some eighteen years previously, this round of fighting was the first case in which *ikkō ikki* involved so many different provinces in the same year.

Some of these conflicts were related. The *ikki* disturbances in Settsu and Kawachi really formed one incident, with members from the two provinces joining together over the same issue and facing off *against* the Patriarch. Those in Echizen and Kaga, as well as those in Etchū and Echigo, similarly transcended provincial borders, and together with the Mikawa *ikki,* they pitted Honganji sectarians against *shugo* who were unfriendly to the shogunal deputy Masamoto. Information on the episodes in Mino, Noto, and Owari is too sketchy to draw firm conclusions, but the trouble in Mino may have been connected to the *ikki* in Echizen.

At one time, the numerous battles of 1506 were seen as attempts by Honganji members and the Kaga *ikki* to expand their power in the region. This interpretation accounted for Mino, Echizen, Kaga, Noto, Etchū, and Echigo, but it ignored the disruptions in Owari and Mikawa, which perhaps had yet to be noticed.[31] A more recent interpretation noticed the large percentage of *ikki* that were fighting against enemies of Masamoto. It took into account that Jitsunyo had ordered members in Settsu and Kawachi to help Masamoto, and theorized that the Patriarch's call to arms addressed Honganji members everywhere, urging them to attack Masamoto's enemies.[32] If Jitsunyo did issue such a formal, widespread appeal, it is curious that no documents relevant to the appeal would survive—curious, but possible.

Holding Jitsunyo responsible for all the warfare obscures other important questions. Although one might reasonably expect that the Patriarch's orders would be obeyed without question, obedience had already been a problem in the past. This time would be no exception, in part because there was no institutional precedent for issuing them. Receiving orders, after all, is different from obeying them.

Despite the institution's hierarchical structure, the Honganji Patriarch seemed to have few tools to enforce or entice obedience short of expulsion from the sect. At least, no Honganji leader attempted to fine members or to order corporal punishment.[33] Furthermore, Honganji leaders had not yet developed the "after-life pardon" (*goshō gomen*), the supposed power of the Patriarch to guarantee rebirth in Amida's paradise, which first appeared in the 1530s.[34] Doubtless some members believed in the Patriarch's power to doom people to hell or send them to paradise well before Honganji's leadership took up those views, but there is no telling how many of them did. Evidently the Settsu and Kawachi followers did not, and they refused Jitsunyo's orders on the basis that no Patriarch had ever ordered followers to fight.

Most of the various *ikkō ikki* conflicts that erupted in 1506 appear to have occurred in support of Masamoto and his allies, but some did not. Even those that did could have occurred without any specific directions from the Patriarch. Honganji followers through much of central Honshu must have heard about the fighting in the Kinai, and probably knew that men from Kaga had gone to Masamoto's aid. Word could spread quickly through a region like the Hokuriku, and although Mikawa, for example, might seem distant from the area, some congregations maintained regular contact with historically related congregations in Echizen.

Indeed, given Jitsunyo's reluctance to send out the first order and the opposition he faced as a result, it seems unlikely that he would send out such a blanket call to arms. The widespread *ikki* battles of 1506 are best seen as resulting not from simple obedience to a Patriarch, but from multiple causes, including an awareness of the Patriarch's sympathies and Masamoto's importance to the sect.

In late 1504 or early 1505, deputy shogun Hosokawa Masamoto, the *de facto* ruler, was faced with the rebellion of Hatakeyama

Yoshihide, one of his subordinates and governor of Kawachi Province.[35] Yoshihide's family had once enjoyed status equivalent to that of the Hosokawa, but it had lost power through a long, catastrophic succession dispute, as had so many other families in the late fifteenth century. Yoshihide's branch of the Hatakeyama had become subordinate to Masamoto by 1494.[36] But then, in one of the bewildering changes of allegiance characteristic of this period, by early 1505, Yoshihide had made peace with his kinsman Hatakeyama Shōjun,[37] one of Masamoto's most tenacious enemies. The two banded together against the deputy shogun.[38]

Nearly a year passed after this change before Masamoto, occupied with other problems, decided to deal with his former Hatakeyama vassal. Finally, on 1505/11/27, his forces attacked Yoshihide's stronghold at Konda castle near modern-day Osaka.[39] The castle held, and Masamoto was hard-pressed to find reinforcements to help bring it down. When one of his advisors suggested appealing to the Honganji sect for help in the campaign, Masamoto seized on the suggestion. He approached Jitsunyo and asked him to order members in Settsu and Kawachi to join the attack on Yoshihide.

Jitsunyo refused over and over again, citing his status as a priest (a person with long sleeves, i.e., one who does not even labor, let alone engage in fighting) and the lack of precedent for such a request, and his belief that the members wouldn't obey even if he issued such an order. Masamoto insisted, citing in his turn the various favors he had done for the Honganji sect over the years, which included helping Rennyo evade the shogun's orders to excommunicate sect members in Kaga for their part in the 1488 rebellion.

Masamoto was so importunate that once, acting on information that he was on his way to see Jitsunyo again, the Patriarch fled from Yamashina to Ōtsu, about four miles away, in effect bolting out through the back door. It was not far enough; Masamoto pursued and found him there. Finally, feeling he had no choice, Jitsunyo gave in to Masamoto's pressure and issued the order to attack Yoshihide. The response bore out Jitsunyo's misgivings: the Settsu and Kawachi members refused, saying the order was unprecedented and that they lacked even the materials—weapons, suits of armor, and so on—necessary to go to war.

This refusal was awkward for the Patriarch, and to satisfy Masamoto, Jitsunyo appealed to Kaga, over a hundred miles away on the other side of the island, for military aid. Kaga responded by sending about a thousand men.[40] Evidently, this was enough to turn the tide. Masamoto's forces finally prevailed, and Konda castle fell on 1506/1/26.[41] Yoshihide then fled, joining his ally Shōjun at another castle nearby, which fell three days later, forcing both Hatakeyama clansmen to flee Kawachi to more distant camps.[42] The temple death register *Tōji kōmyōkō kakochō* estimates fatalities on both sides at Konda castle alone to have been around two hundred, which suggests a scale of fighting small enough for an additional thousand men to have made a significant difference.

The Settsu and Kawachi members did not stop at refusing to attack Yoshihide at Konda castle, however. They were so indignant about the order that they sought to remove Jitsunyo from his office and replace him with his younger half-brother Jikken, Rennyo's ninth son and the region's leader as head priest of the temple at Osaka.[43] Jitsunyo suppressed the movement by dispatching a few hundred guards from the Honganji in Yamashina, not far from the provinces involved.[44] The Honganji guards managed to force Jikken and his associates out of Osaka, and the expelled priests spent years staying at various places in and around Kyoto before Jitsunyo pardoned them.[45]

When the sectarians of Settsu and Kawachi refused to attack Yoshihide, they noted the lack of precedent justifying Jitsunyo's orders. At the time, people accepted the legitimacy of actions and orders in large part because such things had been done in the past, and they tended to see unprecedented activity as unjustified. The sectarians' concern with precedent may have been genuine, but other factors must have influenced their decision. Most important of these was the family relationship between their leader Jikken and the Hatakeyama family, whom they had been asked to attack. Jikken's mother Rennō-ni, Rennyo's fifth and last wife, had been born into the Noto branch of the Hatakeyama family.[46] When she and her son Jikken had to leave the temple at Osaka, her distant relative Hatakeyama Shōjun—the same Shōjun whom Yoshihide joined in opposition to Masamoto—tried to persuade Jitsunyo to allow them to stay, but he was unsuccessful.[47]

Kinship mattered greatly, and in those days of multiple marriages, a new set of ties could bind some family members more tightly while loosening ties for others. However much support Hosokawa Masamoto had offered to Rennyo in his later years (and by extension to the sect), he was not Honganji's only patron. Rennyo must have had a close relationship with at least some of the Hatakeyama as well because otherwise, in an age of dynastic marriages, there is no explaining how Rennō-ni became Rennyo's wife. Jitsunyo had no such association with the Hatakeyama, and does not seem to have been as eager to maintain their good will as was Jikken, half-Hatakeyama himself.

In other words, the sectarians near Osaka chose to disobey the Patriarch rather than attack their regional leader's maternal relatives. When they sought to replace Jitsunyo with Jikken, they challenged the legitimacy of the ninth Patriarch by claiming that his orders were inappropriate, but they may also have thought that Jitsunyo was backing the wrong contender when he chose Masamoto.[48]

Similarly, the positive response from Kaga can be traced to the members' relations with Masamoto, rather than or in addition to faith in Jitsunyo. They were indebted to the warrior for saving them from expulsion, as noted above, and maintained an ongoing military connection, also mentioned previously in this chapter. In both regions, then, the sectarians did not base their responses to the orders solely on their attitude toward Jitsunyo. Rather, they judged Jitsunyo and his orders on the basis of their own political allegiances.

The Kinai was just the first site of the 1506 battles. Beginning just a few months after the fall of Konda castle, *ikkō ikki* uprisings broke out in Etchū, Echizen, and Noto. Because these provinces were all neighbors of Kaga, sectarians from that province played a supportive role in all three conflicts.

Etchū was the first of the three provinces to experience trouble. By the middle of the fourth month of 1506, an *ikki* in Etchū had driven out the deputies who ruled in the name of an absentee governor, forcing them into neighboring Echigo. Contributing to, or perhaps even causing, this attack was the fact that the absentee governor was none other than Hatakeyama Shōjun, against whom Masamoto fought in the Kinai at around the same time.[49]

The deputy governor of Echigo, Nagao Yoshikage, launched a counterattack in the fifth month, attempting to restore the Etchū deputies to power.[50] At least one historian has argued that Yoshikage joined the fight because Hatakeyama Yoshinobu, a relative and ally of Etchū's absentee governor, had asked him to attack the Kaga *ikki* for their part in the fighting in the Kinai.[51] There was no obvious connection between the two men, however, especially given that Yoshinobu was not, apparently, related to the Echigo governor, Uesugi Fusayoshi. Why Yoshikage would respond to his request, then, is unclear. It is more likely that Yoshikage helped Etchū because he wished to avoid having the troublesome *ikki* on his border.

In any case, Nagao Yoshikage soon had cause to regret his decision, though little time to do so. Four months later, on 9/19, the battle went against him, probably because one of the Etchū deputies he was trying to help defected to the *ikki* side, and Yoshikage died in battle.[52] A month after that, the Echigo forces suffered another severe defeat that brought an end to the fighting in Etchū, at least for the time being.[53] Yoshikage's heir Tamekage shifted his attention back to his home province, where he challenged the Echigo governor for power.[54] Warfare between Echigo and Etchū continued sporadically for several years, though the struggle between the Echigo governor and deputy governor took precedence over Etchū for both provinces.

In the seventh month of 1506, nearly six months after the defeat of Hatakeyama Yoshihide in Kawachi and three months after the Etchū *ikki* drove off the Echigo forces, the Kaga *ikki* responded to calls for assistance from within Echizen, where another uprising of Honganji followers was in progress. Kaga sectarians and Kai forces, possibly with help from Noto and Etchū (despite periodic but ongoing fighting in the latter province), attempted an invasion of Echizen.[55] Help came from further to the south and west as well, not just from Kaga's immediate neighbors: a supporting force of at least three hundred troops from the provinces of Settsu and Ōmi joined Kaga in an invasion of Echizen, possibly as early as the third month, though more likely in the seventh month.[56]

The sectarians, however, met with disaster. The Echizen daimyo Asakura Sadakage defeated the invaders in battles in the eighth and tenth months, after which he banned the sect within the province. He exiled the Honganji priests and destroyed the temples, including the one Rennyo had built at Yoshizaki. He also closed his roads, blocking traffic to and from Kaga. The Honganji institution disappeared from Echizen, then, in a decisive defeat. Nevertheless, some of the *monto* failed to capitulate. Although the sectarians never made any headway against Sadakage or his successors, sporadic fighting between the two provinces continued until 1518, when Jitsunyo brokered a peace agreement.[57]

As had occurred in Echizen and Etchū, for reasons unknown, an uprising of some kind broke out in Noto that same summer. The evidence for the uprising gives very little explanation and no details, such as the month in which the rebellion occurred, what its progress was, or how and when it ended. One source notes only, "Peasants in Noto and Etchū dr[o]ve out warriors."[58] There were no visible results of the uprising, such as sectarians punished or exiled, temples destroyed, or changes in the provincial government, as nearly as historians can tell. The Noto governor, Hatakeyama Yoshimune, continued in power.

The Hokuriku *monto,* aware of the episodes in the Kinai, must have known that the leaders of Etchū and Echizen wanted to restore the deposed shogun Ashikaga Yoshitane to his post. They would have readily identified these men as Masamoto's enemies and concluded that attacking them could only help their benefactor. One may infer, then, that the Hokuriku *ikki* were inspired in part by shogunal politics. Noto, however, does not fit this pattern.

The Noto governor, Hatakeyama Yoshimune, had come to power by defeating his older brother some six years previously with help from Hosokawa Masamoto.[59] The deposed brother, who had also supported Yoshitane, found refuge with the Echigo deputy governor, so one cannot think of the Noto governor Yoshimune as an ally of the anti-Masamoto Hokuriku provincial leaders. One would instead expect that Honganji members would aid in the defense of Noto against possible trouble.

At some point the deposed brother returned from exile in Echigo and regained his power by agreeing to name Yoshimune's son as his successor, but there is no way to tell when this occurred. Scholars agree, however, that the rapprochement between the brothers occurred *after* the *ikki*, either soon thereafter and as a result of it, or later, sometime after Masamoto's death in 1507.[60] Either way, Yoshimune backed Masamoto in 1506, even if most of his relatives did not. The uprising in Noto, then, must have been inspired by different motives—motives that may also have contributed to the Etchū and Echizen action.

Quite apart from shogunal politics, one factor in the Hokuriku turmoil may have been the great hardships that afflicted the region at the time. Living conditions in the Hokuriku and Kinai had been especially difficult in the previous few years. *Tōji kakochō* describes widespread disease and famine for the years from 1503 to 1507, after several years of relative freedom from such reports. Sadly for the scholar, it offers little detail:

> [No date, but c. 1504–7] In the five districts and the seven circuits, here and there, especially inside and outside the capital, deaths from famine and disease, several tens of thousands of people. . . .
>
> [1504, 1505] In various provinces, here and there, deaths from epidemics, several tens of thousands of people.

[1506] In various provinces, here and there, death from disease, from the sword, from hunger, from various causes, several hundred thousand people, as well as birds, beasts, fish, and insects.

[1504, 1505, 1506] Various provinces, death from epidemics, several thousands of people.[61]

Tōji's records do not always identify the regions in which these disasters occurred, so possibly they affected places elsewhere in Japan. Other sources also mention famine and disease in those years, however, and some of them locate similar disasters in the Hokuriku. For example, a record kept by a Zen temple in Kaga, the *Yōkōji nendaiki,* also mentions famine in 1504 and epidemic in 1505 in its region, noting that there were many fatalities.[62]

In medieval Japan, years of famine and pestilence frequently were marked by calls for tax reductions or debt cancellations.[63] It would be no surprise if groups in Noto, Echizen, and Etchū made similar demands in 1506. With recent warfare in the Hokuriku tied to the struggle between Yoshitane and Masamoto, leaders there may have been unwilling to grant the usual reductions because of their need to fund military campaigns. In such scenarios, rebellion was a common result. Less directly, the hard times might simply have led to greater dissatisfaction with the leaders, making the *monto* more disposed to attack them on Masamoto's behalf.

For Echizen, as for Etchū, although shogunal politics could have played an important role in the uprisings, the trigger appears to have been local. For the preceding few years, Sadakage had faced several challenges from other Asakura family members who coveted his power, and he had been forced into hard fighting to maintain his position. In order to keep the upper hand, he courted help from some unusual sources, in particular from one of Honganji's greatest religious rivals, the Takada sect of Jōdo Shinshū. The fact that both sects followed the teachings of Shinran (as each school interpreted them) did nothing to decrease the antagonism between the sects. If anything, it exacerbated the rivalry.

Historians have tended to assume that the Honganji *monto* in Echizen were responsible for starting hostilities. Since the cause of the fighting is obscure, however, there are other possibilities. Sadakage might have called on the Takada sect for help in fighting his rivals within Echizen because he saw that the Honganji sectarians supported his enemy, Masamoto, and he did not feel he could count on their support. By openly endorsing the Takada sect, however, he would have inflamed the Honganji supporters. In general, in areas where both sects had a strong following, the presence of one sect in warfare resulted in the other sect joining the opposing side.

Alternatively, after seeing that Honganji sectarians supported his enemy, Hosokawa Masamoto, the Echizen governor Asakura Sadakage might have decided to suppress the Honganji sect or to place some restrictions on it. He would not have wanted to face a sectarian rebellion if he and Masamoto opened hostilities. If so, the Honganji members would almost certainly have fought to defend their religion and temples.

Noto's uprising could not have formed part of a supposed larger movement against supporters of Yoshitane then, because the governor was Masamoto's ally. Therefore, the fighting must have had other roots, possibly related to the effects of the famines and epidemics of recent years. Without more information, such as when the uprising occurred, one cannot work out what connection it may have had with the other uprisings in the area.

Lack of information for the Hokuriku uprisings means that no definite conclusions can be drawn about their causes. Still, it seems safe to posit that fighting in both Echizen and Etchū was related to Masamoto, albeit with additional factors coming into play. By contrast, the Noto uprising was likely related solely to local concerns having to do with the years of recent hardship. Although shogunal politics dominated the fighting in Echizen and Etchū, those local concerns also existed, and may have helped to predispose the sectarians to rise up.

In Mikawa, the disruptions beginning in 1506 lasted for years—three according to one source, as much as eight according to another.[64] They started when Imagawa Ujichika, governor of Suruga province, having successfully taken over Tōtōmi, moved to expand further into the province of Mikawa. In the early sixteenth century, there was no single authority governing all of Mikawa but rather several *kokujin* who controlled smaller regions within the province.

When Ujichika invaded Mikawa in 1506, he found two *kokujin* families in his way: the Makino and the Matsudaira, both commanding able fighters. The Makino held some territory in eastern Mikawa, but the Matsudaira family consisted of several branch families, which together controlled most of western Mikawa. The Matsudaira family head was in the process of building up hegemony over the entire province,[65] though the family would quickly lose it to the Imagawa in 1549.[66]

In the fighting that began in 1506, the Matsudaira were supported by the Honganji members who lived in their region, just to the west of the Yahagi River, which bisected Mikawa. Their support was military in nature, which is what earned this struggle the designation of *ikkō ikki*, even though the *ikki* members were aiding local warriors rather than rebelling against them. The fight was not, however, without broader political overtones, and these involved Hosokawa Masamoto.

In seizing Tōtōmi, Imagawa Ujichika had defeated the former military governor family, the Shiba—the same family that used to govern Echizen and which had received help from Honganji members in Kaga. The Matsudaira, like the Shiba, supported Hosokawa Masamoto and Ashikaga Yoshizumi, while the Imagawa backed the ex-shogun Yoshitane. Hence, the struggle over Mikawa looks different depending on which of the two lenses one peers through: the national shogunal fight or the local expansionist one. Through the former lens, one sees Honganji members in Mikawa choosing to side with the Matsudaira because both supported Masamoto. Through the latter, one sees the sectarians who simply sided with the Matsudaira to repel the invaders.

It is easy to understand why some historians place this *ikki* in the context of shogunal politics and argue that the *monto* chose sides according to that logic. The argument's persuasiveness rests largely, however, on perceiving the *monto*-samurai alliances as odd, lacking internal logic, and thus requiring further explanation. As we have seen, though, that kind of cooperation was the norm rather than the exception: *ikki* and Masachika against Kōchiyo, *ikki* and *kokujin* against Masachika, *ikki* and Kai exiles against the Asakura, and so on. The Mikawa *ikki* is adequately explained as a local struggle against an external enemy, the invading Imagawa army. It is perhaps even more understandable that Honganji followers would support a local *kokujin* against an invading daimyo because daimyo generally exploited the people and resources of their domains more effectively than did their predecessors. It could not have hurt the *ikki*-Matsudaira alliance that both supported Masamoto, and that Imagawa Ujichika did not. Nevertheless, some Honganji members already served as Matsudaira retainers, an allegiance that may well have contributed to the more general willingness of the sectarians to support the *kokujin*.

The Mino and Owari uprisings live on solely in scattered textual references to disturbances in those provinces involving *ikki* or Honganji members. One of the few reports of trouble in Mino attributed the uprising simply to an *ikki*,[67] a vague term. Conceivably, the *ikki* had nothing to do with Honganji members or Masamoto. However, given that the Mino deputy *shugo*'s family was closely related to the Asakura of Echizen,[68] it makes sense to read *ikkō ikki* for *do ikki* and to consider the Mino disturbance within the context of the Echizen *ikki*.

As for Owari, it lay just to the west of Mikawa, and the three most important Honganji sect temples in Mikawa had numerous branches there. Whether there was a separate *ikki* in Owari, or whether the *ikki* of Owari was formed to help Mikawa, is impossible to tell, though the latter seems more likely. The dominant warriors in Owari, the Oda family, were not on good terms with the Imagawa of Suruga either, if only because both had designs on Mikawa, the province that lay between them.

1506: An Evaluation

With the exceptions of Noto and Mikawa, then, the various *ikkō ikki* of Eishō 3 [1506] may well have been linked to Hosokawa Masamoto's situation, even though other factors must have contributed to the sectarians' decisions. Whether or not they were following the Patriarch's direct orders, however, is a different issue.

Even if all the 1506 *ikkō ikki* were clearly formed to support Masamoto, which is not the case, they could have cooperated without explicit direction from Honganji. Sect members in different regions communicated with each other. In some cases, special relationships existed, tying temples in different regions to each other. Mikawa, for example, was connected to Echizen through Hongakuji, which had begun as the offshoot of a temple in Mikawa when a group of residents from the latter province emigrated to the Hokuriku. That connection was never severed. The various sect communities in Echizen, Kaga, Etchū, and Noto, too, were obviously tightly associated with each other, and main temple/branch temple relations there transcended provincial boundaries.[69] The Settsu members who went to the Echizen *ikki*'s aid surely knew of Jitsunyo's orders in their home province. The Ōmi *monto* included many merchants and shippers who traveled to and from the Hokuriku, and could have heard of the orders from members in Kaga. Mikawa temples had branches in Owari. The Honganji members in all these provinces were bound together one way or another, and all could have known of Jitsunyo's orders to Settsu, Kawachi, and, later, Kaga. The timing of the *ikki* and the affiliations of *ikki* targets alone do not adequately prove or disprove that Jitsunyo directed a concerted effort to help Masamoto.

The documentary evidence, too, is inconclusive. There are three letters that some historians have cited to support the contention that Jitsunyo orchestrated all of the 1506 *ikki*. These letters are problematic and unreliable, however. The contents of the first two are very similar, both addressed to Etchū priests and followers congratulating them for their loyalty in protecting the faith and placing them under the jurisdiction of a Kaga temple headed by one of Rennyo's brothers. One was signed by Jitsunyo, the other by two members of a Honganji administrative family.[70]

No extant copies of these letters date from the sixteenth century. They can be found only in an Edo-period war tale called the *Kagaki*. This circumstance alone renders the first two letters suspect since war tales contained some fact and a good deal of embroidery, as do historical novels of any time or place. Because these two letters follow a format that differs from the standard one employed within the Honganji sect at the time, and contain some other discrepancies as well, they can be dismissed as forgeries.[71]

The third letter, thought to be genuine, was written by Rengo (1468–1543), one of Jitsunyo's brothers and an important Honganji leader in the Hokuriku. This letter is dated only by the month and day, 3/16, without a notation for the year. (It was customary in the 1500s for the writer of a letter to date it with only the month and the day, leaving the recipient to insert the year later, if desired. Sometimes the recipient failed to do so, as occurred in this case.) Rengo's letter was originally thought to have been written by Rennyo and only later was determined to bear Rengo's signature. At the time of that reassessment, the document was tentatively dated as "around 1506."

The letter is addressed to "people of good faith" and warns Honganji members of a possible attack from "Nagao" (the deputy governor of Echigo), who had been colluding with "Noto" for a number of years. It concludes by urging members to give up their lives joyfully in defense of the "Buddhist law" (*buppō,* i.e., the Honganji sect, or possibly the Kaga *ikki*).[72]

Remember that in 1506, Noto and Echigo were not, in fact, allies. Although the letter's contents describe the situation in 1506 somewhat, they fit better with events that occurred in 1521 and possibly in other years as well. Any dating (during Rengo's adulthood) is reduced to a guess, and therefore the letter has no great value as a source for any particular conflict.[73]

One piece of textual evidence that tends to absolve Jitsunyo of inciting all his followers to violence is the chronicle called

Yamashina gobō no koto to sono jidai no koto, written toward the end of the 1500s by Jitsunyo's long-lived younger half-brother Jitsugo. He relates the tale of Masamoto repeatedly demanding help and Jitsunyo's reluctance to give it, then goes on to describe the Settsu and Kawachi resistance, and Kaga's response. The next sentence mentions that Jitsunyo had a hard time because of the Echizen *ikki* but does not draw an explicit connection or elaborate.

In all of Jitsugo's writing, he fails to mention Jitsunyo making any broad call for action, only the limited ones to the Kinai and Kaga. It is tempting to discount Jitsugo's testimony as biased, assuming that he wanted to protect the sect and his half-brother, and so was unlikely to include such negative information. The temptation, however, should be challenged.

Throughout his writings on Jitsunyo's tenure, Jitsugo was unremittingly critical of him, with very few exceptions. He heaped praise on the eighth Patriarch Rennyo, the father he could not have known personally—Jitsugo was a small child when Rennyo died—and sharply criticized Jitsunyo's behavior and policies. His accounts were biased, certainly, but not in Jitsunyo's favor. He plaintively noted, "It has been since [1506] that our sect's priests and [those] below [them] started going to war."[74] It seems unlikely, then, that Jitsugo would have passed up such a good opportunity to criticize his brother. Again, however, this is not proof that Jitsunyo had nothing to do with the *ikki* outside the Kinai and Kaga.

It bears repeating that all of Japan, not just the provinces involved in *ikkō ikki,* was convulsed by war. Although war in the provinces may have been driven by shogunal politics, or combatants may have evoked shogunal connections to justify their actions, such conflict was less about the shogunate and more about local power. Most of the various *ikki* incidents of 1506, then, can be seen on one level as directed by one person to attack Masamoto's enemies. On another level, however, they cannot be separated from local conditions.

Among the combatant leaders of the day, one can distinguish two warrior camps: pro-Yoshitane and pro-Masamoto.

One can even hypothesize an overall civil war between the two sides, since warring samurai generally aligned themselves with one side or the other. Yet, governors, deputy governors, and daimyo frequently chose sides according to whichever allegiance their intended opponent had declared most recently. In other words, local agendas had a tendency to determine the nominal national affiliations of most warriors, rather than the other way around.

Not surprisingly, even nominal supporters of a shogun would decide whether or not to obey that shogun's orders based on considerations of their own interests. In one example we have already mentioned, when the ninth Ashikaga shogun and later his successor moved against the Ōmi governor Rokkaku Takayori in 1487 and again in 1491 to reassert their authority and stop his usurpation of estates in that province, many warriors declined to join the campaigns. Others tried to manipulate the shogunate into declaring their own enemies to be the shogunate's enemies. For instance, the ousted governor of Echizen, Shiba Yoshihiro, tried unsuccessfully to get the shogunate to undertake an expedition to punish Asakura Sadakage, a move that Yoshihiro hoped would end with his own reinstatement as provincial overlord.

Whether Honganji members declined to follow Jitsunyo's orders, as those in Settsu and Kawachi did, or agreed to, as the Kaga members did, they followed the same pattern as the warriors they fought with and against. The great significance of Jitsunyo's call to arms was less in the response it received than in how his call legitimated warfare for the sect. Whatever its intent, it seemed to make warfare a legitimate response for Honganji members everywhere, for diverse reasons. His father may have deemed fighting acceptable only when defending the Buddhist law, and perhaps not even then. Jitsunyo's action, limited though it was, implied many things were worth fighting for.

To summarize, *ikki* in Settsu, Kawachi, Kaga, Echizen, Etchū, and Mino occurred for reasons apparently related to Masamoto, though in some instances specific information about the cause and progress of an *ikki* cannot be found. Jitsunyo ordered an *ikki* in Settsu and Kawachi, and then in Kaga, to help Masamoto with a difficult former vassal. The *ikki* in Echizen most likely was related to Masamoto and the assistance given him by the sect. The reason for that in Etchū is still less clear, but also plausibly occurred because of the *monto*'s awareness of events in the Kinai and sympathy for the sect's patron. The difficult years of famine also did nothing to endear the leaders of Echizen and Etchū to the members but probably were not a root cause of the *ikki* in those provinces.

Finally, in Mikawa and Noto, *ikki* occurred for local reasons, primarily unrelated to the battles of the sect's protector, Hosokawa Masamoto. In Mikawa, Honganji members helped defend the province against a neighbor's invasion. The reasons behind the *ikki* in Noto are obscure, but may have been related to several years' suffering from famine and disease.

In 1506, *ikki* occurred in an unprecedented number of places at roughly the same time. In many, the aim evidently was to protect the power of a person of national importance. Whether or not the Honganji leader issued orders to this effect throughout the sect membership, the *ikki* chose their courses of action. For the first time, Honganji members took a step into the center of the national stage.

However able he was as a military leader, Hosokawa Masamoto failed miserably in his familial obligation to marry and beget an heir; indeed, he preferred to keep his distance from women all his life.[75] In more peaceful times, this would have presented little problem, as adoption of an heir was a viable solution to the problem of succession. In *sengoku* Japan, however, adoptions could prove contentious. When Masamoto named an heir in 1502, a son of the aristocratic Kujō family and cousin to the shogun, some of Masamoto's retainers supported this heir, but not all did.[76] In an attempt to placate the opposing side, Masamoto made a major tactical error the following year: he adopted another heir, this one from a branch of the Hosokawa family. Naturally, perhaps, those partial to the first heir resisted the second one. Masamoto could not have set up a succession dispute more effectively had he done so deliberately. The resulting division within the retainer band was an important factor in Masamoto's need for reinforcements in order to defeat Hatakeyama Yoshihide; some of his retainers would not cooperate in the expedition.

Backers of the first heir eventually decided not to wait for Masamoto to die. Instead they killed him in his bath, "slash-[ing] him several times with a sword," on 1507/6/23.[77] That act precipitated a dispute that lasted decades and involved his rival heirs, their successors, and other family members. By 1519, the fighting was between Hosokawa Harumoto and Hosokawa Takakuni.[78] The continuing succession dispute had a modest effect on Honganji and the *ikki* until the later 1520s, during the reign of Jitsunyo's successor, when the protagonists would come to have more importance to the sectarians.

The importance of Hosokawa Masamoto's friendship to Honganji can be seen in Jitsunyo's reaction to his death. Upon hearing that Masamoto had been killed, Jitsunyo promptly departed Honganji headquarters at Yamashina for Ōmi, en route to his final destination in distant Tanba Province. Evidently he thought distance was a better guarantor of safety than the moats, walls, and embankments of the heavily fortified Honganji in Yamashina. A company of fifty or sixty bodyguards, outfitted with armor and helmets, accompanied Jitsunyo on his flight. His son Ennyo followed the next day, bringing with him the sacred image of Shinran that was customarily enshrined in Honganji's main hall of worship.[79] They stayed away from Yamashina for more than a year, waiting until the fighting in the capital wound down.

Jitsunyo, Institutionalization, and More Ikki

Between 1508 and 1520, Jitsunyo made his three most important contributions to the institutionalization of the Honganji sect: he created a standard set of Rennyo's *ofumi*, formalized the family council system, and formulated the "three rules" of behavior for the sect. The first of these contributions, the set of *ofumi,* provided for the first time a uniform text explaining Honganji doctrine to ordinary people. The second clearly defined the leadership hierarchy of the sect and made it more cohesive. The third, the three rules, was a largely futile attempt to correct the behavior that created the worst problems between sectarians and political authorities. These rules were important nevertheless in reaffirming the Patriarch's responsibility for controlling not just the religious messages of the sect but also the behavior of its members in society at large.

Jitsunyo perceived the utility of a standardized text of Honganji's teachings in spreading the faith and maintaining orthodoxy. He turned to Rennyo's more than two hundred *ofumi,* which were written in the second half of his lifetime, and explained basic Honganji sect doctrine in language that most of the members could understand. Not surprisingly, many of these were repetitive, going over the same ground in much the same words for different congregations. Under Jitsunyo's supervision, his son Ennyo chose eighty of these letters as representative of Rennyo's teaching. He then copied them into five fascicles, or volumes, which quickly became one of the primary texts of Shinshū doctrine.

Whether Jitsunyo and Ennyo understood it or not, the importance of their achievement is difficult to overstate. Individual copies and small selections of the letters were made by Jitsunyo and his successors, but the bound sets of the canonical 80 letters were copied in large numbers and circulated widely. Thus, they were used more extensively than the smaller sets.[80] The individual *ofumi* had helped spread Honganji doctrine during Rennyo's lifetime, and thanks to the new compilation, continued to do so well after his death. Arguably they were even more helpful then, when they could be passed around as larger sets, rather than read only a few at a time in isolated congregations. Because they were so easy to read and understand, they came to constitute the basic official teaching and the most authoritative direct exposure to formal doctrinal teaching that many of Honganji's less-educated lay priests—that is, members who oversaw *dōjō* but were not ordained and had not taken the tonsure—and followers would ever have. Finally, the shared religious vocabulary of terms and ideas created by the designation of the canon contributed to the formation and reinforcement of the Honganji sectarian identity.

Jitsunyo's second major contribution to the institution was to formalize the network of regional temples subordinate to Honganji and headed by close members of the Patriarch's family. Initially, temples whose head priests were closely related to the Patriarch, at that time meaning Rennyo's sons, were designated *ikkeshū* or the "one-family group" of temples. Each had jurisdiction over all the temples of its region, as the local representative of Honganji. For example, an *ikkeshū* temple's head could exercise the power to expel members from the sect when he felt it was necessary. As the number of the Patriarch's descendants increased, so did the number of such temples, and that soon made it desirable to define the status more clearly.

In addition to the *ikkeshū* temples, Rennyo had set up an informal family council to advise Jitsunyo, especially on matters of doctrine, should they arise. This first council consisted of four of Jitsunyo's brothers: Renjun and Rengo, who shared the same mother with Jitsunyo; and Renkō and Rensei, whose mother was the older sister of Jitsunyo's mother. All then had family ties closer to each other than to their half-siblings born of other, unrelated mothers. Rennyo may have chosen them for their maturity, however, not because of their maternal relationships. The youngest son Rennyo named to the council was Rengo, who was over 30 when Rennyo died; the next youngest son was no more than 15, not old enough to advise a Patriarch (though old enough to be one). Nevertheless, maternal relationships most likely did matter and should be noted.

In 1519, Jitsunyo took ill and from his sickbed formulated a more precise system of designating temples headed by relatives of the Patriarch. One son of each of Rennyo's sons, Jitsunyo said, was allowed to head a temple of *ichimon* status, a designation that indicated a close relation to the Patriarch. The rest of the children, from second [grand]sons on down, were all to be of just *ikkeshū* status. Jitsunyo identified three exceptions—close relatives who were permitted *ichimon* status—but all of their children would only be able to claim *ikkeshū* status.[81] As defined in 1518 then, *ichimon* denoted a higher status than *ikkeshū,* and members of the family council were drawn only from *ichimon* temples.

By creating two tiers of family temples, Jitsunyo also reduced the number of people who could lay claim to leadership in the sect. The same kind of system was used after Jitsunyo's death, but the definition of *ichimon/ikkeshū* tended to change with each Patriarch. In effect, *ichimon* came to designate the uncles, brothers, and nephews of the reigning Patriarch, whereas *ikkeshū* applied to more distant relatives. Thus, the top leadership consisted of those relatives closest to the Patriarch by blood.[82] The system made the leadership more manageable at first, but it subsequently gave rise to factions that created tensions within the sect with the accession of each new Patriarch. In some cases, the balance of power within the council could shift depending on his mother's family connections.

Finally, there was Jitsunyo's promulgation of the "three rules," which he introduced in 1518 and made binding throughout the sect in 1519. In practice, these were also disregarded whenever they were deemed inconvenient. The three rules were actually prohibitions, banning the following activities:

Item. Taking up arms for offensive or defensive warfare.

Item. Patronage and favoritism.

Item. Failing to send in the *nengu* [land tax or rent].[83]

All three proscriptions, but most especially the first and third, addressed problems that the general population associated with the Honganji sect. On the surface, the rule against warfare seems unrealistic. How could Jitsunyo expect Honganji members to avoid all fighting, given the times in which they lived? Surely he could not have. He may, though, have meant to ban only "private" wars, ones taken up by members fighting on their own initiative rather than under orders from higher authorities.

Another possible interpretation of Jitsunyo's order is that he expected the rules to apply only to full priests in the sect, not to lay priests and ordinary members. In that case, one might object, to whom is the third rule addressed? Wasn't it the ordinary members who were keeping the taxes to themselves? Not entirely. At the time, priests were founding ever more temples and declaring their grounds to have the rights of a *jinaichō* (a temple town, lit., "within the temple"), free from the regulation of other authorities and hence untaxed.[84] An attempt on Jitsunyo's part to curb this kind of behavior, which would have created friction with local warriors and estate owners alike, would have been prudent.

One source, *Hogo no uragaki,* links *jinaichō* directly with hostility directed toward the Honganji sect. It says that the proliferation of new *jinaichō* paradoxically inhibited the sect's growth and strictly following the three rules would promote it:

> After Jitsunyo's death, once again new priests and temples sprang up here and there. Calling themselves *jinai[chō],* they assembled people and ignored the *jitō* and *ryōshu* [warrior authority and landlord] and seemed not to perform corvée. . . . Already in various provinces, *jinai[chō]* were destroyed; we heard about this kind of thing from the north and the south. Because of this, the rules of [Jitsunyo] were strongly re-affirmed. The bad practices of various places were fixed, and this caused a renewal of the sect.[85]

In this sectarian's view, the troublesome behavior of the new temple towns was provoking retaliation from the authorities, and causing difficulties for the Honganji sect in general. When, however, priests and members followed Jitsunyo's orders, paying their rents, taxes, and so on, the authorities left the temple towns and sect members alone, allowing the faith to spread.

At first glance, none of Jitsunyo's contributions seems very important, but over time the first two, at least, grew in significance. The selection of eighty *ofumi* as texts for the teaching of Honganji doctrine helped establish Rennyo as the most important theologian of the sect after Shinran. Indeed, given the dominance of the *ofumi* in lay instruction, one could claim that Rennyo's writings were more important than Shinran's for most members. Rennyo's fame is due to other factors besides the *ofumi,* most notably the numerous memoirs of his tenth son Jitsugo; nevertheless, the preservation of Rennyo's letters and their ready availability played no small part in making him a dominant figure in Honganji's history.

When Jitsunyo created his refined *ichimon-ikkeshū* system of temples, the priests who came to be designated *ichimon* had their jurisdictions and power increased. Yet, as the *ikkeshū* grew in number, they declined in importance. For example, after the rearrangement, Rengo of Honsenji in Kaga had power over Honganji followers in Noto and Etchū as well as in eastern Kaga, where the temple itself was located. *Ikkeshū* temples in the same region deferred to Honsenji. The relative power of temples, especially in the Hokuriku, mattered greatly in the waning years of Jitsunyo's reign and through the early ones of his successors'.

In 1521, Echigo, its ruler, and his policies again became the cause of disorder in the Hokuriku region. In spite of the rule against fighting, Honganji sectarians again found themselves caught up in regional problems, though the Kaga members remained neutral for as long as they could. That turned out to be only a short time.

After the Echigo deputy governor Nagao Yoshikage was killed in Etchū, in the eighth month of 1506, his son Tamekage became the family head. He withdrew his forces from Etchū, less because of weakness than ambition, and he spent the next several years battling his peers and superiors in Echigo to become the dominant power in that province. In 1509, he was defeated briefly and found refuge in Etchū, though he still held one of Etchū's deputy governors, Jinbō Yoshimune, responsible for his father's death. By 1511, he was back in Echigo and had become the *de facto* ruler of that province, though another warrior held the official appointment as governor.[86]

Fighting broke out between Echigo and Etchū again in 1515, pitting Jinbō Yoshimune and his local allies against Nagao Tamekage, who enjoyed the support of the Hatakeyama families of both the Kinai and Noto.[87] That support notwithstanding, Tamekage suffered reverses in the following year and retreated to Echigo. He realized that he needed additional help to avenge his father's death, and after four years, in 1519, he found that help in the person of Hosokawa Takakuni, the deputy shogun. Tamekage won his backing and kept that of the two Hatakeyama families, with the result that Takakuni sent fifty or so of his warriors to assist Tamekage. Just as importantly, either through Takakuni's good offices or through one of the Hatakeyama, Tamekage obtained promises of neutrality from the Honganji members in Kaga in the event of more fighting with Etchū.

Tamekage was more successful in his 1519 venture than he had been previously. Yoshimune and his peers, the other deputy governors of Etchū, defended the province and may have been backed by local Honganji members—one Honganji sect temple was burned down, and its replacement had to move twice. There is, however, no direct evidence of Etchū Honganji members' involvement, and their co-adherents in Kaga maintained their neutrality. Finally, on 1520/12/21, Jinbō Yoshimune launched an unsuccessful counterattack, dying, it is said, along with several thousand of his men.[88]

Despite the Honganji sect's neutrality, Tamekage banned it in Echigo and Etchū in the second month of 1521. The ban was particularly harsh and included the following clauses:

Item. In accord with [Nagao Yoshikage's] order, the *mugekōshū*[89] [i.e., Honganji sect] followers shall be exiled permanently. . . .

Item. As land steward and master, [the local warrior] shall quickly apprehend the suspect[ed Honganji member], and if there is trouble, shall punish [the culprit] physically and execute him. . . .

Item. If an ordinary person, even if he is of another sect, fails to report that there is a *mugekōshū* member in the area, he shall be subject to the same punishment [as the member].

Item. If someone reports an uprising of this sect, he shall be praised and rewarded with household goods and land.

Item. Any warrior lord who tolerates [the sect] shall be replaced.

Item. If an official, because of neglect, has allowed the sect to continue for a long time without reporting it and claims that he knew nothing about it, he has violated the laws of the *kuni* and shall be killed by his assistant.

Item. There is to be no violation of this rule, even by children and grandchildren, and even in land that is not subject to entry by officials.[90]

In punishing those who simply tolerated sect members or failed to report their presence as severely as the members themselves, this ban went beyond the usual bounds of such rules. The sectarians reacted predictably, and there was again war in the Hokuriku, with Kaga against Tamekage, ruler of Etchū and Echigo, and Noto, which sided with Tamekage.

This, most probably, is the context in which Rengo's letter, mentioned earlier in connection with the 1506 *ikki,* was written. If so, on [1521?]3/16, Rengo, the *ichimon* priest of Honsenji, who had recently been given jurisdiction over Etchū and Noto as well as Kaga, wrote an inflammatory letter to Honganji members. It said that "Noto and Nagao," through a long association, had determined to exterminate the Buddhist law (*buppō,* i.e., the Honganji sect) and called on the recipients to defend the faith against this threat, even at the cost of their lives.[91]

Actual fighting did not begin until the seventh month of 1521 when it erupted in Etchū, spreading to Noto in the following year, without decisive victories on either front. Hosokawa Takakuni brokered a peace for the region in 1522.[92]

The war between Honganji sectarians and Tamekage broke the rules that Jitsunyo had put in place only a few years earlier—as did Rengo's incitement to fight. The Patriarch did not punish Rengo, however, nor did he criticize the sectarians. To the contrary, Jitsunyo wrote a letter to the members in Kaga, praising them for their "extraordinary service in Etchū." He further noted that it was "outrageous for the Buddhist law and the everyday world [*seken*] to be at odds" and informed them that Takakuni had arranged a peace, which he hoped they could maintain.[93] In spite of his supposed ban on warfare, Jitsunyo seemed pleased with his followers, further evidence that the rules had a limited intent.

Jitsunyo's Death

The few years left of Jitsunyo's tenure were uneventful, at least in terms of sectarian actions. His son Ennyo died in 1521, leaving a young grandson, Shōnyo (1516–54), as Jitsunyo's heir. By then, Jitsunyo's own health was not good. In the middle of the first month of 1525, one source claims, Jitsunyo summoned Rengo, Renkyō, and Kensei (Renkyō's heir) to his bedside and asked that the rest of the family be assembled. On the twenty-fourth of the same month, he told Renjun and Rengo about a dream he had, which he saw as an omen of his approaching death. In it, Rennyo appeared and beckoned to him, inviting him, as Jitsunyo understood it, to accompany him to Amida's Pure Land. Four days later, on the twenty-eighth, he spoke with Jitsuen, Renjun, Rengo, Renkyō, and Kensei and gave them his dying wishes. He asked them to urge the members to obey his three rules so as to keep the Buddhist law and the world's law working together, and to care for his heir, the 10-year-old Shōnyo.[94] The 68-year-old Patriarch passed away less than a week later, on the second day of the second month.[95]

When Jitsunyo's younger half-brother Jitsugo wrote his memoirs in later years, he primarily recalled what he saw as Jitsunyo's lack of piety, which he contrasted with the extreme piety of their father, Rennyo. He wrote, for example, that Jitsunyo:

> . . . shortened the service from what it used to be. This service, to be done in front of the founder's image, has been handed down for generations. Instead of one hundred verses, Jitsunyo ordered no more than one. Also, in the Amida Hall after reading the Amida sutra, if [the chanter said] the short *nenbutsu* more than once, Jitsunyo would rattle his prayer beads on the floor or a table, as if to say, "Hurry up and finish!" The chanter would stop. . . . What is this?[96]

In this and many similar passages, Jitsugo makes it clear that he thinks Jitsunyo began an era of decline for Honganji.

Yet the biggest change that occurred in the sect during Jitsunyo's stewardship resulted from an action he performed reluctantly, that is, calling members to arms in 1506. That set two precedents: it legitimized warfare by Honganji members and it consolidated the Patriarch's authority to send members into battle. Many other major religious centers, such as Enryakuji and Kōfukuji, were also strong military powers, and Jitsunyo's claim to war-making authority accorded well with the practices of his time. Nevertheless, it was an authority forced upon him by militant Honganji members and the sect's patron, Hosokawa Masamoto.

The path to a warrior-Patriarch probably began in 1473, when Honganji members first fought *as* Honganji members, rather than as warriors bound to a specific overlord. Their successful uprising in Kaga in 1488 put pressure on Rennyo to either legitimate or disavow his militant followers. Those who wished him to expel the Kaga members demanded, in essence, that Rennyo take responsibility for controlling his followers' actions, especially when they organized themselves as sectarian fighters. Similar pressure had prompted him to formulate the eleven rules of behavior he had issued earlier. These rules regulated the congregations themselves by dictating certain actions during meetings. More importantly, they constrained behavior that would antagonize other members of the larger society, especially other religious groups and the military authorities. By doing so, they also protected the sect against repression.

The step from demanding that a religious authority prevent military actions to demanding that he exercise military power was a small one in the context of the time. It was also a fundamental one, and difficult for Jitsunyo to take. It is unlikely that any Patriarch in the same situation would have behaved much differently, though; religious armies were too common, and the sect's debts to Hosokawa Masamoto left scant room for maneuvering. The internal acceptance of Honganji's emerging militarization was probably inevitable.

Most of Honganji's members embraced the opportunity to fight on behalf of the sect. Although initially members were drawn largely from the towns, by the beginning of the sixteenth century, the elite of rural villages had begun to accept the faith, and most of these rural followers were already at least part-time warriors. It cannot have been too difficult to convince them to go to battle on behalf of Honganji (the group of protesters in the Kinai to the contrary notwithstanding). Despite Jitsunyo's reputation for conservatism (a view of the Patriarch not shared by his brother, who regarded him as a degenerate), he had taken a decisive step toward the militarization of the Honganji sect. His successors would seize on his precedent and make heavy use of it.

FIVE

Increasing Secular Power, 1525–1554

The later 1520s and 1530s were eventful years for Honganji. They saw the culmination of the trend, already in progress, that revealed the extent of *ikkō ikki*'s formidable power, especially when led by the Patriarch. For their part, Honganji's leaders created precedents and mechanisms whereby they could mobilize *ikki* if they chose to, though they could not necessarily pacify them when a conflict was already in progress.

Honganji members fought in two wars during those decades: an intra-sect struggle in Kaga and another in which they took on the *de facto* deputy shogun, Hosokawa Harumoto (1514–63). The one in Kaga was a power struggle between the Patriarch and several priests of *ichimon* temples there, a sectarian civil war with overtones from a larger fight between possible successors to Hosokawa Masamoto. When it was over, those siding with the Patriarch won, increasing the Patriarch's strength at the expense of the *ichimon* council. The outcome also left Honganji with a *shugo*'s power in Kaga.

In the second war, Hosokawa Harumoto, the acting deputy shogun,[1] and an *ikkō ikki* faced off. After several years of battles and unsuccessful truces, a negotiated peace produced no decisive victor. After this war, the *monto*'s strength and the Patriarch's ability to command it drew the interest of elite members of society. Courtiers hoped that the Patriarch would help them collect the rents from their shōen, and daimyo saw a potential military ally. In effect, the elite accepted the Patriarch as one of their own.

This war against the deputy shogun also led to ideological changes, specifically the growing belief that the Patriarch had the power to guarantee that a member would be reborn in the Pure Land. An element of such an attitude had existed even during Rennyo's tenure, according to one tale.

It tells of a doctor who claimed to rely on *kami* for aid in this world, and on Rennyo to take care of the next. Supposedly, Rennyo promised that he would see to the doctor's salvation personally.[2] Believers generally assumed that Rennyo would achieve enlightenment and become a Buddha through the Pure Land. That outcome, presumably, would put him in a position to help with the doctor's auspicious rebirth, much as Amida had promised to save all sentient beings. At the time then, this idea may have seemed perfectly reasonable and in line with teachings professing that no human agency could bring salvation. After all, technically the guarantor was not the human Rennyo, but rather the Buddha Rennyo. Still, doctrine specifically assigned the power of salvation solely to Amida.

Members already believed that the Patriarch had the power to condemn someone to hell because they perceived that expulsion, somehow, necessarily meant the offender would fall into hell. The Patriarch could, of course, expel unruly followers and therefore could send people to hell. It was then only a short step to believe that he could also guarantee their rebirth in the Pure Land. Some Patriarchs, beginning with the tenth, Shōnyo, would not discourage that belief, and they may have used it consciously to manipulate believers.

Shifting Leadership and the Dai-shō Ikki

Dynastic and territorial tensions both contributed to civil war in 1531. When Jitsunyo neared death in 1525, his grandson and heir Shōnyo was only 10 years old.[3] So Jitsunyo appointed as guardians a five-man council of regents, all of them heads of *ichimon* temples: Jitsuen (Honshūji of Mikawa), Renjun (Ganshōji of Ōmi), Renkyō (Shōkōji of Kaga), Rengo (Honsenji of Kaga), and Kensei (Kōkyōji of Kaga). Renjun (1464–1550) and Rengo were Jitsunyo's full brothers, Jitsuen (1498–1555) was his son, and the others were the heirs of two of Jitsunyo's half-brothers. All, then, shared close family ties to each other and to Shōnyo. Renjun had a particularly close relationship to the new Patriarch because he was Shōnyo's other grandfather through his daughter Chin'ei. The young Patriarch's grandfather and mother dominated Honganji's leadership at least until the boy was old enough to rule by himself.[4]

Shōnyo's accession, then, changed the balance of power within the Patriarch's extended family. Before Jitsunyo's death, the priests of Kaga's so-called "three temples"—the *ichimon* temples of Honsenji, Shōkōji, and Kōkyōji—had been especially influential because the Hokuriku had so many Honganji members. Renjun, despite being Jitsunyo's full brother and overseeing temples in the provinces of Ōmi, Ise, and Kawachi, had enjoyed less influence because of the Hokuriku's great importance in the sect.

In dynastic institutions, power derives from proximity to the family head, in this case the Patriarch. The closer one's relationship to him, the greater one's influence. It was only natural, then, that Shōnyo's mother and grandfather would dominate the other council members when their child became Patriarch. Their ascendancy detracted from the influence of the Kaga *ichimon* temples, whose heads had previously enjoyed the most power within the *ichimon* council. This situation resulted in friction between Renjun and the priests of the Kaga temples.

Other factors in Kaga exacerbated the tension between the *ichimon* priests and the Honganji clique of Shōnyo, Renjun, and Chin'ei. Specifically, the three temples had rivals in Kaga, the two "Echizen temples," so called because they had originally been founded in Echizen. As a result of losing the 1506 fight to the Asakura, the priests of these temples were forced to flee the province. They had re-established their temples, Chōshōji and Hongakuji, in the more hospitable province of Kaga, where they already had several branch temples. They had many followers, drew more still, and also formed connections with local warriors. In consequence, the power of the transplanted Echizen temples in Kaga grew, threatening that of the *ichimon* temples.

Further, the head priests of these temples were also related to Renjun and Chin'ei. The mother of Chōshōji's main priest, Jikken, was another of Renjun's daughters, and so the priest was another of Renjun's grandsons.[5] Thus, in spite of the temple's lower status—it was not *ichimon*—Chōshōji's priest Jikken suddenly had the ear and support of the dominant regent, as it were, whereas the three Kaga temples had no comparable relationships to counterbalance Jikken's advantage.

The provincial civil war that scholars have termed the *dai-shō ikki* (lit., large and small *ikki*) took place in Kaga in 1531, and grew out of the increasing friction between the province's two Echizen and three *ichimon* temples. Partly because of Jikken's relationship with Renjun and the now 15-year-old Patriarch Shōnyo, and partly because of tension between Renjun and Honganji's conciliar advisors, that is, the Kaga *ichimon* priests, Honganji took Jikken's side in the struggle. Ultimately, it became a war of overlapping issues: between the main Honganji leaders and the three *ichimon* temples over power within the sect, and between the Echizen and *ichimon* temples over power within Kaga.

The term *dai-shō*, "large and small," refers to the two *ikki* that did most of the actual fighting for the two sides. Both chronicles and historians apply the labels inconsistently, however. In some cases, the Honganji side is called the large *ikki* and the three temples' side the small. In other instances, the terms are switched, making Honganji's side small and the three temples' side large. For clarity and simplicity, we will ignore "large" and "small" in favor of labeling the two sides as "Honganji" and the "three temples."

Although the friction between Honganji and the three temples had begun after Jitsunyo's death in 1525, it took six years to fully ignite. It did so over a small issue that united the three temples' rivals and forced a confrontation between the Honganji and three temple factions. This issue, the immediate cause of the war, was linked, if only tangentially, to the ongoing struggle over who should be deputy shogun and shogun.[6] Hosokawa Takakuni and his would-be shogun Ashikaga Yoshitane fell out in 1521, after which Takakuni championed Yoshitane's rival and came to dominate Kyoto.

By 1526, Takakuni faced competition in the persons of Hosokawa Harumoto and his ally Miyoshi Motonaga. The newcomers attacked, and after five years of warfare, Takakuni lost, dying on the battlefield. Harumoto and Motonaga then seized Takakuni's lands in order to redistribute them to their retainers.

As it happened, some of this land was in Etchū, with its substantial population of Honganji sectarians under Honsenji's jurisdiction. Two of the Patriarch's retainers, Shimotsuma Raishū and his brother Raijō,[7] had designs on that land and seized it before Harumoto allotted it to others. Jikken of Chōshōji supported their claim, but the three *ichimon* temples, Honsenji, Kōkyōji, and Shōkōji, opposed it. They argued that the brothers' actions violated Jitsunyo's rule against taking up arms.

Partly because of Jikken's relationships with Renjun and Shōnyo, partly because the Shimotsuma family served the Patriarch, and partly because Honganji headquarters saw an opportunity to undermine the *ichimon* temples, when it weighed in on the question, it did so on the side of Jikken, Raishū, and Raijō.[8] The three temples stood firm in their disapproval, however, asserting their regional authority. Ironically, they took up arms to punish the Echizen temples for disobedience. On the ninth day of the intercalary fifth month, the three *ichimon* temples attacked and destroyed the Echizen temples, forcing their priests to flee. The refugees regrouped in southwest Kaga, in a region called Yamanouchi. The *ichimon* temples' victory was, however, only temporary.[9]

When the Echizen temples counterattacked, their strategy focused, logically, on the three temples and their priests. They started with Shōkōji in Hasadani, which they destroyed, and then went on to burn Honsenji to the ground. The Echizen temples' forces captured the priests from Shōkōji—Renkyō and his sons Jikkyō and Kyōjo—and took them back to Yamanouchi as prisoners.[10] These were the opening battles of the *dai-shō ikki* war.

By the seventh month, Honganji had sent Chōshōji reinforcements from several other provinces, including Ōmi, Hida, and Mikawa, making their *ikki* forces numerically superior to anything the three temples could field.[11] Thus strengthened, the Honganji-Chōshōji forces attacked Gantokuji, another *ichimon* temple, because it was under the care of Jitsugo, the adopted son of Honsenji priest Rengo. On 7/23, the Honganji *ikki* attacked Gantokuji.[12] The *ichimon* temple, unable to defend itself against such a force, fell, and the enemy forces set fire to it as they had to Honsenji and Shōkōji, burning it to the ground.[13] At that point, the Honganji side had only one important target left—Kōkyōji temple—and they did not wait long to deal with it.

Less than a month later, the Honganji-led army arrived in force at Yamada, where Kōkyōji lay. One source says Honganji could boast seven thousand horsemen.[14] Although such sources exaggerate routinely, sometimes wildly, the Honganji *ikki* must have nonetheless greatly outnumbered any *ikki* force that Kōkyōji could muster. Battle commenced on 8/17, and in a surprise turnaround, Kōkyōji's forces repulsed the attackers. That temple's head priest Kensei knew, however, that he needed assistance to prevail and turned to Asakura Norikage, a powerful local samurai of Echizen who was related to the daimyo.[15]

Echizen samurai, along with those from Noto and Etchū, agreed to collaborate and help the three temples. On 1531/8/19, Norikage set off with his troops to invade Kaga, which they did three days later. Noto and Etchū forces arrived in the tenth month and camped on Kaga's northern border, where the remainder of Honsenji's forces joined them.[16] News of one or more of these expeditions must have reached Kyoto quickly, as Shōnyo wrote a letter on 8/23 to the Ishikawa-gun *ikki,* which evidently opposed the three temples, urging its members to fight conscientiously.[17]

Throughout the war, the existing *ikki* that helped administer Kaga had failed to act in unison, their individual members responding to different loyalties. Followers from the Ishikawa and Nōmi *gun ikki* tended to support the Honganji group, whereas most of those in the Enuma *gun ikki* supported the three temples, allying them in this case with the neighboring daimyo.[18]

Norikage and his men from Echizen attacked the Honganji forces near the end of the tenth month and succeeded in pushing them back for the time being. A few days later, on 11/2, the Noto and Etchū forces also took to the field, but they were routed and withdrew from Kaga.[19] This was a critical defeat for the three temples' side, and Asakura Norikage decided to leave as well. He started back to Echizen the next day, and within the week all his forces had left Kaga.[20]

Some *ichimon* priests continued to fight for a while, but their defeat was finally confirmed on 11/18, when the head priest of Shōkōji, Renkyō, killed himself at Yamanouchi. He was joined in death by his two sons, Jikkyō and Kyōjo, and by three members of the Shimotsuma family, Raisen, Raikō, and Raikei, who had remained with the *ichimon* side. Renkyō's father Renkō had died of illness one month previously, to the day.[21]

The other *ichimon* priests scattered. Rengo, formerly of Honsenji, had a friend in the Noto governor, so he and his son Jikkyō fled there. Some time later, Jikkyō died of poisoning for reasons that are unclear. Kensei fled to Echizen, and others went even further, to the Kinai and elsewhere.[22] Shōnyo pardoned all those who were still alive in 1550 on the occasion of Renjun's death, but sixteen years after that, Kensei suffered expulsion again and died without a pardon. The bitterness of the 1531 war lasted for decades.

In addition to Honganji's support of the Echizen temples, a number of other factors contributed to the three temples' defeat. Perhaps the most important of these reflected the differences in status of the Echizen and the *ichimon* temples. Within the sect, of course, the *ichimon* priests enjoyed a higher status than the others, although the *dai-shō ikki* war reduced their power. The priests also held higher status in the society at large, but that had unforeseen liabilities.

Ichimon temples reported directly to Honganji and acted as the main temple's representatives in the field. As Honganji's representatives, they stood outside the pyramid of temples and branch temples, and they lacked branches of their own. These circumstances underscored their singular positions. Although the *ichimon* priests theoretically had jurisdiction over the temples in their regions, that authority derived from Honganji, so when, as in this case, the *ichimon* priests quarreled with Honganji, they were quite on their own.

The *ichimon* temples thus lacked independent connections to local temples. They also lacked relationships with local warriors because temples formed such relationships through branch temples and patrons, which *ichimon* priests did not have, or through marriage. *Ichimon* priests tended to marry within the sect to descendants of other *ichimon* temples or to members of the main Patriarchal family, thus preserving an elite religious status. The few warriors with whom the *ichimon* priests of Kaga had connections were usually daimyo, reflecting, perhaps, the priests' relatively high status, their supposed power over Honganji members, or both.

As allies, however, daimyo had limitations. Because of the uncertainty of *sengoku* daimyo rule, no one understood better than they that status by birth, title, rank, or position did not guarantee real power. When those considerations did accompany power, they might not do so for long, as a valuable ally one day might be a mendicant refugee the next. Under these conditions, it was a foolish daimyo who backed an underdog for long. Thus, although the *ichimon* priests' allies had great strength, when things went badly, they had no choice but to cut their losses in battles undertaken on behalf of others. When the daimyo and Asakura Norikage left Kaga, the three temples had no allies left.

By contrast, the Echizen temples expanded their influence and power by building up a local base of support. Both Chōshōji and Hongakuji had many branch temples in Kaga, and they cultivated ties with local warriors as well. One of Chōshōji's earliest supporters was a warrior family, the Sugawara, with whom the main priest's family intermarried for several generations.[23] When they were chased into Kaga, the priests of the Echizen temples probably sought the same kinds of patrons. In short, both temples could draw on a wider following than the Kaga *ichimon* temples could. Their supporters included their own members, members of branch temples, warriors, and *jizamurai.* None of these sources of assistance depended heavily or directly on Honganji. When Honganji also joined with the Echizen temples, and even arranged for reinforcements from other provinces like Mikawa, Chōshōji and Hongakuji had a winning edge.

The *dai-shō ikki* episode wrought a number of changes, aside from strengthening the Patriarch's hand relative to the *ichimon* temples. More importantly, it strengthened Honganji's place in political and military affairs on a national level, which contributed to the next war. Other consequences primarily concerned Kaga.

Two of the five men Jitsunyo chose for Shōnyo's advisory council—Rengo and Kensei—were expelled from the sect as a result of the civil strife, and a third, Renkyō, had died. Their Kaga temples lay in ashes. In effect, Honganji's triumph over the Kaga temples destroyed the council as Jitsunyo had constituted it. Although there were still *ichimon* temples, and they still wielded power as Honganji's representatives, the Patriarch no longer needed to listen to their advice.

More basically, Honganji's support of the temples at war fully legitimized military actions taken by priests for political reasons, that is, for reasons other than self-defense. Of course,

Jitsunyo's call to the membership in the 1506 *ikki* to assist Hosokawa Masamoto set an important precedent, but Jitsunyo soon backed off from it. Such second thoughts would not occur this time. Shōnyo and his supporters gave their blessings to still more fighting before long.

The *dai-shō ikki* gave extensive battlefield experience to members of the Shimotsuma family, who acted as generals and warriors for Honganji temple. It also demonstrated to the temple that it could call on followers everywhere for specifically military support by utilizing the powers of the remaining *ichimon* temples.[24] The 1506 *ikki* conflicts had nudged the sect closer to militarization; the *dai-shō ikki* war left it a full-fledged military power.

The issues that precipitated the *dai-shō* war were political, concerning power within the sect on one level and national struggles on another. To the extent that it was a religious war, it was institutional rather than doctrinal. The winners criticized the losers for disobeying Honganji's top leaders. The losing side had refused to accept the Patriarch's decision when, in their view, it ran counter to temple precedent and policy, in this case condoning the actions of people who broke Jitsunyo's rules of peace. The Honganji-side victory made it clear that no *ichimon* temple had authority to pass judgment on the Patriarch's orders, and it reaffirmed Patriarchal supremacy.

The disruptions in Kaga resulting from the *dai-shō* war also exposed the lack of coherent provincial governance. Indeed, they contributed to it. As the dust settled, Honganji took over governance of Kaga and established the Kanazawa *gobō,* an office to manage the province's affairs.

Under Honganji rule, the four Kaga *ikki* became much more involved in such administrative matters as collecting taxes, but even then they did not completely replace unaffiliated warriors, many of whom continued to exercise local power. In the most significant change, authorities and landholders outside Kaga accepted Honganji as Kaga's new *shugo,* in effect, and communications were subsequently sent to Honganji in the same way they went to daimyo elsewhere. This configuration of government functioned for more than 40 years, many times as long as duration of the Yamashiro *kuni ikki*, described in the introduction. Had Kaga not been overseen by one authority – Honganji – the province's government, and the *ikki*'s important role within it, probably would have gone the way of Yamashiro and been dissolved within a few years.

The Tenbun War, 1532–1536

The Tenbun War, so called after the name of the era in which it was fought, was a four-year-long episodic conflict. It required the Patriarch to coordinate all his resources in order to defend the sect against Hosokawa Harumoto, the acting deputy shogun. Once again, a Patriarch needed to exercise the kind of military authority that he had used during the *dai-shō ikki*, but this time on a much larger scale. He succeeded and thereby demonstrated the great strength Honganji had achieved.

The early stages of the Tenbun War in 1532 resembled the beginning of the 1506 *ikki* conflict, in that the acting deputy shogun, Hosokawa Harumoto, asked Shōnyo for military backup in much the same way that his predecessor Masamoto had done. In the course of building power in the 1520s, Harumoto had acquired a vassal, Kizawa Nagamasa, a powerful provincial warrior from Kawachi. Nagamasa had formerly been an official for one of Harumoto's enemies, Hatakeyama Yoshinobu, who naturally disapproved of his vassal's defection.[25]

Yoshinobu attacked Nagamasa twice at Iimori, the latter's castle, which was in Kawachi near Osaka. Nagamasa alone was no match for his former lord's army, so when Yoshinobu attacked the first time, Harumoto provided troops to help his new vassal. They repulsed Yoshinobu, who withdrew, but then he regrouped and attacked a second time. That time Harumoto could not send his own forces, so he sought assistance from others. As his predecessor Masamoto had done when faced with a similar situation, Harumoto asked Honganji, with its many followers in the Settsu/Kawachi area, to support Nagamasa.

Back in 1506, the earlier Patriarch Jitsunyo had tried to refuse Masamoto's request and faced a revolt by local sectarians when he finally did send the orders. By contrast, in 1532, Shōnyo readily agreed; after all, unlike Jitsunyo, he had a precedent. On the night of 1532/6/5, Shōnyo himself left sect headquarters at Yamashina for Osaka, leading a small force that included the temple's military leaders, members of the Shimotsuma family.[26]

This time, Settsu, Kawachi, and Izumi sectarians responded to the Patriarch's call, ten days later following the Shimotsuma men into battle. On 6/15, they attacked and drove Yoshinobu's army away from Nagamasa's besieged castle, thereby fulfilling Harumoto's request.[27] The prominence of Honganji fighters in the battle is revealed, perhaps, by one diarist who described the attackers as a *do ikki*, a designation we have already seen in other documents referring to an *ikkō ikki*.[28] The *ikki* and Nagamasa's allies pursued Yoshinobu to his stronghold at Konda castle, where, after the defeat of his forces, he committed suicide a few days later.[29]

Apparently encouraged by that success, Harumoto asked Shōnyo for help with another of his problems. For some time there had been friction between two of his top officials, Ibaraki Nagataka and Miyoshi Motonaga. Of the two, Nagataka enjoyed the higher status, but Motonaga commanded more military power and, it seems, wanted to be raised to a status reflecting his strength.

Motonaga had been working toward concentrating power into his own hands, and in doing so he had made enemies in the city and surrounding countryside. The need to find adequate supplies to maintain his troops also contributed to his unpopularity in rural areas; he had already levied additional taxes and, worse yet, could not make his troops stop pillaging.[30] Notwithstanding his sizeable army, then, Motonaga was unusually vulnerable.

Motonaga's rivals tried to drive a wedge between him and Harumoto, succeeding so well that fighting broke out between the two. As a result, Motonaga fortified himself within the city of Sakai. Facing a well-entrenched enemy, Harumoto again asked Honganji for help, and again, the help was readily forthcoming.[31] The *ikki* joined Harumoto's forces, along with reinforcements that had become available five days previously, with Nagamasa's rescue. Motonaga was outmatched, and on or about 6/20, Sakai fell.[32]

During the two weeks between the departure of Shōnyo and his assistants from Yamashina and the fall of Sakai, the Patriarch was able to find a remarkable number of Honganji members willing to fight at his request. Accurate estimates of the scale of fighting are impossible to come by. For example, sources give troop estimates for the battle of Sakai at anywhere from 30,000 to 210,000. Not only do these numbers vary a great deal, but the estimates are also unreasonably high.[33] Information about the earlier battle at Iimori is no better, as one account claims some 3,000 killed on the fifteenth alone.[34] In this fighting, as with the 1488 uprising in Kaga, all that can be said with confidence is that the size of the Honganji *ikki* surprised and impressed observers.

Why did many sectarians from Settsu and Kawachi agree to help Harumoto, when 26 years earlier their forebears rebelled rather than serve? In the Tenbun fighting, the Hatakeyama factor no longer meant as much as it had before. The regional sectarian leaders who had been related to them, Rennyo's wife Rennō and son Jikken, had first been exiled from Osaka and later died, in 1518 and 1532, respectively. No Hatakeyama kin replaced them. Furthermore, this new generation of sectarians evidently did not share the reluctance to fight that had been expressed in 1506. Just the previous year, men from Mikawa had gone to fight in support of the Patriarch in Kaga, and even then it would have been difficult to claim a lack of precedence for the request.

Easier still to understand is why Shōnyo would respond to Harumoto's request. It had been standard policy at least since Rennyo's times to accommodate the secular authorities, though within limits. In 1488, when the shogun wanted the Kaga sectarians expelled for overthrowing their governor, through

Masamoto's good offices Rennyo had negotiated a reduction in the punishment, but nevertheless responded to the shogun's desire to chastise the Kaga *monto*. Jitsunyo initially had resisted Masamoto's request for military help in 1506 because he felt it was inappropriate, and he gave in only when it became clear he could not refuse without losing Masamoto's vital support.[35]

A small factor contributing to Shōnyo's decision may have been that Ibaraki Nagataka, Harumoto's top vassal and Motonaga's top rival, was related by marriage to the Shimotsuma, Honganji's family of administrators and military leaders.[36] The Shimotsuma were servants to the Patriarch, of course, and theoretically had less say in matters than he. Practically, however, their influence within the sect was particularly strong during Shōnyo's youth, and that may have had significant bearing on the decision. The importance of such marriage alliances can be overestimated, of course, so it may have mattered only a little. Nevertheless, it is a factor worth noting.

Finally, perhaps Shōnyo's youth and the recent civil war had their influence as well. Shōnyo was still only sixteen and victorious in the warfare of the *dai-shō ikki*. His faction's success may have given him confidence in the military capabilities of his sect and also in his close subordinates' skill as military leaders. Furthermore, the distinction between priest and warrior seems not to have been as clear to him as it appears to have been to Jitsunyo, who at first refused to help Masamoto because of his "long-sleeved status," that is, his status as a priest, that is, one who did not labor with his hands.[37] In 1532, if Shōnyo had tried such an argument, it would have seemed laughable after his activities in the *dai-shō ikki*.

By then, Shōnyo and his advisors evidently saw no good reason to deny Harumoto's request, and no doubt they felt that much could be gained by retaining his good will. Unlike Jitsunyo, who had feared that the members would not obey his orders—and indeed, some did not—Shōnyo had proven he could exercise military authority. The *dai-shō ikki* had resulted in tighter control of the organization by the Patriarch and his associates. In particular, it gave them a stronger hand with the *ichimon* temples, which had weakened relative to Honganji, yet still enjoyed considerable power over local temples. Should the Patriarch desire people to fight for him, the *ichimon* temples would be compliant and assist in organizing fighters. The *ichimon* temples might even single out temples or individuals for punishments if they resisted. Shōnyo and the *ichimon* temples increasingly applied the punishment of expulsion during his tenure, and he exercised a more coercive authority than his predecessors had.[38] All in all, the leaders in 1532 seem to have felt that they could rely on their organization. They could and did, but, as it turned out, the membership still had a few surprises in store for them.

After the successful assault on Sakai, Shōnyo and his aides returned home to Yamashina, as the sect members were expected to return to their provinces. The episode of fighting seemed to be over. Less than a month later, however, on 7/17, an *ikkō ikki* in Nara attacked and burned down nearly all the buildings of Kōfukuji, the ancient temple that held the official appointment of *shugo* of Yamato Province.[39] In addition to destroying the buildings, the *ikki* had sacked them and killed priests; they also took sutras, discarding them in stacks in the streets. They spared most of nearby Kasuga shrine, but broke into its storehouse, removing and destroying its sacred objects.[40]

If the reactions that courtiers recorded in their diaries are any gauge, the attack horrified the capital's elite population. *Nisui-ki* reported the author's shock at this "unheard-of" catastrophe. Former *kanpaku* Konoe Hisamichi wrote of a "Honganji *ikki* [that] . . . killed several priests, set fires, etc." in Nara, concluding, "This is outrageous."[41] Another claimed the attack occurred because of "Honganji instigation,"[42] though we can't know whether he means Shōnyo, or that the Honganji members started it, but then other non-Honganji rioters joined in.

It is now generally believed that the attack occurred without encouragement or leadership from Honganji headquarters.[43] Even though the leadership did not plan the attack, however, the sect as a whole was to be held responsible for it. Six days later, on 7/23, the exiled shogun Ashikaga Yoshiharu sent out a call asking members of the Nichiren sect to attack and punish Honganji for the *ikki*'s actions.[44]

Yoshiharu's choice of ally is noteworthy. The Nichiren sect had been founded in the thirteenth century, and like Honganji, it made many converts among the urban merchant and artisan communities, most especially in Kyoto, which boasted more than twenty Nichiren temples and their branches. The doctrines of the two sects were mutually incompatible. Nichiren adherents worshipped the Lotus Sutra instead of Amida, and they were even more convinced than the True Pure Land groups that their approach to Buddhism was the only right one. During the 1530s, the Nichiren sect members, too, would form *ikki* that had a dramatic impact on their world. Yoshiharu, in effect, wanted the *ikkō ikki* punished by another religious group.

The acting deputy shogun Harumoto echoed the call in a letter dated 8/2, that was addressed to yet another temple. In a nice example of *sengoku* politics, he claimed that Honganji's "selfishness and treachery are well-known" and requested the same type of aid.[45] Although the Honganji *ikki* had just finished helping Harumoto out of a tight corner, he thus acted to distance himself from them. Harumoto had been currying favor with the old establishment to which Kōfukuji belonged, that is, the esoteric temples, the court, and its aristocrats, and evidently he wanted to position himself as their champion. Moreover, in spite of the damage the *ikki* had visited on Kōfukuji, that temple, like most of the older ones, boasted its own army, and Harumoto may have seen more danger from the old sectarians than from the new ones.

Meanwhile, in Yamato, the Kōfukuji officials responsible for administering the city of Nara had fled for safety to the stronghold of a powerful local warrior family. The *ikki* pursued them on 7/30, but finally lost the battle on 8/8, fleeing in their turn to a section of Yamato that harbored some of their co-adherents. When the Kōfukuji priests emerged from hiding the following day and returned to Nara, they reportedly found the city completely burned with nothing but empty fields.[46]

A later chronicle suggested that the attack occurred because of the sect's dissatisfaction with the supposedly tyrannical rule of Kōfukuji's administrators.[47] Kōfukuji had, in effect if not officially, outlawed the Honganji sect in Yamato, at least in the north, and punished members when they were discovered.

Despite Kōfukuji's hostility to the Honganji sect, it had gained a foothold in the south of the province, especially in the Yoshino district, and an *ikkeshū* temple had been founded in 1495 in a town called Iizuka.[48] Although the sect had spread more successfully in areas at some distance from Nara, the city itself housed a number of believers—though not if the authorities could help it. As early as 1458, at least 28 houses had already been inhabited by Honganji adherents, which we know because city officials raided them, confiscating the houses and everything in them.[49] In spite of this and similar shows of power, however, the sect continued to spread.

The leaders of the *ikki,* or at least the men killed and whose severed heads were exposed as leaders of the *ikki,* were primarily wealthy merchants, with some *jizamurai* among them.[50] At least one of them, a man named Kariganeya Minbu, was wealthy enough to have owned a famous tea ceremony utensil and even entertained the Honganji Patriarch's heir in 1521.[51] Honganji adherents in Yamato, especially but not only in the Nara area, included many merchants who had probably been exposed to the teachings of the sect in their dealings with merchants in Sakai and Osaka, not to mention *jinaichō* closer to home in Iigai and Shimoichi.[52]

It is difficult to estimate the harshness of Kōfukuji's rule as of 1532. Only eleven years later, however, in 1543, Honganji established a *jinaichō* that later became one of its more powerful temple towns in Imai-chō, now within the Nara city limits.[53]

Another explanation that historians offer for the assault on Kōfukuji is that local Honganji members had discovered their own power on the battlefield and decided to exercise it further. According to this view, they did it essentially because they knew they could; the choice of target mattered little.[54] Others look less at Kōfukuji as the problem than at the local warriors in power in Yamato, who had been allied with Harumoto's enemies. According to this view, the sect members in Yamato were overly enthusiastic in following their leadership's wishes to attack Harumoto's enemies, and so went after Kōfukuji and its warrior supporters.[55]

The three factors—Kōfukuji suppression of the Honganji sect, *ikkō ikki* capability, and Yamato warriors' opposition to Harumoto—probably worked together, though the last seems particularly influential. Doubtless, Kōfukuji and its administrators would have been unpopular with the sect, though they may not have enforced the anti-Honganji laws frequently or broadly enough to provoke an uprising on those grounds alone. However, the persecution—in combination with the *ikki*'s consciousness of their power, and their hope that Harumoto might not only tolerate but also applaud the actions—could have tipped the balance. But if the *ikki* participants did think Harumoto's Sakai shogunate would approve, they made a serious miscalculation.

As we have seen, Harumoto was alarmed, not pleased, by the Kōfukuji attack. First of all, he was in the process of changing his support of shogunal contenders by negotiating a relationship with Yoshiharu. He did so because his former shogunal candidate had fled and Yoshiharu's backer had been killed. Yoshiharu was much closer to the old interests represented by the court and esoteric Buddhist temples, like Kōfukuji, than Harumoto had been, and it did not serve Harumoto's interests to antagonize Yoshiharu or his friends. Even if it had, the independent rampage was shocking in its sheer unaccountability.

Unlike his adoptive grandfather Masamoto, who 45 years earlier had continued to protect the sect after an *ikki* had toppled Kaga's governor, Harumoto turned on the sect. In 1488, the shogun had demanded that Rennyo expel the members responsible for the uprising, and Masamoto interceded on the sect's behalf. In 1532, by contrast, neither Harumoto nor the shogunal candidate sought to have the members expelled.

Instead, Harumoto was determined to punish the adherents more directly, by attacking them himself.

Some historians have suggested that the mere existence of Honganji's now well-demonstrated power, combined with the fact that it was independent of warrior control, made it necessary for Harumoto to turn next to the destruction of the sect.[56] According to this view, Harumoto would have turned on Honganji even if sect members had not attacked Kōfukuji; the attack merely offered him the ideal pretext to proceed.

There can be no doubt that in 1532, the Honganji sect's military potential was clearer than it had ever been. Although the sectarian armies had cooperated with warriors in helping to defeat Harumoto's two enemies, their presence was perceived as overwhelming. If the *dai-shō ikki* had left any doubt as to the sect's military power and prowess, the two battles in the summer of 1532 erased them.

Harumoto had reason to be concerned about the Honganji sect's power, if only because it existed outside his direct command; the Patriarch could be an ally but not a vassal, and alliances were fluid. The sect leaders had chosen to support him this time, but could they be counted on to do so in the future? If Harumoto was unsure about Honganji's threat, the attack on Nara must have relieved him of uncertainty. It proved that Honganji's military power was unpredictable as well as independent, which gave the ambitious deputy shogun ample motive for reducing or eliminating it.

Within a few weeks of the assault on Kōfukuji and before the fighting between the *ikki* and the Kōfukuji priests died down, word of Harumoto's calls to attack Honganji started to reach the ears of the Patriarch. On 8/3, an *ikkō ikki* took the offensive by attacking Sakai, only to be quickly defeated. Overall, the eighth month was a bloody one, with no fewer than eight engagements taking place, not counting instances of organized burning and looting. During the first week of the eighth month, warfare centered around Osaka and Sakai. Honganji was a steady loser in these battles, in spite of its support by *ikki* from the provinces of Izumi, Kawachi, Settsu, and Yamato.

By the second week, the fighting had spread north and east to Kyoto and Ōmi, as Nichiren adherents, forming their own *ikki*, began to respond to Yoshiharu and Harumoto's call. The daimyo Rokkaku Sadayori (1485–1552), who controlled southern Ōmi, contributed by attacking an *ikkeshū* temple in his province on the twelfth,[57] while others, probably the Nichiren *ikki*, burned down Honganji sect temples and *dōjō* within the capital.[58] It must indeed have seemed, as one Kyoto diarist lamented, that the whole world had become overrun with *ikki*.[59]

The disruptions of the *ikki* went beyond the physical attacks on Honganji sect targets, as the Nichiren *ikki* held processions called *uchi-mawari*. Sometimes these ended with the destruction of property, as when a similar procession of Honganji adherents set fire to places near the capital,[60] but they seem primarily to have acted as displays of strength and unity.

Scholars debate the full meaning and implications of the phrase *uchi-mawari*, though all agree that it refers to a commoners' procession of some kind, preceding (by as much as several days) an attack by the participants on a given target. Some hold that the marchers intended the procession to encourage other people to join the group as it passed through the streets on its way to battle.[61] Since not all *uchi-mawari* occurred as immediate preludes to battle, however, this explanation is not quite complete.

Other historians point out that the character used to write *uchi* means "to strike" or "to hit," and might refer to the ritual beating of a drum or ringing of a bell, perhaps accompanied by chanting. In this case, an *uchi-mawari* could have been a religious procession of some kind, especially one using practices of the Nichiren sect.[62] Imatani Akira largely rejects this explanation, however, partly because the phrase appears in earlier documents designating actions taken by other groups, before it was applied almost exclusively to the Nichiren *ikki*. Thus, he argues that it could not have referred to practices exclusive to the Nichiren sect. Furthermore, Honganji adherents also sometimes held *uchi-mawari* processions, and their rituals differed from Nichiren practices.

Imatani instead suggests another interpretation for *uchi* by relating it to a different usage, as a prefix that makes the following verb more forceful, even belligerent. For example, *uchi* added to *deru*, meaning "to go out" (pronounced *uchi-izu*), refers to an army going out to engage an enemy.[63] Therefore, an *uchi-mawari* could have described non-samurai people using the procession to prepare themselves for the same purpose: making an attack.

This does not necessarily preclude a religious aspect to *uchi-mawari*. For centuries, it had been believed that ritually striking a metal object, usually but not always a bell, summoned the gods. Cultivators did this when organizing themselves for a protest because they wanted the god(s) present to witness oaths and make them more binding.[64] Beating an object, then, need not have been related to specifically Nichiren sect practices. Commoner armies may have wanted to call on the gods for help in battle, for example, or simply to intimidate prospective opponents. Groups probably attached a number of different meanings to drum beating or bell ringing, and it may not always have indicated the same thing in any given *uchi-mawari* as it did elsewhere or even in other *uchi-mawari*.

It would seem, then, that an *uchi-mawari* was most importantly a display of strength during the days leading up to a battle. Even if it was meant to attract more supporters, more importantly it helped forge a common bond among participants, creating a more cohesive fighting band.

The second and third weeks of the eighth month saw a lot of localized fighting between Honganji forces and the Nichiren *ikki*, who were sometimes reinforced by Rokkaku Sadayori's men. Most of the battles were in and around the capital, though the Nichiren *ikki* also traveled as far as Settsu to attack Honganji sect targets. Honganji tended to lose these encounters, sometimes heavily, as in a battle at a mountain pass called Shirutani, between Settsu and the capital, where an estimated two or three hundred Honganji men were killed.[65] These actions were only a prelude to a devastating attack on the Nichiren *ikki*'s main target: Honganji itself.

Despite its heavy fortifications and prior warnings of the attack,[66] the Yamashina Honganji fell quickly on 1532/8/24. The forces arrayed against the temple were daunting, including the Nichiren *ikki*, Rokkaku Sadayori's army, and people from, allegedly, "more than 50 villages."[67] On the night of the twenty-third, these forces had all moved into position to attack the following day, and some had already begun to burn villages in the area. The force was so large, it seemed "as if there was an army camp in every field."[68] One courtier estimated the attacker's at 30,000 to 40,000 men.[69]

The forces advanced on Honganji from all sides, beginning early in the morning of 8/24. Honganji's defenders evidently realized the hopelessness of their position and decided to sue for peace. No sooner had they opened the gates to send out a hostage, however, than the enemy's forces came pouring in. Within two hours, there was little left to defend. One of the priests fled, taking the sacred image of Shinran to safety, but otherwise "everything in the temple had burned."[70] In the end, not a single house was left standing in the temple town.[71]

The victorious forces did not remain long at Yamashina. The men from Kyoto left immediately, and the Rokkaku forces returned to Ōmi the same evening.[72] Only looters stayed through the following day, picking valuables out of the debris of Honganji temple and its once-flourishing town.[73]

Patriarch Shōnyo's absence from Yamashina and the intensity of the fighting southwest of the capital no doubt contributed to Honganji's unsatisfactory defense. Most of the sect's best military leaders had probably gone with Shōnyo to Osaka, and they may have counted on the temple's moats and embankments to keep it safe. No accounts of Honganji's collapse mention help for the temple from the nearby villages, with which the temple and its *jinaichō* must have had extensive dealings. Nevertheless, those villages became targets of Honganji's enemies, and a number of them were also attacked, before and after Honganji's fall.

After the attack, shogunate officials tried to hunt fugitives in the villages, which strongly opposed their attempt. Honganji had been located in the midst of a group of seven villages that formed a *sōgō*, a cooperative unit made up of neighboring or nearby villages. This one called itself the "seven villages"; it came under the emperor's exclusive jurisdiction and consequently had been granted the right to refuse entry to warrior officials. On the basis of that right, the villagers appealed to the court to support them against the officials, promising to conduct their own investigations and punish any fugitives they found. The villages prevailed, and the officials withdrew.

The seven villages had always been vigilant and even militant in protecting their rights, so the intensity of their opposition is not surprising. Fifty years previously, for example, they had defended themselves successfully against efforts by one of Hosokawa Masamoto's top vassals to take control of the *sōgō*.[74] Their victory in 1532, though, might also have served to protect some of the Honganji fugitives.

The destruction of the Yamashina Honganji did nothing to stop the war. The sect moved its headquarters to Osaka, where the Patriarch had already taken up residence. It would be another year before Shinran's image was installed in the new location, making it the official seat of the religion, but functionally Osaka filled that role immediately.[75]

Honganji persevered in the war despite losing battle after battle in the first two months. Although they defeated Harumoto's forces and Nichiren *ikki* in Settsu once, late in the ninth month, their record otherwise was dismal.[76]

During the second month of 1533, the *ikkō ikki* pushed Harumoto back to his home base in Awa, marking the sect's most notable victory in the war thus far.[77] By 4/26, a little more than two months later, however, Harumoto had returned and, with the help of the Nichiren *ikki*, pushed Honganji's forces out of Sakai and back to Osaka.[78] That defeat put Honganji on the defensive once again. Although it had managed to defeat Harumoto's forces occasionally, it now seemed that the sect would not prevail as they could never press their advantage home. At that point, however, Honganji benefited from the arrival of a new ally, Hosokawa Harukuni.

Harukuni was the younger brother of Takakuni, who had been defeated by Harumoto in 1531. Like his brother, he had ambitions to supplant Harumoto. To that end, he began attacking Harumoto's allies, the Kyoto Nichiren *ikki*, and other targets in the fifth and sixth months, while many members of the Nichiren *ikki* and Harumoto's army were occupied with Honganji. By then, Harukuni had made the entire area around the Osaka Honganji into a battlefield, and the temple was struggling to survive.[79] Harumoto's side clearly had the upper hand, but he had attained it only by committing substantial resources to the fighting. Evidently, Harukuni perceived this and took advantage of the distraction to hit Harumoto where he was vulnerable, in the capital itself.[80]

Harumoto responded to the assault by ordering forces from Ōmi to assist his men in Kyoto. Nevertheless, Harukuni defeated them, killing one of Harumoto's top generals and, reportedly, several hundred of his men.[81] Harukuni's successes apparently created the necessary conditions for negotiations between Harumoto and Honganji because within a few days of his victory a peace was arranged between the warring factions, including both *ikki*—Honganji and Nichiren—and both warrior factions, Harukuni's and Harumoto's.[82] The agreement allowed Harumoto, finally, to enter the capital with his new shogun, Yoshiharu.[83]

In these battles of 1532–33, the first phase of the Tenbun War, one cannot say that Honganji held its own against Harumoto. The temple scored a few victories, to be sure, but it wound up losing most of the battles, and the peace was forced by the danger posed when Harukuni joined the fray.

The military reverses notwithstanding, evidently, one faction within Honganji disliked the settlement and wanted to pursue the war further. In the year following the peace agreement, this faction arranged for one of Honganji's best military leaders to leave Kaga for Osaka and even went to the trouble of orchestrating that transfer in secret. The secrecy implies that military, not just administrative, reasons lay behind the move, which appears to have been a part of preparations for renewed warfare.

The peace arrangement of mid-summer 1533 stopped the fighting between Harumoto and Honganji, but not all interested parties honored it. Two of Harumoto's allies attacked Honganji temples in Settsu at the end of the eighth month and again early in the ninth.[84] In a demonstration of force to intimidate Honganji, Harumoto's vassal Kizawa Nagamasa once brought his men to the surrounding area and had them set fire to various places.[85] Four months later, in 1534/3, Kizawa was back attacking towns close by the city, starting with Mikuriya, where, for unknown reasons, an *ikki* had formed in the tenth month of the previous year, 1533.[86] Nagamasa went on to attack Morikawachi, then circled Tennōji to attack Kōzu and Watanabe.[87]

In the context of the times, this kind of activity was not unusual. Quite possibly it demonstrated Nagamasa's concern that Honganji, which was near his own castle, or its members might encroach on his lands. Maybe they did. In any event, Nagamasa's quarrel with Honganji went beyond Harumoto's, and eventually its resolution would require a separate peace agreement.

At Honganji, in the meantime, the militant faction had gained ascendancy. In the eighth month of 1534, the leader of the Honganji peace faction, a prominent and relatively independent priest of a temple called Kōshōji, departed from Osaka on unfriendly terms with the Patriarch.[88] Some other members of the peace faction stayed at Honganji, but their influence was diminished by his departure. Even with the militants dominant, though, it took several months—and Nagamasa's provocation—before Honganji re-opened hostilities.

Presumably in response to the attacks being conducted by Nagamasa's forces near Osaka, on 4/4 a letter went to a leading Honganji sect priest in Hida Province, requesting his assistance in Osaka. Similar letters had gone out to priests in Mino, Owari, and Mikawa already, the letter said, and the need was urgent.[89]

Honganji leaders decided on 5/29 that the war should resume.[90] Nagamasa's continued harassment of the sect contributed to that decision, of course, but another factor had enhanced Honganji's military potential: the sect had made some new friends, in particular local warriors of the castellan or deputy shugo level. These included Hatakeyama Motonobu, a member of the Miyake warrior family, and Miyoshi Naganao of Settsu.[91] All of these men had bases near Osaka, opposed Hosokawa Harumoto, and provided troops to help Honganji in 1534 and thereafter.

The second stage of the Tenbun War differed from the first in three interrelated ways. First, all the fighting took place outside the capital, though not far away, occurring in Osaka and its environs. Second, Harumoto lacked the help of the Nichiren *ikki,* which had its own concerns in Kyoto. Finally, Honganji had more allies and began this second stage with a series of victories, though ultimately it could not sustain them.

On 1534/6/5, shortly after the decision to resume the war, Honganji solidified its alliance with Miyoshi Naganao by sending him gifts while his army was camped at a small village near the temple.[92] By the end of the month, Honganji and its allies had captured at least one of Harumoto's castles, and they continued to prevail in battles through the tenth month.[93] Then, however, Harumoto and the Miyoshi family came to an agreement and ceased fighting each other, thereby depriving Honganji of a valuable ally. Harumoto and the Miyoshi did not, however, join forces against the sect. Rather, the Miyoshi maintained neutrality for the remainder of the war and stayed out of subsequent battles.[94] Despite losing an ally, the sectarians maintained their military advantage over Harumoto until the end of the year and possibly a little longer.[95]

For unknown reasons, the Kōshōji priest, the peace faction leader who had left Honganji in the eighth month of the previous year, returned to Osaka at the end of the eleventh month and petitioned the Patriarch for forgiveness. He was reinstated in the sect on 11/28.[96] Exactly one month after that, he went down to Kii Province, one of Honganji's strongholds, where he stayed for seven months, evidently assisting the sect in arranging for reinforcements.

During the first few months of 1535, the war faction seemed to weaken. There was relatively little fighting, and on 3/25 a rumor surfaced that the Shimotsuma military leaders had been told to resign.[97] This rumor turned out to be false, but only a few weeks later, on 4/9, two more important members of the peace faction, an *ikkeshū* priest and his son, came to Osaka as well.[98]

Weakened though it may have been, the war faction maintained the upper hand. The *ikki* kept fighting, but the sect's position in the war deteriorated. Honganji lost ground throughout the fourth and fifth months,[99] and the sixth month was one long catastrophic battle, as the sect's enemies burned their way through villages close to Honganji temple itself.[100] In one battle on 6/12, Honganji is supposed to have lost 500 to 600 people, leading one diarist to wonder if this marked the end of the *ikkō* sect.[101] In the latter half of the sixth month, possibly as many as 900 more members came to Honganji's aid from the province of Kii. Nonetheless, at the end of the seventh month, Honganji lost Settsu Province to Harumoto.[102]

The losses that undermined Honganji's position in the war also undermined the influence of the Shimotsuma military leaders in the sect. Throughout the war, they had failed to maintain a military ascendancy over Harumoto. Any arguments they could bring to support continued fighting must have sounded increasingly weak, and arguments urging peace took on greater strength.

Early in the ninth month, the Kōshōji priest negotiated the safety of roads in Settsu, a project he successfully concluded in less than two weeks.[103] The militant Honganji faction seemed displeased with these talks, and for a few days, the town of Osaka was put on alert against some danger associated with that faction's Shimotsuma leader.[104] In the end, no such trouble came. Instead, on 9/14 the three Shimotsuma military generals who had led the Honganji forces for so long, both in Kaga during the civil war and in the Tenbun War, were forced to resign and left Osaka.[105] With the leaders of the militant faction gone, the peace faction expanded its influence.

Formal peace negotiations began through the good offices of Shōren'in, a branch of the Tendai temple Enryakuji, and were concluded around the beginning of the twelfth month.[106] The sect achieved peace first with Hosokawa Harumoto, on 11/26, but evidently separate arrangements were necessary to end the fighting with Kizawa Nagamasa and other generals who had sided with Harumoto.[107]

In some areas, the fighting continued longer, but the temple leaders had not encouraged the continuation of hostilities. Hosokawa Harukuni, for example, took on one of the generals forced to leave the sect, and together they continued the battle from Nakashima, a Honganji temple town in Settsu Province. Harukuni was finally defeated by Kizawa Nagamasa in the seventh month of 1536. The former Honganji general fled after the fall of the town; over 800 other people were supposedly killed, and Harukuni retreated to Tennōji, where he killed himself.[108] Later, Shōnyo congratulated Nagamasa on his victory, an act that further disassociated Honganji from Harukuni and confirmed the sect's renewed friendship with Harumoto.[109]

Although Honganji had ended hostilities with most of its opponents by the end of 1535, it received a pardon from the shogunate only eight months later, on 1536/8/19.[110] The final negotiation of this war, however, concluded when the Ōmi governor Rokkaku Sadayori agreed to peace on the condition that Honganji *monto* in his province be expelled from the sect. Shōnyo acceded to this request in the eleventh month of 1536, and the Tenbun *ikkō ikki* was, at last, over.[111]

The Nichiren Ikki *and* Ikkō Ikki*: A Comparison*

Although the Nichiren *ikki* disappeared from our narrative with the first peace settlement in 1533, it continued to be active in Kyoto on other business until 1536, when it was destroyed by a number of forces, among which the still-powerful Tendai temple of Enryakuji predominated. The Nichiren *ikki*, which ruled Kyoto for a few years, is a topic worthy of separate and extensive treatment, and lies beyond the scope of this study. Nevertheless, as another religion-based *ikki* contemporary with the *ikkō ikki*, some comparison between the two is enlightening.[112]

As we have seen, the Nichiren *ikki* was initially called up by Hosokawa Harumoto, who asked them to attack Honganji temples in Kyoto and the sect headquarters at Yamashina. The *ikki*, however, quickly developed its own momentum and aims. When the sectarians began to assemble and conduct their *uchi-mawari* processions, they apparently did so under the direction of warrior leaders. But roughly two months after the attack on the Yamashina Honganji, they started to assemble and parade on their own.[113]

From the second to fourth month of 1533, when Harumoto had been pushed back to his home province of Awa, the Nichiren *ikki* began to exercise increasing power in the capital. In particular, *ikki* members began to conduct trials and punish criminals, though there is no evidence they were granted the relevant powers officially; they simply began to exercise them.[114] One factor that made such a move easier for them was Harumoto's absence from the capital, which left it with no credible warrior authority. A more important factor, however, was the Nichiren members' desire for more control over their world, and perhaps a growing sense of their own importance and strength in it.

Broadly speaking, the disorder of the *sengoku* period afforded greater scope of action to the kinds of people who formed *ikki* than had earlier periods. The chaotic political situation demanded new ways of achieving and upholding order, perhaps the most successful of which was the daimyo domain. Daimyo armies began to draw on the same people of local influence that *ikki* did, especially *jizamurai* in rural areas. As we have seen repeatedly, warriors recruited *ikki* as their allies, especially utilizing sectarian *ikki* to fight against other religion-based groups. Warriors disliked it, however, when *ikki* acted on their own initiative, which they were prone to do.

Gradually, the Nichiren *ikki* began, in effect, to administer the capital city's government. At first adherents tried to extend their power into the countryside and estates, seeking official appointments, which—not incidentally—usually carried various tax exemptions.[115] For a time, the shogunate seems to have been content to let the Nichiren *ikki* control the city because it had more urgent problems elsewhere. In 1536, however, that situation changed. By then, the *ikki* had alienated the court and older temples, in part because of their interference with the administration of their estates. Finally, the Tendai temple Enryakuji decided to address the matter. Historian Imatani Akira argues that the shogunate not only allowed Enryakuji to destroy the Nichiren sect in Kyoto, but also encouraged it to, which is quite likely.[116]

Enryakuji did not undertake the destruction of the Nichiren *ikki* by itself. After soliciting support from other temples (including Honganji; Shōnyo sent money but no participants), Enryakuji also gained the backing of the Ōmi governor, Rokkaku Sadayori. On 1536/7/27, the battle was joined. The *ikki* lost, and in the fighting, much of Kyoto was burned to the ground. Surviving Nichiren members, both *ikki* participants and non-participants, scattered, many fleeing to Sakai. There was to be no repetition of the Nichiren *ikki* phenomenon in Kyoto.

There were, of course, many differences between the *ikkō ikki* and Nichiren *ikki*, not the least being that the former was largely a provincial phenomenon and the latter an urban one. Additionally, unlike the Kaga *ikkō ikki,* which continued to fill a variety of roles for decades, the Nichiren *ikki* lasted only a few years, though it was remarkably effective while it did.

Along with these and other differences, there were also some striking similarities in both *ikki* and the ways they got started. The Nichiren *ikki,* like the *ikkō ikki* that coalesced in 1473, 1506, and 1532, formed initially at the request of warriors requiring military assistance. Furthermore, more than once, warriors approached a religious group specifically to have it fight against another one. Sometimes members agreed to assist a warrior because of other sectarians assisting his opponent. In Kaga in 1473, for example, the Takada sect was already helping Togashi Masachika's opponent, a situation that seemed to give Honganji members even more reason to respond to Masachika's plea. Similarly, Hosokawa Harumoto apparently exploited inter-sect rivalries when he wrote to several religious institutions asking them to punish the Honganji sect in 1532.[117] When it came time to break the Nichiren *ikki*'s power in 1536, Harumoto may well have gone to Enryakuji to do the job. He certainly allowed Enryakuji, with assistance, to get it done.

A critical similarity between the *ikki* was the exclusive nature of their belief systems. Functionally, both Nichiren and Honganji sects appear to have encouraged the idea that their members constituted a special group, different from—and possibly superior to—other Buddhists. Formally, Honganji's teachings explicitly rejected the notion of superiority and urged believers to respect other sects and Buddhas, as all were encompassed within Amida. Nevertheless, they also asserted that salvation came only through Amida's *tariki* and that only Honganji Patriarchs were able to transmit Shinran's thought accurately. Therefore, there were insiders—Honganji adherents—and outsiders—those who followed distorted teachings. Furthermore, Amida insiders could be saved and outsiders could not. These beliefs necessarily fostered a strongly shared identity that was strengthened by regular religious services. Some adherents, perhaps many, seem to have equated expulsion from the sect, in other words, becoming an outsider, with damnation.

Much more overtly, Nichiren *did* preach that he alone understood Buddhism and Japan's relationship to it. Some of his followers even extended the concept of exclusivity, forbidding believers to have any interaction with non-members at all and forming the so-called *fuju fuse* (do not receive, do not give) group of believers. Although few Nichiren adherents joined the more extreme *fuju fuse* faction, the main sect's teachings nevertheless created a clearly delineated group, distinct from other people. For both Honganji and Nichiren sectarians, then, the sense of a shared and exclusive truth may have helped their *ikki* to stay cohesive.

Of the two creeds, Honganji's teachings lent themselves to more efficient military operations because there was only one "fundamental" temple (*honzan*, a temple that was the seat of a sect or teaching line) and one Patriarch. The Nichiren sect in Kyoto had many divisions, and as many as 21 fundamental temples. In the Tenbun War and some later incidents, the Honganji sect also benefited from having a relatively unified command based on a pyramidal structure. By contrast, the Nichiren *ikki* lacked a sole focal point, not to mention an easily unified leadership.

Ikki members of both sects seemed to want a greater degree of governmental power in their worlds than they previously had, although they may well have envisioned their local power fitting within a hierarchical political context. This growth in political ambition seems related to the type of people attracted to the two sects, specifically merchants, artisans, and elite villagers. Economic growth probably helped these groups recognize their increasing importance, or at least realize that their growing numbers might give them clout. Developments in warfare—for example, the increasing use of foot soldiers—may have given elite villagers a greater appreciation for their collective military potential. Finally, a long tradition of *ikki* or *ikki*-like groups supplied a ready model for organization. All of these factors influenced the appearance, formation, and ambition of the two sectarian *ikki*.

Some components of the Nichiren *ikki* experiment appeared radical only because of their urban setting; the community exercise of police and judicial rights, for example, was unremarkable for a rural village but unusual in cities at the time. The sectarians' attempts to become appointed estate officials in villages near the capital failed, although not necessarily because such appointments were unheard-of. They failed in part because the estate proprietors had succeeded best at maintaining direct control in those same villages. Direct control benefited both the owners and cultivators by eliminating the warrior overseer, who exploited the villagers more harshly than temple representatives, and who might fail to forward to the owner the taxes that he had collected. Therefore, incursions in these estates invariably encountered stiff resistance.

The *ikkō ikki* were more widespread than Nichiren *ikki* in part because the membership was both larger and less concentrated in particular cities. Therefore, there was a larger territory in which *ikki* could form. In addition, the Honganji sect's one fundamental temple, with a national network of branch temples, allowed its leader to appeal to members everywhere through their local representatives. The relative fragmentation of Nichiren leadership limited the sect's ability to collect members from disparate regions, but their concentration in the capital mitigated this organizational drawback when that was the site of their activities.

Broadly speaking, then, the Nichiren *ikki* came about because of several circumstances, many of which it shared with one *ikkō ikki* or another. It began with a warrior's call to arms and was possible because of the number and concentration of Nichiren adherents in Kyoto. Their physical proximity helped overcome the disadvantage of having multiple fundamental temples because it allowed word to spread rapidly without the need for a network like Honganji's. Similarly, their hostility, as Nichiren adherents, to rival Buddhist sects inclined them to cooperate with the warrior.

There were, of course, other factors that affected the formation, activities, and defeat of the Nichiren *ikki* than can be assessed in this context. It is to be hoped that another scholar will take on the topic. Nevertheless, many identifiable similarities more or less peculiar to the Honganji and Nichiren sects help to explain why they, rather than other religious communities, formed so many *ikki*.

Honganji's Strategies for Control of the Ikki

The Honganji members' tendency to take independent action was an old problem for Honganji's leaders. The shogunate looked to the Patriarch to regulate the sectarians' militant behavior, so when an *ikkō ikki* attacked Kōfukuji in 1532, Hosokawa Harumoto decided to retaliate on the Patriarch Shōnyo and the Honganji temple itself. It was, thus, in the Patriarch's interests to facilitate his and his priests' control over sect members. Even before the 1530s, Patriarchs had tried a number of mechanisms to restrict members' behavior. Perhaps foremost among these was the strengthening of the organization's hierarchical structure through the creation of the *ikkeshū/ichimon* system, which emphasized direct and coherent communication from a Patriarch through priests to local followers. The new temples were intended to assure the cooperation and orthodoxy of local priests, whose range of action had been wider without such oversight. The Kaga civil war further subordinated the *ikkeshū/ichimon* temples to Honganji's authority, making them that much more an instrument of the Patriarch. Some ideological changes also enhanced the Patriarch's power. These mechanisms, however, were all more successful at mobilizing the followers than they were at restraining them.

As we already have noted, in 1532, Honganji raised an *ikki* army through this chain of command. That is, Shōnyo employed *ikkeshū* and *ichimon* priests to collect and coordinate the *monto* of their region, and sometimes even to lead them to the site of battle. It is not clear what mechanism Jitsunyo had used in 1506 to notify Honganji sectarians of his two calls to arms, whether he utilized the *ikkeshū* temples or wrote letters to be circulated through congregations. In the second call, sent to Kaga, he appears to have addressed *ikki* organizations directly, rather than communicating through priests. In 1532, by contrast, we have the letter cited above, from the Shimotsuma leader to the priest at a Hida temple, asking for assistance, with its reference to similar letters having gone out to priests in Mino, Owari, and Mikawa.[118] We see a similar process when the Kōshōji priest led several hundred members from Kii Province to help Honganji in the last days of the war.[119]

Honganji seems to have worked especially through the *ichimon-ikkeshū* temples (except for the ones in Kaga during the *dai-shō ikki*) and those headed by Honganji's direct branches.[120]

Since priests, arguably, were most vulnerable to the negative incentive of expulsion—it would deprive them of their very livelihoods—the sect leadership had even more leverage over them than it did over its lay members. There is at least one documented case of a priest and members of his household starving to death after he was expelled.[121]

Another factor that helped Honganji both in maintaining the chain of command and mobilizing troops in the event of trouble was the practice of drawing its own temple guards from provincial congregations on a rotating basis.[122] Everybody involved had become used to the idea of sharing responsibility for protecting the temple headquarters. The members' common experience as temple guards probably made it easier for priests to gather men for military duty, as both levies must have drawn from the same pool of able-bodied men.[123]

In the case of the Tenbun War, the fact that Harumoto issued orders to destroy the sect, not just to punish members involved in the attack on Kōfukuji, surely did its part to help mobilization efforts as well. Fighting in defense of the sect itself, as opposed to fighting for the sect's allies, was a powerful reason to show up for duty. Shōnyo was able to play on the religious aspect even further, as he did in the following letter written to members in the village of Noda, near Osaka: "Twenty-one people died in today's battle. This is necessarily a painful thing, but it is certainly [a] blessed [thing] to be called an ally [*mikata*] of the saint [Shinran]. There is no doubt that the people who died in battle achieved rebirth in the Pure Land. More than ever, I ask your help. Please pass on this message to the relatives of those who died."[124]

This letter is particularly significant because it represents a distinct ideological shift that appears to contradict the orthodox Honganji doctrine. That doctrine holds that only faith guarantees rebirth in Amida's paradise and that no action of one's own can lead to that rebirth. Shōnyo implies, however, that by fighting on behalf of Shinran, or rather for the sect his descendents led, and dying on the battlefield, one would certainly achieve an auspicious rebirth. Thus, one's own action *could* establish rebirth in paradise. This is clearly one step closer to a banner used in the war against Nobunaga that read, "Advance and be reborn in paradise; retreat and fall immediately into hell." Such a slogan would, no doubt, have had tremendous potential to motivate believers. The letter is thus also a link in the process by which Shōnyo eventually claimed for himself the power to guarantee rebirth in paradise, the *goshō gomen*.

Shōnyo had not mentioned a posthumous reward in a letter he had written previously in 1531 to members of the sect in Mikawa who had gone to fight for him in the *dai-shō ikki*. That letter simply praised their loyalty and thanked them for enduring the hardships of a long campaign.[125] It is unclear when Honganji began to claim that the Patriarch could guarantee members rebirth in paradise—our best source only dates it to the Tenbun era (1532–55)[126]—but Shōnyo's letter to his followers in Noda was surely one of the steps that furthered its development. By the time of the war against Nobunaga, many members believed the claim, but ironically Kennyo (1543–92), then the Patriarch, backed off from it in his letters.

Thus, in tightening the organization's hierarchy and developing an ideology that could motivate believers to do what was required, the sect leadership succeeded in improving its ability to mobilize the sect members. None of these developments, however, improved the sect's ability to prevent its members from acting independently. For that, there was still nothing available but the negative incentive of expulsion, which the sect leaders had traditionally refused to apply to communities for actions against provincial and local nonsectarian authorities.

Shōnyo's agreement to expel the members in Ōmi Province for their part in opposing Rokkaku Sadayori demonstrates clearly the weakness of Honganji's position at the end of the war. It was a departure from tradition and highly unusual, to say the least. Had the Patriarchs consistently applied this sanction to *ikki* participants, it is probable that they would have succeeded in training their members to form *ikki* and fight only when a Patriarch or priest asked them. In practice, however, Patriarchs remained neutral in such situations more consistently than they punished their followers. The *monto*'s penchant for violent methods did not reflect a rejection of the Patriarch's right or ability to punish them severely, then, but rather their expectation that, though the Patriarch *could* do these things, he would choose not to. It seems that to the members, their independent *ikki* were simply unrelated to the sect's business, and the Patriarchs' neutrality would only reinforce their attitude.

Analysis of the Kaga Civil War and the Tenbun War

It would be nearly another 35 years before Honganji found itself embroiled in such another large-scale conflict as the Tenbun War. That conflict would be Honganji's famous conflict with Oda Nobunaga, which began in 1570. Because the Tenbun War of the 1530s was a sustained conflict against the established authority, it resembles the war against Nobunaga enough to justify calling it, as at least one historian has, the first Ishiyama War.[127] The similarities are superficial, but the scale of the 1530s warfare proved that Honganji wielded considerable power, perhaps as much as Harumoto's rival Harukuni, who also failed upon losing his allies. If the Settsu and Kawachi members' resistance in 1506 demonstrated to Honganji that it needed to manage its members better in future, the 1532–36 war showed that the temple had made considerable progress towards that goal.

Much had changed since 1506. The sect had continued to grow in membership, wealth, and power, especially through the Kinai *monto* and their flourishing temple towns. As centers of commerce and shipping, it is likely that these towns directly helped the sect maintain and supply the *ikki* that made up its army, though we have no proof. We do know the towns were an important financial resource for the sect in general.

The experience of the *dai-shō ikki* in Kaga in 1531 also had an impact on Honganji. Afterward, the Patriarch no longer shrank from military involvement, and the sect no longer tolerated open dissension within the upper ranks of its leadership, although less severe factional disputes continued. The struggles of the peace faction during the Tenbun War show that Honganji's internal politics remained lively. Nevertheless, the *dai-shō ikki* gave the Patriarch the upper hand over the *ikke-shū/ichimon* temples, and thereafter the council was more compliant than ever.

The Patriarch had also demonstrated a willingness to use the sanction of expulsion against his opponents in the sect, however highly ranked. Even some *ichimon* priests—direct descendants of Shinran, close relatives of the Patriarch—incurred that punishment. Less well-connected priests must have feared it greatly, making them even more willing than before to support Honganji in peace or war.

When the first military encounters of 1532 took place, observers were surprised at the size of the forces under Honganji's command. The subsequent uprising at Nara, and the attack on Kōfukuji, reinforced their alarm at the *ikki*'s power. Sect members repeatedly showed their readiness to fight for Honganji, for example, by the speed with which nearly a thousand people from just one province went to Honganji immediately after its defeat in the sixth month of 1535. In short, the sect's leaders found it easy to assemble an *ikki* army drawing on members from such provinces as Kii, Echizen, Mino, and Owari, in addition to those recruited locally.[128]

The task of identifying exactly who these fighters were, what kinds of people pursuing what kinds of occupations, is as difficult here as it has been for other *ikkō ikki*. Certainly, priests were mobilized this time, as the memoirs of one priest attest; he mentions that his son, also a priest, was responsible for commanding the watch in the temple town at Osaka.[129] In addition, there were wealthy merchants and village warriors leading the independent strike on Kōfukuji.

In some ways, any attempt to determine the status of the fighters is problematic at best. A single member of the village elite could play the roles of cultivator, merchant, village leader, and warrior, depending on what was required of him at different times. None of these roles precluded any other. Nevertheless, when battles occurred during the planting and harvesting seasons, it would seem either that those fighting represented a small number of men from any one village, or that they had other people who could do the farming work for them. At these seasons of peak activity, generally speaking, every member of the village, including women and children, performed a vital function; there was no group of people engaged in less important work who could take over for absent cultivators—except for landlords. So the most reliable indication we have of peasant activity is the timing of the battles.

As with the uprisings in 1506, no pattern emerges in the timing of the battles that can easily be traced to the rhythms of agricultural life. Engagements occurred during the winter, when anyone could have participated, but then continued through the planting and growing seasons, and sometimes even at harvest time. Only wealthy farmers would have been able to leave their fields in other hands for so long, especially during the harvest, while they went to war.

The description of those executed for the Nara uprising shows that Honganji drew participants from a lower level of the population than an average warrior general would have. Still, the bulk of the Honganji sect's armies appear to have been drawn from the village elite and, in the Kinai, from merchants. As we have noted, warriors also increasingly called on the village elite—witness the participation of "more than fifty villages"[130] in the attack on the Yamashina Honganji. We must remember, however, that even if villagers would have seen the participants as members of an elite, to the warriors they were still lowly commoners.

After peace was reached in 1535 and 1536, the Honganji sect entered a long period of relative prosperity when it co-existed with the authorities. Although *ikki* did occur regionally in 1536 and later, the episodes did not seriously affect Honganji itself, which generally denied any connection with the uprising in question, a denial that was accepted.[131]

The fact that Shōnyo could disavow responsibility for *ikkō ikki* without further difficulties shows how much power he had attained;[132] Rennyo had not been able to do so. The 1532–35 *ikki* proved that Honganji wielded considerable power on the battlefield, more perhaps than warrior leaders had expected and quite possibly more than they wished to provoke. Furthermore, by actually expelling the Ōmi members in 1536, Shōnyo gained some credibility for what might otherwise seem disingenuous responses to regional *ikki.* He usually told the warriors that he would do something if all the *ikki* participants were Honganji members; since they were not, he would do nothing. Finally, by following through with the promised expulsion of Ōmi members and maintaining a neutral stance with other *ikki,* Shōnyo may have reassured those intimidated by Honganji's power that he was now serious about avoiding conflicts.

Kujō Hisatsune, a former imperial regent (*kanpaku*) and brother of one of Hosokawa Masamoto's adopted heirs, sponsored Shōnyo at the young man's coming-of-age ceremony. Apparently, by then Honganji was well-enough established, and the Patriarchs sufficiently well-regarded, for the imperial elite to accept them more closely within their circle. Honganji Patriarchs prior to Shōnyo had been sponsored by members of the Hino family, also courtiers, but only of the middle rank, with close ties to the shogunate. Hisatsune also had enjoyed an intimate connection with the warrior government through the deputy shogun Masamoto, and in addition, he held an exalted rank at court.

Power and court rank did not necessarily go together, although the former could lead to the latter. The highest courtier ranks were available only to those born into certain aristocratic families, but if lesser individuals became powerful in a practical sense, courtiers often welcomed intimate connections with them. So it was with Honganji and its Patriarch.

During the remainder of Shōnyo's life and into that of his son Kennyo, many elite or powerful men approached them, hoping to establish closer ties to the sect. In 1541, for example, the Echizen daimyo Asakura Takakage asked Shōnyo to admit him to the sect, most likely because he hoped to gain more power with Honganji sectarians in the Hokuriku. Although Shōnyo turned him down, a little more than two decades later, Takakage's granddaughter would marry Shōnyo's grandson.[133] Shōnyo's son had married Hosokawa Harumoto's daughter, thereby making the highest-level warrior marital connection that had yet occurred in Honganji history.[134] Also in the 1540s, Honganji finally ceased paying dues to Enryakuji, signaling its independence from and full acceptance by other elite institutions. The Tenbun War gave Honganji a confirmed seat, though not a prepossessing one, at the tables of both the high and the mighty.

Kaga under Honganji

In its ascent to grandeur, it did not hurt that Honganji gained its own domain in Kaga. Historians disagree about when Honganji really began to rule Kaga with the Patriarch acting as *shugo*. The relevant documents are ambiguous and have been interpreted in ways that are mutually exclusive. Beginning in the 1530s, however, Honganji temple began to keep records of requests from estate owners and of warrior holdings that had been granted in Kaga, indications that it had taken over the direct administration of that province. The shogunate also evidently recognized Honganji as *de facto* governor of Kaga. At least, it ordered the temple to resolve questions of back rents and taxes.[135] Whenever it started, by the 1530s Honganji, not *ikki*, ruled Kaga.

Honganji continued to work with the *gun ikki*, so the leagues did not disappear. Instead they found a place within government as district agents of Honganji. The *gun ikki*, in turn, worked through groups called *kumi*, which served as agents between the *ikki* and the villages.[136] These groups were not new; some *kumi* appear as early as 1495, playing a role in forwarding rents to estate owners.[137] Their importance in ruling Kaga, however, dates from the Tenbun years. Historian Inoue Toshio, after analyzing entries in Shōnyo's diary and other sources, suggests a division of responsibilities between *gun*, which had some jurisdiction over *kumi*, and the *kumi* themselves.

In addition to performing such functions as collecting some taxes, taking care of confiscated lands, settling some kinds of disputes within the *gun* area, and meting out punishment to enemies, the *gun ikki* passed on Honganji's orders to the *kumi* for action. They also suggested leaders for the *kumi* (Honganji actually appointed them) and divided guard duties among the different *kumi*. The *kumi* collected rents (*nengu*) and Honganji sect dues and donations, and sent them to Osaka. They supplied contingents of guards for Honganji temple, and Honganji also used them to assess taxes. Disputes within villages were settled by the villagers themselves, but when a dispute went beyond a single village, the responsibility for resolution fell to the *kumi*. Only if the dispute involved more than one *kumi* did the *gun* step in. Both *kumi* and *gun* reported news and intelligence to Honganji.[138] Honganji maintained an office in Kanazawa, known as the *gobō*, to oversee provincial matters. It was located on the site that would be used for Kanazawa Castle.

Shōnyo and his successor Kennyo came as close to achieving daimyo status as any religious leaders of the time. The Patriarchs did not achieve the kind of fully independent and extensive authority over Kaga that scholars associate with *sengoku* daimyo and their domains, and the Patriarchs seem to have acknowledged that their powers in Kaga depended on the permission of the shogunate. In 1536, for example, while the sect was at war with the shogunate, Shōnyo turned down requests to confirm fiefs in Kaga because, he claimed, he had no authority to do so. After peace was restored, however, Shōnyo again took up such petitions.

For the most part, aside from its involvement with Kaga, Honganji stayed away from politics and military activities for the rest of Shōnyo's tenure and through much of Kennyo's, contenting itself with its considerable gains. Sect members still took up arms locally, but perhaps because of the Patriarch's non-involvement, any *ikki* of Shōnyo's latter years and Kennyo's earlier ones left scant documentation beyond a notation somewhere that something happened. One *ikki* that occurred under Kennyo, however, left behind enough records and memoirs to yield a reasonably complete description of itself, though it may not have been typical of the *ikki* conflicts of its time. That was the Mikawa *ikkō ikki,* which took up arms in an uprising against an emerging daimyo, as the Kaga *ikki* had done in 1488.

SIX

From Peak to Defeat, 1554–1580

By the end of Shōnyo's reign and the beginning of Kennyo's, the elite of medieval Japan—leading daimyo, high-ranking priests, and the court—recognized the Honganji sect as a major power and treated it with respect. Shōnyo and Kennyo themselves were accepted as members of the elite. Although Shōnyo and his predecessors had at times involved themselves and their retainers in warfare, for several decades after 1536 he and his successor maintained the peace. They were able to distance themselves from the disruptions that periodically occupied members. In the disordered times of *sengoku*, however, such an interlude could not continue indefinitely.

During the years of Kennyo's reign, two of the most famous *ikkō ikki* occurred. The first was the Mikawa *ikki*, a localized struggle against an ambitious young warrior (Tokugawa Ieyasu) and an uprising that Kennyo and the *ichimon-ikkeshū* priests evidently ignored. The second was the lengthy war between Honganji and Oda Nobunaga (1534–82), who set out to destroy the sect's autonomous power in the course of his bid for hegemony over all Japan.

In the Mikawa *ikki* of 1563–64, Tokugawa Ieyasu (so early in his career that he was still using the family name of Matsudaira) faced an uprising that nearly prevented that career from getting underway.[1] His opponents included some powerful warriors and disgruntled high-ranking members of his retainer band, but the conflict revolved around four Honganji sect temples and their followers, whose numbers also included some members of the lower stratum of Ieyasu's own followers. The uprising lasted roughly six months, ending in a negotiated settlement that nonetheless meant defeat for the temples.

The struggle with Nobunaga, by contrast, involved every level of the sect throughout central Honshu, rather than just a small number of local temples, and it was directed by Honganji headquarters. These battles are often referred to as the Ishiyama War, which is a problematic label insofar as it conceals the broader context of the fighting.[2] In reality, Honganji was just one party in wide-ranging alliances that made two attempts to destroy Nobunaga.[3]

In spite of the radically different scales of the Mikawa *ikki* and the anti-Nobunaga war, the two share a number of similarities. In both cases (as with other *ikkō ikki*), the Honganji or its temples had warrior allies, and the warriors had similar goals but different motives than the Honganji adherents. Both uprisings also began with the warrior abrogating traditional rights of temple towns. Moreover, both opponents of the *ikki* were working to consolidate power in their own hands—Ieyasu on the provincial level and Nobunaga on the national one—and Honganji temples and their followers sought to frustrate that process. In neither case, however, could the *ikki* halt it.

Arguably, then, the most significant difference between the two uprisings was simply one of scale. Yet that difference in scale was enormous and, consequently, required different methods of mobilization, wartime strategies, and, perhaps, ways of encouraging members to fight. In Mikawa, one province was at stake, whereas the other war involved a reordering of the entire political and economic landscape of Japan.

Mikawa

The forces opposed to Ieyasu in 1563 can be seen as a loose coalition with three basic components. One consisted of powerful warriors who did not belong to the *ikkō* sect but who resented Ieyasu's ascendancy. The second component involved some less powerful warriors who were still relatively high-ranking members of Ieyasu's retainer band. Some, though not all, of these men were Honganji sect members. Finally, there were the Honganji sect temples themselves, backed by their members, whose ranks included many of Ieyasu's lesser retainers.

Ieyasu, too, drew on a variety of forces. Throughout the period of fighting, he enjoyed the support of most of his top retainers, including those who were Honganji sect members. Several non-Honganji sect temples also joined the fighting on his behalf, chiefly from Pure Land and a rival sect of True Pure Land Buddhism. The pre-existing animosity between the Honganji sect temples and those who aided Ieyasu may have reinforced the bonds among Honganji sect members by giving the struggle an element of a religious war.

Despite the involvement of temples on both sides, and despite the fact that the aftermath of the uprising brought about the abolition of the Honganji sect in Mikawa, this was not a religious war in the sense that it was fought primarily over doctrine or ideology. As with most *ikkō ikki,* the role played by religion was complicated and difficult to isolate, but this uprising appears to have been chiefly a fight over the control of the region and its revenues. The *ikkō* sect temples and their allies were defending their own material interests against incursions by the ambitious Ieyasu.

What was Mikawa Province is today the eastern two-thirds or so of Aichi prefecture. It lay between Owari to the west and Tōtōmi to the east with Shinano to the north. The bulk of the province consisted of mountains and steep hills, with the flattest land to be found in the southern reaches of the Yahagi River basin between the city of Okazaki and Mikawa Bay. Today, much of this area supports rice farming but only as a result of extensive irrigation projects carried out toward the end of the nineteenth century.[4] The sixteenth-century landscape would have looked quite different.[5]

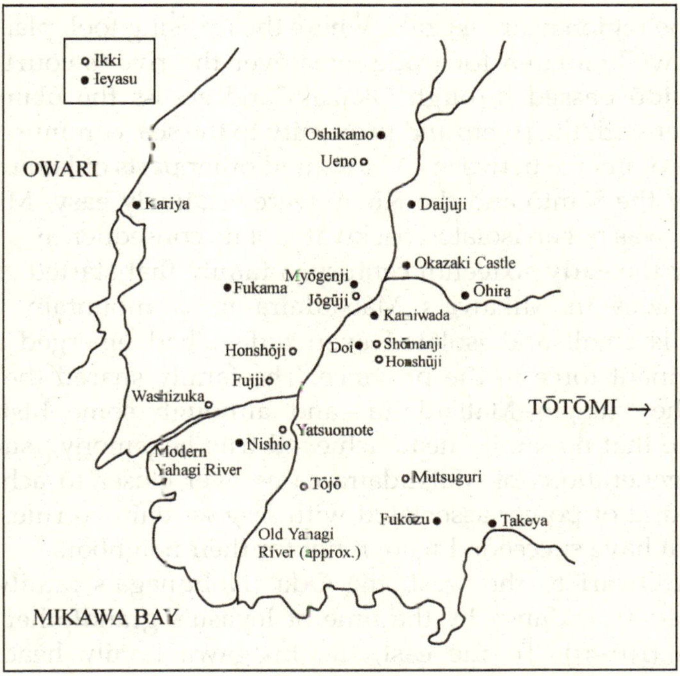

Map 3 Medieval Mikawa Province

Most importantly, the course of the Yahagi River itself has changed substantially. The modern Yahagi runs southwest from Okazaki. Above Nishio it forks, with a branch called the Old Yahagi River flowing into the bay to the southeast of the modern Yahagi's mouth. The northern branch did not exist at the time of the uprising, however; it was created in the early seventeenth century. Even the Old Yahagi, despite its name, probably no longer runs along the course of the sixteenth-century river. Geological surveys indicate that the stream split into several branches between Okazaki and the bay, flowing even further to the southeast than the Old Yahagi's course. Unfortunately, we have no maps from that time, and the geological evidence is imprecise, making more accurate mapping impossible. This makes it difficult to judge the old river's navigability and its possible contributions to irrigation, both of which would have affected the economy of southern Mikawa.

The region near Okazaki, where the uprising took place, was also well situated for trade, whatever the river's course. The Tōkaidō passed through Okazaki and across the plains. Together with the rivers and proximity to the sea, communication and commerce between Mikawa and other parts of Japan, especially the Kantō and the Kinai, were relatively easy. Mikawa, then, was not an isolated backwater of no consequence.

By the early sixteenth century, a family that started as local magnates in Mikawa's Matsudaira-gō, a mountain village that is small and isolated even today, had emerged as the dominant force in the province. The family shared the name of the village—Matsudaira—and although some historians argue that no family head achieved true hegemony,[6] succeeding generations of Matsudaira came ever closer to achieving the kind of power associated with *sengoku* daimyo rule.[7] They might have succeeded were it not for their neighbors.

In Owari to the west, the Oda (Nobunaga's family) had gained ascendancy by the time of Ieyasu's grandfather Kiyoyasu (1511–35). To the east, the Imagawa family heads had already established themselves as daimyo and expanded from Suruga into Tōtōmi. Caught between these two more efficient regimes, the Matsudaira found themselves increasingly embattled and outclassed as fighters. As the Oda repeatedly invaded from the west, Ieyasu's grandfather Kiyoyasu and father Hirotada (1526–49) turned to the Imagawa for help. Indeed, Hirotada had little choice but to accept Imagawa Yoshimoto (1519–60) as his overlord since he was only 10 years old when his father was killed. With his retainers' help, Hirotada was still able to maintain a semi-independent rule until his death at the age of 24 in 1549, leaving 8-year-old Ieyasu as his heir. At that time, Mikawa came under direct Imagawa rule.

The daimyo Imagawa Yoshimoto worked through Matsudaira vassals where this was useful, but he instituted several changes in the governing of the province, especially in taxation practices. In some cases the Imagawa were able to bypass the warriors and collect taxes directly from the peasants, thereby depriving the warriors of various tax exemptions as well as their own take from the collection. There is some doubt, however, that the Imagawa were able to do this on a significant scale.[8] They also conducted land surveys, which resulted in increased taxation because it included newly opened lands, and assessed some lands more heavily than before.[9] The tax burden on cultivator and warrior alike, then, was no doubt heavier than it had been under the Matsudaira, especially for the relatively poor.[10]

After his father's death, Ieyasu grew up as a hostage of the Imagawa. His name, Motoyasu, indicated his subservience as it took the character for "moto" from the Imagawa family head, Yoshimoto. Although he remained a hostage after he reached maturity and was therefore a kind of prisoner, Ieyasu wielded some power as an Imagawa retainer and warden of Okazaki castle, on a level roughly equivalent to Yoshimoto's other castellans.

In 1560, Ieyasu's situation changed when Imagawa Yoshimoto fell at the battle of Okehazama, defeated by Oda Nobunaga. He left a hapless heir, Ujizane, and Ieyasu took this opportunity to assert his independence and claim the land his father and grandfather had ruled, albeit precariously. He returned to his base at Okazaki, gathered his retainers, and set about the task of subduing Mikawa.[11] At first, he continued fighting Nobunaga, but by early 1561, he had arranged a peace, probably through the good offices of his uncle, Mizuno Nobumoto, who had long been on good terms with the Oda.[12] Ieyasu went on to gain control of the northern mountainous region of Mikawa, then turned, or was forced to turn, his attentions south.

Turning south meant facing powerful warriors still loyal to Imagawa Ujizane or, even more likely, eager to strike out on their own much as Ieyasu had, specifically Kira Yoshiaki (dates unknown) and his supporter and distant relative, Arakawa Yoshihiro (dates unknown).[13] Kira Yoshiaki had good reason to believe he had a claim to Mikawa, much as Ieyasu did. Yoshiaki's was a very old family, a branch of the Ashikaga. The first Kira came to Mikawa in the early Kamakura period, serving as *jitō*, or land steward. When the shogun's power declined after the Ōnin War, so did the Kira family's, and they ultimately lost out to the upstart Matsudaira.[14] Much like the Matsudaira, the Kira had earlier been caught up in the struggle between the Imagawa and the Oda, only the family evidently was unable to agree on an ally. The Kira divided into two branches, one based at Saiijō castle and the other at Tōjō castle, each branch supporting a different side. Over the years, the two branches switched sides frequently, making their history somewhat bewildering. That maneuvering probably reflected the two branches' perceptions of who had the upper hand in the area at any given time because each branch would have sought the ally best suited to help it maintain its diminishing power. Eventually, the two branches combined under Kira Yoshiaki's leadership and became dependent on the Imagawa.[15]

Yoshiaki had shown no interest in subordinating himself to Ieyasu, and his presence and power in southern Mikawa meant that Ieyasu would eventually have to contend with him. As it turned out, Yoshiaki may have been the one who opened the fighting between them. Urged on by Ujizane, he attacked Ieyasu's forces at Ueno castle in the fourth month of 1551.[16] Fighting between Ieyasu and Yoshiaki continued over the next five months, mostly in Yoshiaki's home territory, near what is now Nishio. Ieyasu finally prevailed in the ninth month, after Arakawa Yoshihiro changed sides and allowed his castle to be used as a base against Yoshiaki. After his victory, Ieyasu pardoned Kira Yoshiaki and rewarded Arakawa Yoshihiro with marriage to his, Ieyasu's, half-sister. Two years later, both Yoshiaki and Yoshihiro would again join hands in opposition to Ieyasu. In the battles of 1561, they may have been loyal to Imagawa Ujizane and fighting Ieyasu on his behalf, but in the battles to come Yoshiaki, with Yoshiro's support, would fight as Ieyasu's direct rival for dominance in Mikawa.

Throughout 1562, Ieyasu continued expanding his power over the province, and by 1563, he had most of western, central, and northern Mikawa under his control with only the southeast remaining to be conquered. The campaigns thus far had been successful, but they also left the young warrior with further problems. Since Ieyasu created his domain by taking over land previously controlled by the Imagawa—and since that alliance was defunct—he needed to find a different way to confront the continuing threat from the Oda to the west. In addition, fighting was expensive, and he had to collect as much funding and as many supplies as he could to sustain his campaigns.

Ieyasu's response to the threat posed by the Oda family was simple if somewhat controversial among his advisors: he made peace with them and concluded an alliance. Sakai Tadanao, one of Ieyasu's most trusted retainers, whose family had served the Matsudaira since the fifteenth century and had served as high officials for generations,[17] was particularly displeased with Ieyasu's choice. He spoke out strongly against the Oda alliance when Ieyasu first proposed it, though it is unclear how he expected his lord to maintain the Imagawa relationship under the circumstances.[18]

Ieyasu strengthened the Oda alliance still more in the third month of 1563 when he and Nobunaga arranged the betrothal of Ieyasu's 5-year-old son Takechiyo to Nobunaga's 5-year-old daughter Tokuhime.[19] Four months later, the new Mikawa hegemon emphasized his independence from the Imagawa by dropping "moto" from Yoshimoto's name and changing it to the name by which he is best known: Ieyasu.[20]

In establishing his own rule, Ieyasu continued most of the Imagawa policies, particularly in taxation, which must have disappointed any of his followers who hoped he would roll back at least some of the Imagawa increases.[21] His decision to maintain the higher level of taxation made sense, given his continuing need for funds. That need contributed to his choice of policy with regard to the Honganji temples and helped prompt him to take the steps that sparked the uprising in the fall of 1563, attacks on four Honganji sect temples and their exemptions from taxation and warrior interference.

The four temples involved—Jōgūji, Honshōji, Shōmanji, and Honshūji—had been affiliated with the Honganji sect for nearly a century.[22] All had developed temple towns—local commercial centers connected with the temples—and all enjoyed special rights, including *funyū*, the right to bar warriors from entry. This right prevailed even during wartime, when the temples could function as sanctuaries for non-combatants.[23] They also investigated crimes and administered justice within the town precincts.

The *funyū* rights included tax exemptions, though the temple continued to be responsible for paying certain specified taxes on some holdings.[24] In effect, the temples and their *jinaichō* were self-administering and self-policing. The Imagawa had recognized such rights and exemptions for many temples when they ruled Mikawa, and these four temples and their members would have expected Ieyasu to recognize them as well. Evidently, Ieyasu had other plans.

The autonomous nature of the Honganji temples and *jinaichō* posed a problem for Ieyasu both politically and economically. Although their *jinaichō* were not the only commercial temple towns in the area—Ieyasu's family temple Daijuji also had a temple town—they were the most important in the region. Together with the lands that supporters had donated to the temples, they constituted a significant portion of southern Mikawa and its economy that was not subject to Ieyasu's rule—at a time when Ieyasu needed all the wealth he could find.[25]

The Honganji temples even had a kind of military power because their followers included many lower-level samurai and *jizamurai* who might respond to a temple's call for help. After all, there was precedence for such a situation: the head priest of Honshūji had led a group of warriors from Mikawa to Kaga to aid Chōshōji in the civil war of 1531.[26] So in these ways—economic, political, military—the temples were similar to the warriors that Ieyasu had to subdue in order to build his domain.[27]

In the fall of 1563, then, there were several sources of tension in Mikawa. Kira Yoshiaki still nursed ambitions to take over the province, and some others of his kind continued to look for a chance to overthrow Ieyasu in favor of Yoshiaki, the Imagawa, or themselves. Sakai Tadanao, one of Ieyasu's most important advisors, thought the Oda alliance was a terrible mistake and was unhappy that the alliance was continued in spite of his remonstrance. Finally, Ieyasu was on the brink of his campaign to take the Imagawa-controlled eastern portion of Mikawa, and he needed warriors and funds to undertake it successfully. The actual uprising, however, started with the temples.

The dating of the uprising is unclear. Although we have been dating its start in 1563, there is a dispute about whether it occurred then or in 1562. The two most reliable war tales, both written well after the events but by authors with access to relevant records, put the incidents at the temples in the fall of 1562. Contemporary documents related to the *ikki*, however—such as Ieyasu's letters rewarding vassals for their part in the fighting and death registers recording warriors' deaths—are dated 1563 and 1564. Therefore, either more than a year separated the temple incursion(s) and the uprising, which seems unlikely, or the war tales are off by a year in their dating of events.[28] Given the nature of the documentary evidence, the latter explanation seems more likely.

There are also two versions of the uprising's beginnings, one involving Jōgūji and the other Honshōji. Both versions agree that the conflict between Ieyasu and the temples had its origins in his threats to their *funyū* rights. They also say that it began when Ieyasu's forces attacked a temple, with some provocation, and the people defended it.[29]

The Jōgūji version claims that one of Ieyasu's warriors[30] seized rice for military provisions from that temple, and its priests took offense on the grounds of the temple's *funyū* rights (including tax exemptions). The priests rallied nearby villagers, who attacked the warrior's castle and retrieved the rice, returning it to the temple and barricading themselves inside. Messengers sent by Ieyasu to Jōgūji to inquire about the incident were beheaded, so Ieyasu ordered a retainer[31] to investigate and punish the perpetrators. That act constituted a further infringement on the *funyū* rights that gave the temple jurisdiction over crimes in its own precincts. The priests of other Honganji branch temples and their members joined in the defense of Jōgūji, and the uprising became general.[32]

In the Honshōji version, one of Ieyasu's warriors held a grudge against a merchant living in Honshōji's temple town. One supposes that the warrior owed him money. Whatever the grievances, the warrior sacked the merchant's home and was in turn attacked by town residents who came to the merchant's defense. The warrior fled the town and later complained to Ieyasu, who authorized a punitive raid on Honshōji's *jinaichō*. That order infringed the temple's right to investigate and deal with crimes, so the temple and its townspeople fought back against Ieyasu's men, sparking the uprising.[33]

One further commonality of the versions stands out: both say that Ieyasu went after the temples because of injuries inflicted on his retainers—in the latter case the rambunctious warrior who may have deserved it, and in the former the beheaded messengers who did not. Obviously, Ieyasu needed his warriors' support, which could have been obtained in several ways but not by failing to avenge his retainers' death or injuries. Ieyasu had to act.

Neither of the attacks on the temples can be corroborated by documents contemporary or near-contemporary to the events. The Honshōji version has some credibility because it appears in chronicles written by both a staunch supporter of Ieyasu and someone from the temple's side. The Jōgūji version, however, names the participants, all but one of whom really were Ieyasu's warriors. The exception was a man who could not have participated in these events because he would have been much too young. It seems hasty to reject the account on the basis of one incorrect name that may have reflected a simple error in transmission.[34]

If we cannot document either version, then, we also have no concrete reason to discount them. In sum, it is likely that one of the Honganji sect temples or their townspeople somehow injured one or more of Ieyasu's men and tried to evade the consequences by standing on their right to bar entry to officials. No matter what incident moved Ieyasu to take on the Honganji sect temples—one of the two described or some other one—the temples' autonomy and their supporters' determination to fight for it, combined with Ieyasu's goals and his unwillingness to compromise, made a clash inevitable.

In any case, the priests at all three Honganji sect temples joined with those at the injured one, and what began with them soon spread to other parties with grievances against Ieyasu. Kira Yoshiaki, so recently subdued, quickly joined the opposition from his base at Tōjō. Moreover, he was supported by the warrior who had betrayed him two years previously, Arakawa Yoshihiro of Yatsuomote, despite his new standing as Ieyasu's brother-in-law.[35] Another retainer, Natsume Yoshinobu, also broke with Ieyasu, though his father had followed the Matsudaira since Kiyoyasu's day.[36] Sakai Tadanao favored the Imagawa over the Oda and rallied his own forces in revolt at Ueno, even while other members of his family remained loyal to Ieyasu. Even some Matsudaira branch families rebelled, in particular the Ōkusa and Sakurai branches, whose relations with the main branch had often been strained.[37]

As the uprising spread, hundreds of Honganji members, including many from Ieyasu's own retainer band, rose to the temples' defense, though the actual number of sectarians is unknown. The most reliable sources provide what amount to roll calls of warriors at Ueno (Sakai Tadanao's base), at the four temples—Jōgūji, Honshōji, Shōmanji, and the *ichimon* temple Honshūji—and on Ieyasu's side. Combining their lists yields 177 on Ieyasu's roster and 146 on the *ikki*'s. This count includes only those combatants listed by name.

In addition to those warriors, there were many other supporters of the *ikki* at the temples and elsewhere. For example, we are told that at Jōgūji, there were "over one hundred horsemen and [an] unlimited [number] of small samurai" with similarly vague descriptions of lesser combatants at other *ikki* strongholds.[38] Often, historians have understood these "small samurai" to be *jizamurai* who were Honganji members. They emphasize the "cultivator" component of their daily lives rather than the "warrior" one, thereby equating them with peasants.

The sources contribute to the perception insofar as they do not mention such humble combatants within Ieyasu's forces. This omission implies that all the "small samurai" must have been Honganji members. Yet Ieyasu's forces, too, must have been supported by numerous fighters too unimportant to mention by name. Sakai Tadanao at Ueno enjoyed such support, and it is not clear that his "small samurai" were Honganji members at all; they could have been local recruits or part of Tadanao's network of supporters. Surely Ieyasu had comparable ways to raise foot soldiers and similar lowly troops. Of course, the implication that Ieyasu's loyal retainers were able to defeat hordes of *jizamurai* all on their own enabled warrior chroniclers to give us a more dramatic story of triumph. It also put forth a suitably derogatory view of the members of *ikkō ikki*.

The number of combatants is as difficult to determine as matters of status are; trying to estimate the number of participants by looking at the number of Honganji sect members does not help. Among Ieyasu's retainers, as reflected in the numbers of warriors at the various temples, the Honganji sect as a whole must have counted more members than any of the other sects individually. The three temples—Jōgūji, Shōmanji, and Honshōji—together boasted as many as 170 branches.[39] Branch temple figures do not translate easily into membership figures, however, because some branch congregations may have numbered as many as a hundred members and others as few as two or three.

Okazaki castle remained Ieyasu's base of operations during the *ikki* uprising, and he also placed forces led by his most dependable hereditary retainers close to all the *ikki* bases. Most of these retainers held defensible positions between the *ikki* strongholds and Okazaki castle, which the *ikki* fighters tried to attack repeatedly. Combatants from Honshūji and Shōmanji at Toro and Harisaki had to get past the forces under the Ōkubo family at Kamiwada, backed up by Honda Hirotaka at Doi. Sakai Masachika at Nishio could readily check both Honshōji at Nodera and Arakawa Yoshihiro at Yatsuomote. (At the time, there was no river flowing between Nishio and Nodera.) Jōgūji at Sasaki had to contend with Matsudaira Chikatoshi at Fukama, as well as with the anti-Honganji Takada branch temple Myōgenji at Kuwako. The Jōdoshū temple Rinshōji served as a base of operations for Ieyasu's forces near Ueno, used by Sakai Tadanao. Natsume Yoshinobu faced the Fukōzu Matsudaira, and so on.[40]

Reliable dates for specific battles do not exist, but there are descriptions of battle given in vivid, personal terms. For example, the following quote comes from an account by a warrior who had fought on the *ikki* side: "Ōkubo Yoichirō came out of the castle toward Hanzō, who was ferociously shooting off arrows. When Hanzō took up his spear, Yoichirō was forced to retreat toward the fortified gate. Hanzō gave chase, saying, 'I'll fling [the spear] and run it through you!' But it did not reach [Yoichirō's] body, and he withdrew into the castle. Then Hanzō returned to the temple."[41] The war tales often tell us who was killed, even how, but rarely whether the battle as a whole went for or against Ieyasu. They emphasize individual combat and often, as in this case, give the impression of small-scale fighting rather than of armies clashing. Some sources supply dates, but these rarely confirm each other's dating. The basic outlines, however, are in agreement.

The fighting began in the ninth or tenth month of 1563 and continued until the third month of the following year. The uprising's leaders, focusing accurately on the source of their troubles, made Okazaki castle, Ieyasu's headquarters, their main target. At least once and possibly repeatedly, Sakai Tadanao left Ueno castle to attack Okazaki,[42] while the Honganji members from Toro and Harisaki made repeated attempts to do the same. The hilliness of the terrain made it impossible for the *ikki* forces to get to Okazaki without first getting past the

Ōkubo stronghold at Kamiwada. The difficulty in doing so accounted for the many engagements that took place there.[43] Once, the *ikki* participants tried to go around the hills that prevented them from easily bypassing Kamiwada, choosing to approach Okazaki from Ōhira, but they were intercepted and turned back.[44]

Ieyasu's defense relied heavily on the retainers whose own bases were close to the rebellious temples and castles. In addition, he had a communications system that easily warned him in Okazaki castle of *ikki* activity at Jōgūji, Shōmanji, and Honshūji. Ieyasu's ally, the Takada sect temple Myōgenji, located only a mile or so from Jōgūji, built a watchtower, the better to keep an eye on the temples. At any sign of dangerous activity, the watchers would ring the temple bell, whose sound reached Okazaki, alerting Ieyasu.[45] Similarly, when the Ōkubo at Kamiwada saw *ikki* forces coming from Harisaki or Toro, they blew on a conch shell to summon their forces. Kamiwada was also close enough to Okazaki that Ieyasu's men could hear the alarm and respond with reinforcements.[46]

Ieyasu and his forces did not simply wait for the *ikki* to attack, however. He turned his attention to some non-Honganji warriors early on and forced Sakai Tadanao, his rebellious advisor, out of his castle at Ueno,[47] perhaps as early as 1563/9/6. Then, in the tenth or eleventh month, Ieyasu's forces attacked and defeated Kira Yoshiaki, who either fled or continued fighting elsewhere. Although he survived the battle, Yoshiaki lost possession of his castle and control of his lands.[48]

This is not to say that Ieyasu's side ignored the temples. The Ōkubo repeatedly attacked Shōmanji at Harisaki, and sometimes Ieyasu joined them, reportedly leading the assault.[49] Ieyasu's side also attacked Jōgūji repeatedly, on at least one occasion getting help from the people of Kariya, a town almost eleven miles distant on the border of Owari.[50]

Around the first month of 1564, Ieyasu's men defeated their leader's former retainer Natsume Yoshinobu at Mutsuguri, leaving only Arakawa Yoshihiro at Yatsuomote and the temples to fight on.[51] Yoshihiro then faced heavy fighting from

Ieyasu's retainer Sakai Masachika at Nishio. Masachika also continued attacks on Honshōji at Nodera and *ikki* forces at Washizuka.[52] Not long after Yoshinobu's defeat, however, the two sides entered into peace negotiations.

In the fighting, the *ikki* side was at a disadvantage. It lacked a central command, and its segments had limited communications among themselves, leaving them unable to coordinate attacks or pool information. Only forces from Shōmanji and Honshūji at Harisaki and Toro could often act in concert, probably because they were so close—within a mile of each other. Signs of cooperation among other *ikki* groups, however, are hard to see.

To the extent that Ieyasu had a discernible strategy, it was to isolate and defeat the *ikki* components separately. He concentrated first on picking off the most powerful warriors, such as Kira Yoshiaki, who might have been able to provide leadership. After that, his forces attacked lesser warriors and the temples. The *ikki*'s overall inability to coordinate its efforts may not be traceable to any lack of will to cooperate but rather to Ieyasu's success at arraying his own forces in ways that pinned the *ikki* supporters down while denying them effective leadership.

Much as there were two versions of the opening of hostilities, so are there two versions describing the subsequent peace overtures and negotiations. According to *Mikawa monogatari,* the first overtures came from Hachiya Hannojō Sadatsugu, a relative of the Ōkubo and a Honganji member who had fought hard for Shōmanji.[53] *Matsudairaki,* the earliest chronicle of the uprising, says the Ōkubo family itself, concerned that enemies from Suruga (Imagawa Ujizane) or Kai (Takeda Shingen) would take advantage of Ieyasu's troubles and invade, made the first moves.[54] Either way, the talks seem to have begun at Kamiwada, the Ōkubo family base. The negotiations themselves would have involved others in addition to Hachiya Sadatsugu, and some *ikki* combatants probably communicated through family members who had remained loyal to Ieyasu.[55] Neither source mentions the non-sectarian allies in connection with the peace talks at all. Indeed, the tales imply that only the *ikki* supporters who had defected from Ieyasu's retainer band figured in the negotiations.

The *ikki*-side negotiators advanced three conditions—two, according to *Matsudairaki*—for their surrender: one, that warriors who had joined the uprising be pardoned and reconfirmed in their original fiefs; two, that the temples remain as they were before and retain their exemptions; and three, that the ringleaders' lives be spared.[56] *Mikawa monogatari* contended that Ieyasu balked at sparing the lives of the ringleaders, but the *ikki* representatives insisted, with support from an unlikely ally. A member of the Ōkubo family, one of the warriors who had fought for Ieyasu particularly tenaciously, also pressed for the ringleaders' lives to be spared. He pointed out that if Ieyasu pardoned the retainers who had joined the uprising, apparently including the unnamed ringleaders, he could use them to easily defeat hold-outs such as Arakawa Yoshihiro.[57]

Ieyasu finally agreed, writing up a peace contract that was circulated by the temples. Evidently he had agreed to pardon most of his former retainers who had joined the uprising, but not all, for reasons that are not always clear. For example, he pardoned Watanabe Hanzō Moritsuna, the author of *Watanabe Chūemon oboegaki,* a personal memoir that includes a description of the fighting during the uprising. By contrast, Moritsuna's cousin, Watanabe Genzō Sadatsuna, had his fief confiscated by Ieyasu and was forced to leave Mikawa.[58] Matsudaira Ietsugu surrendered and was pardoned, perhaps because he was a Matsudaira, even though his branch of the family had often opposed the family head. Unlike Ietsugu, however, Kira Yoshiaki and Arakawa Yoshihiro were not permitted to surrender and fled, Yoshiaki to Ōmi and Yoshihiro to Kawachi. Sakai Tadanao had already fled to the Imagawa in Suruga after his defeat.

At first, Ieyasu restored the temples' exemptions, albeit with some restrictions.[59] Later, however, once the most powerful of the rebels were out of the way, he turned against the temples and banned the sect, offering to let the temples and priests remain, provided they changed their affiliation to another branch or sect.[60] If they did not, Ieyasu would exile the priests and destroy the temples. When the chief priests refused to renounce their sect, Ieyasu made good on his threat. As *Mikawa monogatari* puts it: "[Ieyasu had] promised to 'let them be as they were originally,' then said, 'originally they were fields, so let them be fields, as originally,' so they were destroyed, and the priests fled, scattered."[61]

This time, no one rose to the temples' defense. Indeed, some former Honganji sect priests—none of the leaders, though—even joined Ieyasu's retainer band.[62] Some twenty years later, starting in 1582, Ieyasu gradually lifted the ban, allowing lesser priests and temples to be restored in Mikawa. He allowed the four major temples to return only in 1584, after the defeat of the *ikkō ikki* holdouts from the war against Nobunaga.[63]

As is the case with so many of the *ikkō ikki* incidents, the role of religion in the Mikawa uprising is difficult to pin down, though we have enough information to suggest an answer. It would be quite easy to discuss the Mikawa uprising without mentioning religion *per se* by focusing on economic issues and problems with institutions that happened to be religious ones. Such an argument would point out that the temples defended their political and economic rights against Ieyasu's incursion just as any institution would have done. In that case, many Honganji sect members would have joined the fight—partly because if their temples lost income they as members would have to make it up, and partly because they had similar rights themselves that they feared Ieyasu might terminate next. In other words, one could argue that they fought because of rational economic considerations. One could further suggest that they remained quiet when Ieyasu finally destroyed the temples because they perceived that victory without more powerful allies was impossible. After all, they had not really succeeded before, even with such allies. Besides, Ieyasu had confirmed them in their holdings, and it may have seemed better not to risk losing them.

Indeed, those pragmatic considerations surely played some role in motivating the Honganji members to take the temples' side at first and to stand aloof later when Ieyasu razed them. Yet given how integral religion appears to have been to life in the sixteenth century, the influence of beliefs must not be ignored, and the chronicles associated with this *ikkō ikki* give us information that we lack for other outbreaks. The *Mikawa monogatari* and *Matsudairaki*, with their lists of combatants on both sides of the uprising, together with genealogical records for Ieyasu's retainers, allow us to see some of that influence on the participants.

For some, primarily the more elite warriors, religious issues played little if any part in their calculations, as far as one can determine. None of the strongest of the rebels—Kira Yoshiaki, Arakawa Yoshihiro, Natsume Yoshinobu, Sakai Tadanao, Matsudaira Ietsugu—were members of the Honganji sect, with the possible exception of Yoshinobu, whose religious affiliation is unknown. The Kira, Arakawa, and Sakai families were affiliated with the Zen sect,[64] and the Matsudaira family, including Ietsugu, supported Jōdo temples, which in turn supported them. Some Matsudaira branches also supported Zen, whose temples and temple personnel generally stayed away from warfare, as they did during the Mikawa uprising.[65] Indeed, it would have been difficult for Zen temples to participate, even if the sect had a history of intervention, since they had patrons on both sides of the conflict.

By contrast, religious affiliation mattered greatly at the lower levels of Ieyasu's retainer band, which divided cleanly along sectarian lines. Honganji members chose the *ikki* side, and those of other religions chose Ieyasu's. A few Honganji members of lower status joined other sects in order to support Ieyasu, and a number of families split along class or status lines.

Within the divided families, those who remained with Ieyasu were primarily family heads or members of the main branch. Those who went to the *ikki* side belonged to subsidiary branches or were less powerful family members of the main branch. Among Ieyasu's closest retainers, only one family, the

Watanabe, broke this pattern by not splitting between sides; all joined the *ikki*. Particulars of warrior status, or maybe proximity to Ieyasu, seemed to matter a great deal in determining which side a person would choose.

One example serves to typify a divided family. One of the most important kin groups among Ieyasu's retainers was the Honda family, who were also Honganji followers. When the uprising began, members of one of the two main branches[66] of the Honda changed to Jōdoshū to remain with Ieyasu, including the family (or branch) head, Honda Tadakatsu. The head of the other main branch, Honda Hirotaka,[67] also remained with Ieyasu but refused to abjure his religion and so, as a guarantee of his loyalty, handed over his son as a hostage instead.[68] Honda Masanobu, who sided with the *ikki*, was from the same family as Hirotaka, but he was not the family head. Consciously or not, these families hedged their bets, ensuring that prominent relatives might help their more humble—and rebellious—relatives to reconcile with Ieyasu, if he won. Similarly, the more prominent relatives would have some representatives on the other side, if he lost. As we have seen, something very like the former occurred during the peace talks when loyal relatives of rebel families contributed to the success of the negotiations by urging Ieyasu to be magnanimous in victory.

For Ieyasu's lower retainers, then, and with the temples as central belligerents, sectarian bonds overrode military ones when the two were in conflict. When the temples were not involved in the fighting, Honganji members, indeed members of the same temple congregation, could be found on opposite sides of combat. In 1549, the Honganji sect temple Honshōji had some difficulty in deciding on an appropriate heir to become its leading priest. A letter on behalf of a particular candidate circulated among the members, pledging him the support of 115 signatories from 38 families. At least one historian has argued that this letter proves the existence of an *ikkō ikki* that dominated Mikawa.[69] If that were the case, it follows that the *ikki* members would be on the same side in battle since members of an *ikki*, by definition, act together.

Yet that was not the case in 1549. At the time the letter circulated, the Matsudaira were at war with the Oda, during one of the latter's periodic invasions.[70] Signatories to this letter could be found on both sides of the fighting, so there cannot have been one dominant *ikkō ikki* in Mikawa. The letter does show, however, that a large Honshōji congregation existed and drew members from different military organizations.[71] In the 1563 uprising, the economic foundations of the temples, even their continued existence, were at stake. The crisis provided a basis for Honganji sectarians to rally, forming an *ikki* to defend themselves. Ieyasu's quarrel with the temples seems to have had nothing to do with doctrine and everything to do with temporal power and finances. Religious solidarity and the desire to protect their temples motivated the lower-level retainers to band together. In some sense, doctrine played a role, but only insofar as the temples were the guardians of that doctrine as well as the ritual centers of the religious community.

For Ieyasu, the local temporal power that derived from the *funyū* rights of the four temples mattered more than doctrinal issues. His concerns were political, not religious, in nature. For the temples that supported him, however, that was not always the case. Among Ieyasu's defenders were temples of at least three different affiliations: the Takada branch True Pure Land sect, Jōdōshū, and Nichiren. Further, some of Ieyasu's allied temples seem to have been assisting their patrons. The local Jōdoshū owed its regional growth to Ieyasu's ancestors, and a Jōdoshū temple, Daijuji, was Ieyasu's family memorial temple, so it is no surprise that they participated in the fighting on Ieyasu's behalf.[72] The one Nichiren sect temple known to be active was the Ōkubo family temple in Kamiwada, Myōkokuji, also understandably supporting its sponsors.[73]

The most active temples that took Ieyasu's part, though, were the Takada branch temples, especially Myōgenji and Manshōji, and their concerns appear to have been religious. As we have seen, Myōgenji was especially well situated to help defend Okazaki from Jōgūji.[74] Unlike the Jōdoshū and Nichiren temples, whose support was a result of long-standing and mutually beneficial relationships with warriors, the Takada sect temples' support for Ieyasu was based firmly on their enmity for the Honganji sect.[75] In Mikawa, as in Kaga and elsewhere, they could be counted on to join the side of anyone at odds with their archrivals. As has been noted elsewhere, the friction between the two True Pure Land sect branches owed something to doctrine—the Honganji sect's doctrine basically invalidated the Takada sect's—and something to the ongoing competition for members.

Thus, a few combatants had religious motivations to fight as they did. For others, like Ieyasu himself and his retainers, secular power meant more than any religious belief. That Ieyasu's retainer band split along status levels as well as along religious ones reflects on the structure of the band itself, rather than on the power of Honganji faith. The warriors of higher status must have felt that their bonds with Ieyasu outweighed their connections to specific temples. Because of this closeness, their relationships to Ieyasu were probably personal—and quite strong. Lower-status warriors, by contrast, followed a chieftain they did not know personally, and utilitarian concerns may have dominated their choices. Their sense of obligation to him evidently could not overcome their devotion to the temples and religion that were so much a part of their lives.

When Ieyasu later destroyed their temples, however, they acquiesced, a lack of action also requiring explanation. For that, though, we must return to rationality. The negotiations in early 1564 strengthened Ieyasu's organization when he agreed to pardon the Honganji members with prominent roles in the uprising. He had initially refused to make this concession, but by so doing he tacitly acknowledged the importance of those warriors to the success of his enterprise. Surely the members also felt that they had managed to impress Ieyasu with their power—and thereby strengthened their positions with regard to him. They may even have been impressed by his magnanimity in pardoning them for fighting against him.

When Ieyasu repudiated the agreement to allow the temples to continue as they had, why would the Honganji sect retainers not return to the field to protect them? They may have realized that they could not succeed so well again, especially without more powerful warrior allies. In the earlier days of the uprising, they had benefited from the participation of Kira Yoshiaki and others, who then had been either banished from the province or killed. Without these more powerful warriors, the retainers had no chance against Ieyasu at all and stood to lose everything. It seems unlikely that he would pardon them again. Honganji's supporters in Mikawa, then, were not religious fanatics, ready to sacrifice themselves for the sake of the temples in the face of certain failure, but rather men of faith who recognized *de facto* defeat.

The Mikawa *ikkō ikki* occurred during a long period of peace for the main Honganji temple in Osaka. The uprising ran its course without involvement from the Patriarch or even from the *ichimon* priest who was nominally in charge of Honshūji. He had a dual appointment with another temple in Harima (near modern-day Himeji) and spent most of his time there rather than in Mikawa. He was not even present during the episode.

The Mikawa temples did benefit from assistance from their co-religionists in nearby provinces, such as Owari and Ise. The temples had branches there, which most likely were the source of the outside help. Therefore, it is difficult to see the Owari and Ise reinforcements as evidence of otherwise undocumented pressure or support from Honganji leadership. Seven years later, when they fought Nobunaga, the situation would be different.

Nobunaga and Honganji

In the ninth month of 1568, Oda Nobunaga rode triumphantly into Kyoto as the champion of the last Muromachi shogun, Ashikaga Yoshiaki (1537–97). At first, Kennyo showed interest in cultivating Nobunaga's good will. He sent Nobunaga a letter and gifts to congratulate him on recent successes in Mino and Ise, and on his imminent entry into the capital.[76] Just over a year later, with his New Year's greetings on 1569/1/11, Kennyo again sent Nobunaga gifts. Four days after that, on the fifteenth, he sent another letter and still more gifts congratulating Nobunaga on his recent return to the capital.[77]

Despite his early cordiality, the interests of Nobunaga and Honganji diverged. After all, Nobunaga's ultimate goal was to force other powers in the archipelago to submit to his rule. Temples, with their independent economic and military power, were no exception. The Honganji sect also had power that was more than independent: it was enormous. Although records of the time provide no way of quantifying the sect's membership or economic power, clearly Honganji and its members were a dominant force throughout much of Japan. The main temple ruled the entire province of Kaga, and members had strong influence in Echizen, Noto, Etchū, southern Ōmi, Kii, and Owari. Financially, at least one report claims that the Patriarch controlled most of Japan's economy, especially because of its temple towns of the capital region.[78] Although the extent of Kennyo's power over the economy may have been exaggerated in the report, he certainly controlled a significant portion of it. Furthermore, a number of warriors with whom Honganji maintained close relationships—Takeda Shingen of Kai, Asakura Yoshikage of Echizen, and Asai Hisamasa of Ōmi, to name just a few—were already fighting strenuously against Nobunaga. It should not be surprising that Kennyo eventually joined them.[79]

On 1570/9/6, more than a year and a half after Kennyo's cordial New Year's greetings to Nobunaga, the Patriarch sent out a call to Honganji followers throughout Japan:[80]

About Nobunaga's arrival in the capital: he is causing us trouble. Ever since the year before last, he has given us many problems. This is horrible treatment. Even if we respond to him, it would be useless, as there would certainly be an order to destroy us. On top of that, our strength does not suffice. Nonetheless, at this time, in order that our founder's line does not die out, we must all fulfill our duty without consideration for our own lives. This would be most gratifying. In short, I ask for your help. Anyone who does not respond will not be a sect member.[81]

Kennyo left unspecified the troubles that Nobunaga caused, but they certainly included the 5,000 *kan* special tax the hegemon had levied on Osaka, Honganji's temple town, which had previously been exempt from such taxation. For Osaka, as for the temples in Mikawa, the money itself mattered less than the repudiation of the town's privileges, the beginning of losing its traditional independence. Whatever additional reasons he may have had, Kennyo joined the many warrior and religious groups that already opposed Nobunaga in what would come to be called the first anti-Nobunaga league.[82]

The hostilities between Kennyo and Nobunaga began later that month and did not conclude until 1580. Warfare was interrupted by two periods of peace; the first began in 1571 and the second in the tenth month of 1575, though both were short-lived. Part of the reason for the protracted fighting is that the Honganji sect presented a special military problem for Nobunaga. Kennyo and the other members of the first, and later the second, anti-Nobunaga leagues tried to coordinate their efforts, engaging Nobunaga on multiple fronts at the same time. Honganji was better positioned than a daimyo to do that because a daimyo tended to draw troops from one region: his own domain. In contrast, Honganji had no real territorial home base, not even Kaga, important though it was. Instead, its fighters and revenue sources were widely dispersed in Kaga, Ise, Kii, Echizen, and elsewhere—all of which Nobunaga needed to isolate and defeat before Honganji itself would fall. It finally did, in 1580.

Nobunaga's long struggle with Honganji and the sect's *de facto* defeat have been treated extensively elsewhere.[83] Here, the record of Nobunaga's efforts to destroy the Honganji stronghold at Nagashima, in Ise Province, should suffice to describe the kind of fighting that took place during this war.

The most remarkable feature of the fighting at Nagashima is how long it took Nobunaga to subdue the temple and its followers: nearly four years. In the eleventh month of 1570, two months after Kennyo had sent out his call to arms, Nagashima members went to attack Ogie castle in Nobunaga's home province of Owari. The *ikki* fighters apparently coordinated their attack with the Asai and with Honganji members in Ōmi, who had previously attacked Nobunaga and at the time were occupying his attention. Nobunaga's younger brother Nobuoki defended Ogie castle, but he could not fend off the *ikki*. Within days he committed suicide in defeat.

After the Nagashima *monto*'s successful foray into Owari, together with some of Nobunaga's other defeats in late 1570, he asked the shogun and imperial court to arrange a truce with his enemies, including Honganji. Perhaps he wanted a little time to regroup as the truce was short-lived. In the fifth month of 1571, Nobunaga resolved to destroy the Ise *ikki* and advanced with land forces as far as Tsushima, in Owari.

On 5/12, Nobunaga ordered his army to attack Nagashima from three separate directions. Some of his best generals led the attack, including Shibata Katsuie, who would later pacify Kaga. The campaign did not go as planned, however, and the *monto* instead routed Nobunaga's forces. By the sixteenth, Katsuie had retreated with his greatly depleted army, while another general had been killed along with many of his retainers.[84] Katsuie's defeat was especially remarkable because the individuals who formed the *ikki* were of comparatively low status—"worthless beings," according to Nobunaga's sixteenth-century biographer Ōta Gyūichi.[85] The defenders were aided by their surroundings; the temple stronghold was situated in a delta through which branches of eight or nine substantial rivers flowed into the sea. Practically speaking, they formed a series of moats that hindered Nobunaga's land army.

Following that setback, Nobunaga shifted his focus to northern Ōmi Province, where he was again under attack, this time by the Asai. It took him more than two years to return his attention to Nagashima.

The next battle in Ise took place between 1573/9/26 and 10/8. Again Nobunaga sent in land forces from several different directions, and again they were led by some of his most able generals, this time including Toyotomi Hideyoshi, who would succeed Nobunaga less than a decade later. Nevertheless, in

1573, as in 1570, the Nagashima *monto* drove off the attack, demonstrating that they could not be overcome as easily as Nobunaga evidently thought.

In neither battle did the Nagashima *ikki* face Nobunaga's full forces; rather they were pitted against just a few divisions. In theory, they should have easily defeated the *ikki*. One problem was that, despite the delta terrain, Nobunaga only sent land forces both times. Probably it was difficult for him and his exalted samurai generals to believe that a bunch of farmers and *jizamurai* could resist so effectively. After this second defeat, however, Nobunaga realized that his navy would be necessary to destroy the *ikki*.

On 1574/7/13, a much greater deployment of Nobunaga's army attacked Nagashima by land, and by the fifteenth, his navy had joined the battle. If the *ikki* felt safe because they had the sea at their backs and their bases were surrounded by rivers, they soon learned they were mistaken. The sea was thronged with warships, so thick that "one couldn't see the water" any more, just the ships.[86] Ships also assisted the land forces by moving them ever closer to the temple stronghold.

There were, in fact, several fortified areas in the delta, not just the big fortress at Ganshōji, and Nobunaga's army went after these others first. Progress was slow, however. On 1574/8/2, the weather was dreadful with wind and rain, probably the result of a passing typhoon. Under the cover of night and storm, people who had barricaded themselves in tried to leave the lesser fort and escape to Ganshōji. Although some succeeded, the army managed to kill hundreds of others, both men and women.

Elsewhere in the delta, the attackers managed to cut off a fort's water supply, forcing those inside to surrender. As the defeated opened the gates to the victors, men, women, and children fled for other forts, but the siege director, Hideyoshi, saw to it that most were killed.

Other fortresses kept their water supplies but ran short of food as Nobunaga's forces besieged them on land and blockaded them at sea. These holdouts surrendered a few months later at the end of the ninth month. Many of the defenders had already died of starvation; Nobunaga's men slew the rest, forcing several thousand of the vanquished into one fort and setting fire to it.[87] Overall, the victors took and exposed as trophies the heads of many priests and others of higher status, though not those of "worthless beings," whose deaths were proven with dismembered noses or ears. Although the warriors intended that there be no survivors, a few *ikki* members managed to escape.

Sources credit Nobunaga's forces with killing as many as 40,000 people at Nagashima. These numbers are almost certainly inflated, but many thousands must have died, and news of the hegemon's triumph spread so far that even a death register kept at Tōji temple in Kyoto described the commoners' losses.

The *ikki* at Nagashima had fought long and hard but finally lost. Its defeat took two years, in part because of Nobunaga's miscalculations; his first attempts clearly underestimated the sectarians' strength, and the *ikki* stood no chance with the greater forces deployed the third time. The defenders' achievement must not be ignored, however. Even when Nobunaga let loose both his army and navy against them, it took more than two months before the *ikki* surrendered. The Honganji members at Ise had fought far more effectively than the warriors expected. None of Nobunaga's victories against *ikkō ikki* were easy, though often they were total. In the war overall, Honganji was able to persevere for so long in part due to help received from daimyo allies. But there would have been no daimyo allies if Honganji members had not made significant military contributions to the struggle.

Justification and Incentives

Honganji's leaders saw Nobunaga and his approach to governance as a threat to the sect's very existence, not just to its power. Kennyo and his advisors understood that if Nobunaga succeeded in breaking the sect's independence, its continued existence would rest wholly on Nobunaga's sufferance. No one knew what he might do with the sect or what demands he might make. Like his predecessors, Kennyo was caught between protecting the sect as he thought best and cooperating with this particular warrior and his shogun. He chose to protect the sect, no matter the price, as Shōnyo, Jitsunyo, and even Rennyo had done before him.

No doubt the Honganji leadership also recognized that defending the sect amounted to defending their own privileges, power, and wealth, as these could not exist without the Honganji institution that supplied them. No one can say to what extent this realization influenced their actions; whatever the balance of motives, from their perspective, they had no good option other than to resist Nobunaga.

What of the members, though? Through what inducements did they rise to fight the unifier, and why did some of them decline to do so? Kennyo's initial call to arms and subsequent letters to members in different regions justified the war simply as one of survival. Nobunaga, wrote the Patriarch, threatened the *buppō*, the "law of the Buddha," and the continuance of their teaching line was at stake. Therefore, all good members should devote themselves to fighting and defending the faith.

Given that Buddhism prohibited the taking of any life, animal or human, one might suppose that Kennyo would explain how warfare—that is, wholesale killing—could be justifiable, but his letters fail to discuss the issue at all. In part, the question of justifiability or, possibly more to the point, the effect that killing had on a member's chances for an auspicious rebirth, had already been addressed in the sect's insistence that faith in Amida would guarantee rebirth in the Pure Land regardless of sins committed in this life. Kennyo's silence suggests that fighting itself was not problematic for him, other priests, or even the followers. And why should it be? It had not bothered his father Shōnyo either. Fighting was so much a part of *sengoku*, and so many Buddhist temples engaged in warfare, that killing in the context of war may have required no special excuse.[88]

However, Kennyo did see the utility of strengthening the followers' bonds with the sect. It has often been argued that he promised his followers that if they fought for the temple, after death they would be reborn in Amida's Pure Land.[89] The most dramatic evidence of this pledge is the banner that read: "Advance and be reborn in paradise. Retreat and fall immediately into hell." This banner actually seems to have been used by forces led by the Mōri family of western Honshu, a circumstance that provokes some questions. Did the army's use of the banner mean that the injunction applied to everyone, member or not? Or was it just an expression of how an outsider understood Honganji teachings?

Some Pure Land sects taught that, in exchange for a member's obedience, the leader could and would guarantee salvation, that is, rebirth in the Pure Land.[90] Possibly, other people—Honganji members, warrior allies—understood the Patriarch's power in a similar way. Honganji teachings rejected this idea, but they also allowed Patriarchs to identify behavior that did or did not reflect faith. Both Shōnyo and Kennyo exploited this belief. The Patriarch did not grant heavenly rebirth; rather, the act of fighting demonstrated that a member had faith and therefore could rely on rebirth in the Pure Land.

The question of whether or not Kennyo actually made this claim is especially important because it contradicts Honganji's core teaching about "other power" (*tariki*), which explicitly asserts that no action taken on one's own initiative can lead to rebirth in the Pure Land. Only Amida can grant such salvation, according to sect doctrine, and he grants it only to those who rely on him utterly. The question is this: did the eleventh Patriarch deliberately preach heresy in his efforts to defeat Nobunaga? If he did knowingly spread the heretical doctrine, it would imply that he did not genuinely care to preserve Shinran's and Rennyo's teachings. One can argue, then, that he cynically manipulated the believers for his own personal gain: to defend the institution, yes, but also to maintain his own wealth and power. If Kennyo did not wittingly teach heresy, if he stuck to Honganji's teachings about *tariki* clearly and consistently, then even in wartime he remained faithful to the doctrine as expounded by Rennyo.

As with many accusations of heresy, the answers are less clear-cut than the questions. Kennyo's language was always carefully in line with Honganji sect doctrine, and he rarely wrote anything with which his ancestor Rennyo, who defined the orthodoxy, would disagree. His first call to arms, in which he threatened unresponsive members with expulsion, skirted heresy, if only because he did not threaten members who transgressed established sect rules. One must acknowledge, however, that Kennyo meant to expel only those members who failed to come to the aid of the sect when its very existence was threatened (as he saw it). We have seen that the Patriarch had an accepted right to identify certain actions as demonstrating a member's lack of faith. This thinking was behind Rennyo's original rules of behavior. It is not much of a stretch, then, to say that failing to defend the sect demonstrated a lack of faith in its teachings.

Usually, Kennyo finished his letters with phrases urging the members to heed the teachings and place their faith in Amida, as Rennyo had done. A letter written in 1572 warning the Etchū followers of an imminent attack from Echigo ended by saying, "[Y]ou must not neglect the teachings. It is necessary to cherish the fact that there is no doubt of auspicious rebirth if you quickly settle your faith."[91] A 1576 letter to followers in Mino concludes, "Human life is uncertain, and sudden death does not occur only in battle. This is all the more reason to settle one's faith in Amida quickly and look toward rebirth in paradise."[92] A fuller expression of Kennyo's teachings can be seen in letters addressed to the Kaga, Etchū, and Noto followers in 1578: "Faith is when one puts one's own existence aside, abandons the many paths of our self-power, and relies wholeheartedly on Amida; then certainly one will be reborn in paradise. There is no doubt of this. In addition to settling this faith, one must say the *nenbutsu* in daily life, out of gratitude to the Buddha."[93]

These three letters are representative of Kennyo's communications with his followers during the entire course of the fight against Nobunaga. In one, and only one, surviving letter, he did write that helping in battle would show that the member had a fundamental desire for rebirth in Amida's paradise.[94] Here, he takes a shaky step toward heresy by implying that having a fundamental desire results in an auspicious rebirth. This seems to contradict Honganji orthodoxy, which claims that salvation comes only from Amida, not from any action a person takes. In earlier writings, however, a fundamental desire for salvation had been identified as an indication that faith had been achieved, so again Kennyo falls short of actual heresy.

One cannot just leave the issue there, however. Kennyo must have known of the popular belief that fighting in Honganji's defense, or receiving a dispensation from him, would guarantee rebirth in paradise. Writing in the 1580s, Kennyo's great-great-uncle Jitsugo, one of Rennyo's particularly long-lived sons, criticized this widespread belief repeatedly, tracing its origins to Shōnyo's tenure as Patriarch.[95] If Kennyo was indeed aware of the misperception, he did nothing to correct it. Although Kennyo's letters do not encourage this heretical idea, neither do they try to dispel it. They do nothing to identify and correct members' misapprehensions, the way his ancestor's letters did.

Honganji's power in the 1570s, which allowed the sect to continue resisting Nobunaga for so long, came from three sources that its leadership had been cultivating for decades. One was the members. By allowing the blurring of the lines between action resulting in salvation and action as a demonstration of the faith that resulted in salvation, Kennyo and other Honganji leaders were able to draw on exceptionally motivated forces.

The second source of Honganji's might was its daimyo allies, men whose amity Kennyo had courted well before Nobunaga became a serious problem. The daimyo's interest lay in the military power that the sect could command. No single military organization had the wherewithal to resist Nobunaga for long without the support of others, and the Honganji sectarians had repeatedly demonstrated their fighting abilities. Honganji and daimyo needed each other to face Nobunaga.

Finally, Honganji had friends at court. At least since Rennyo's time, members of the Patriarch's family had intermarried with courtiers, and Honganji's leaders showed homage to the emperor early in every new year.[96] Courtiers were not necessarily influential, however. Factions split the court, and power depended on which was in ascendancy at any given time. One indication of Honganji's importance, though, is that Niwata Shigeyasu, one of the courtiers sent by the imperial court to negotiate peace between Honganji and Nobunaga, was closely related to the Patriarch's family. He was Shōnyo's second-cousin and his brother-in-law as Shōnyo had married Shigeyasu's sister, who bore Kennyo. Shigeyasu, then, was Kennyo's uncle. Shōnyo also had been adopted by a former regent, Kujō Hisatsune.[97]

The war between the unifier and the Honganji sect finally ended by order of the court, which sent two representatives to aid the negotiations. This helps explain why Nobunaga accepted terms of peace instead of holding out for total military victory. The emperor and his courtiers may not have wielded direct political power, but Honganji's case suggests that their moral weight still mattered. If so, it is easy to understand why Nobunaga would settle because he, too, depended on the court's backing and did not wish to lose it. When Honganji's daimyo allies could no longer help the sect, and its members no longer prevailed in battle despite their enthusiasm, it was Honganji's connections at court that helped keep the sect intact.

Honganji's prominence and power had enabled Kennyo to stay aloof from the Mikawa *ikki* uprising, thereby keeping the sect as a whole at peace. That same prominence and power, however, also brought the sect to its confrontation with Oda Nobunaga in 1570. Eight decades earlier, Rennyo had been vulnerable to outside pressure, as was Jitsunyo in 1506, because the sect was not yet so forcefully established.

Aside from the level of sectarian involvement, the Mikawa *ikki* and the anti-Nobunaga war had much in common. Both were fought to protect the sect from leaders who infringed on the temples' privileges. Both were settled through negotiations rather than abject defeat, although Ieyasu quickly reneged on his promise to accept the temples as they had been. Both, on their face, could be characterized as anti-authoritarian because protecting the sect meant opposing the kind of authoritarianism represented by Nobunaga and the daimyo.

Yet even these *ikki* were not anti-authoritarian on principle but only so to the extent that concentrating power in the hands of one national leader was seen as putting the sect at a disadvantage. The Muromachi shogunate, with its system of sharing power among *shugo*, temples, and the court, posed no problem. Furthermore, Honganji followers accepted the authority of the Patriarch. In fighting Ieyasu and Nobunaga, the sectarians acted not out of dislike for authority, even for a new kind of authority, as much as they acted in defense of their threatened temples.

It has been suggested that Nobunaga hated the *ikki* so much simply because he had no way of absorbing them into his military organization. The problem was not merely a matter of including Honganji members in the organization but rather of the continuing unreliability of their behavior. For instance, Ieyasu had absorbed many Honganji believers into his organization, but in the Mikawa *ikki* most of them broke with him to side with the temples. The real problem, then, was one of loyalty and solidarity. For what would the sectarians fight when the time came? The Mikawa *ikki* gave a crystal-clear answer: religious loyalties overcame military ones. Nobunaga had learned from that conflict too and so chose not to bring the *ikki* members into his army. Ieyasu's experience also contributed, I think, to the unifiers' subsequent concerns that Christians would join an invading Christian force rather than defend Japan, an important factor in the decision to outlaw that faith. The Christian religion, like the Honganji and Nichiren faiths, preached exclusionary doctrines that fostered dangerous cohesion within the group and alienation from others. The *ikkō ikki* showed what could happen when military and religious identities collided—and military leaders did not like it.

After the settlement with Nobunaga, a small number of Honganji members continued their opposition to unification until Hideyoshi defeated the last hold-outs in 1585. The sectarians' reputation for military prowess lingered; at one point Hideyoshi even asked Honganji members to fight as his allies.[98] Nevertheless, the phenomenon of *ikkō ikki* died, along with Honganji's independence, in 1580.

Conclusion

The political activities of Honganji members, undertaken as *ikki*, or leagues, ranged from local uprisings (such as Kaga in 1488 and Mikawa in 1563) and widespread battles coordinated loosely if at all (the 1506 *ikki* battles) to all-out wars waged by Honganji Patriarchs (e.g., the Tenbun War in 1532–35). Understanding the *ikki* involves establishing what those activities were and sorting through many underlying issues and themes. These include the creation and growth of the sect's military power, the role of religion in forming the *ikki* and in carrying out their activities, and the apparent motivation of the members in fighting.

None of these issues has a single explanation. None can be wholly separated from any of the others. Nevertheless, each must be analyzed as if it could be separated or else we may become hopelessly entangled in the intertwining themes.

The Honganji sect became a military power, led by the Patriarch, through a series of incremental stages involving pressure from Kyoto authorities who reacted to the members' actions. When sectarians from Katata in Ōmi tried, unsuccessfully, to defend the Ōtani Honganji in 1465, the authorities seem not to have cared. Indeed, sectarians in Katata joined with other townspeople in a number of actions (see Chapter 2) without anyone in authority singling out the sectarians, as such, involved in the fighting. In none of these incidents, however, did the people attack the warriors who ruled the province.

A similar *laissez-faire* attitude seems to have prevailed when Honganji members agreed to help Togashi Masachika gain control of Kaga Province in 1473. That situation changed in 1488 with the overthrow of Masachika and his consequent suicide. With the destruction of a *shugo*, the Muromachi shogunate took notice and forced the then-Patriarch Rennyo to punish the Kaga sectarians. Although Rennyo managed to avoid leveling the worst punishment—expulsion—against the Kaga sectarians *en masse*, he still was forced to bow to the shogunate's will. His tacit acceptance of responsibility for the behavior of Honganji members led him to institute rules of behavior, the violation of which merited expulsion from the sect.

Until 1506, the Patriarch's authority over the members was a kind of negative authority, consisting of the responsibility to punish members who broke his rules. He could, of course, order priests to take certain actions, such as stepping down from office, but apparently the Patriarch did not exercise that power over members. Certainly, he never asked them to take up arms. Once the sectarians had taken up arms themselves, however, warriors evidently saw them as at least potential combatants, leading the deputy shogun Hosokawa Masamoto to ask the ninth Patriarch, Jitsunyo, for military assistance. Once again, the actions of Honganji members had brought pressure from Kyoto to bear on the Patriarch, changing the character of his authority. From 1506 on, Patriarchs had precedent to order lay sect members into battle.

Both kinds of pressure on the Patriarch had been responses to the success of the Kaga *ikkō ikki* in overthrowing Togashi Masachika, despite the fact that in that fight, they had been only part of a coalition army that included some of Masachika's top retainers. Still, that uprising created a lasting perception of Honganji members as both anti-*shugo* and militant/military activists. It is impossible to know for certain how much that perception affected sect members outside Kaga, but clearly members elsewhere took to arms using the shared religious affiliation as an organizing principle. Even though Rennyo's and Jitsunyo's response to the pressure from Kyoto authorities changed the relationship between Patriarch and lay members, the militarization of the sect began with and was fed by those members, not by the Patriarch.

It was not until the accession of Shōnyo as the tenth Patriarch that the full power of the sect as an army became manifest. Shōnyo's war with the *ichimon* temples of Kaga drew on Honganji members from throughout central Honshu and helped to establish other *ichimon* temples as recruiters for sectarian combatants. With the Patriarch recognized as a military leader both by members and daimyo, the sect was poised to be a full-fledged political force.

There are many different ways to assess and interpret the role of religion in the *ikki*. Did the egalitarianism that arguably exists in Shinran's doctrine affect the formation of *ikki* and create an anti-authoritarian ideology? Did the regular meetings of Honganji sect congregations provide a unique space for members to discuss all manner of issues, especially grievances with warriors, making the temples and *dōjō* breeding grounds for radicalism? Might the war against Nobunaga properly be understood as millenarian? After all, the slogan "Advance and be reborn in paradise" might suggest that victory would lead to a Pure Land realized on earth. Did Honganji sectarians ultimately follow the Patriarch's orders without question in blind obedience to his authority? Or did the religion have some other effect?

A religion can be understood as a combination of theology, institution, and ritual.[1] In the case of the *ikki*, the institutional structure contributed greatly to the phenomenon and the theology somewhat less so, at least at first. Furthermore, the theological influence might better be called ideological because ideology is less tied to orthodox doctrine. The understanding of *ikkō ikki* as manifestations of Shiran's egalitarian doctrine and the anti-authoritarianism inherent therein has been largely rejected by secular Japanese historians though it lingers in the

English-language literature.[2] There is no reason to believe that Japanese people had formulated a concept of social egalitarianism in the sixteenth century any more than Europeans had. Both Christianity and True Pure Land Buddhism have doctrines that lend themselves to an egalitarian interpretation when viewed with modern eyes, yet in the 1500s, neither had done anything to subvert the social hierarchy. A distinction must be made between doctrines that preached "everyone must answer to God" or "anyone can be reborn in the True Pure Land" and ideologies that preached social equality. The former can, and did, exist without the latter. Even the Protestant Reformation, which attacked the Roman Catholic Church and the authority of the Pope, did not threaten European monarchies or aristocracies. That had to wait for the Enlightenment thinkers, most of whom saw the Catholic Church and organized religion as agents of repression.

The Honganji sect was itself a hierarchical institution, and the Patriarch had a clearly defined doctrinal authority. Over time, as the wars against Hosokawa Harumoto and Oda Nobunaga amply demonstrated, he also achieved a military authority, which members resisted only the first time it was used, in 1506. Honganji followers accepted the Patriarch's power to expel members from the sect, a power common to leaders of sects, and believed that expulsion equaled being condemned to hell after death.

Although all Honganji believers might have equal access to Amida's Pure Land, they did not have equal access to the Patriarch. Except for the head priests at a select number of temples, members usually communicated with the Patriarch through a secretary. Capable or ambitious people might achieve some power in the sect through administrative appointments, which they obtained only after being adopted into the Shimotsuma family. The religious leadership, though, was still defined by heredity, and no outsider could even dream of becoming Patriarch. Concepts of egalitarianism or anti-authoritarianism did not apply to Honganji members or *ikkō ikki*.

The concept of the league as an organization of people who shared a status and enjoyed an equal right to express their views, however, had a long tradition in Japan. Members of the Honganji sect, whatever their social position, shared the status of co-religionists, which conferred a basis for forming *ikki*. Regular monthly meetings also reinforced that fellowship and shared identity as a distinct group apart from others.

Religious identity created strong bonds among the members, which is why the *ikki* formed along sectarian lines rather than through other possible shared connections. Exclusivist religions like Honganji's create a powerful sense of cohesion among members, especially when they are persecuted, as Honganji sectarians were in some regions. There were other places to gather and exchange gossip besides monthly meetings, such as markets, and different ways of defining groups with common interests. None, however, could match the bonds felt among members of an exclusive religious group, so it is only natural that when action was required, Honganji members first looked to each other. Furthermore, the sect had spread to the extent that in some regions a majority of people—some historians say all people, but that seems excessive—were Honganji sectarians. Therefore, when Honganji members joined with others in a group defined in other ways, they were likely to dominate nonetheless.

A similar phenomenon was at work in the Nichiren *ikki*. Members of the Nichiren sect, too, relied on the conviction that their path was the only effective one to enlightenment, but they substituted the Lotus Sutra for the Amida of Honganji's sectarians. Of course, although the difference between Honganji beliefs and Nichiren sect beliefs was not nearly so simple, they shared both the phenomenon of *ikki* and the satisfaction of belonging to an exclusive group of "saved" people living in a world filled with those who were "lost."

It is possible to see millenarian overtones in Honganji's war against Nobunaga because of the slogan "Advance and be reborn in paradise, retreat and go straight to hell." One can read the first phrase to imply that by advancing—and winning—

Honganji followers would bring about a paradise, a Pure Land on earth. The second phrase, then, would mean that failure condemned all to the hell that already existed on earth, the hell that was *sengoku* Japan.

The idea is not, perhaps, outlandish, since people interpret the same text in different ways, often all the more so when the text is brief. The millenarian theory also relies on concepts of *buppō* (lit., Buddhist law) and *buppōryō* (the realm of Buddhist law). Both terms are somewhat vague. Most historians take the first to designate a sect or its teachings. A threat to the *buppō*, when used by Honganji, meant a threat to the sect and its teachings. When used by Enryakuji, *buppō* meant Tendai. *Buppōryō* then refers to the land or the jurisdiction of the sect or its temples, which are presumably under the general protection of the Buddha. This is in line with the documents that temples employed to threaten peasants by equating failure to pay rents with disdain for Buddha.

According to the millenarian theory, by contrast, *buppō* means literally the law of Buddha, not of his priests. *Buppōryō* then becomes land ruled over by the Buddha himself, in this case Amida. The land ruled over by Amida is the Pure Land, and therefore, land taken by sectarians would become the Pure Land itself. The reading is interesting, but one might expect then that war tales and other documents from non- or anti-sectarian sources would attribute this marvelous way of thinking to Honganji members. They do not.

More to the point, there is a simpler explanation, that is, the one described previously. *Buppōryō* or no, Honganji teachings do not allow for becoming a Buddha in this life or even for one to enter Amida's paradise before death. Nothing, except possibly the reading of this banner, suggests that the members believed in an earthly Pure Land, not even mistakenly. On balance, the simpler interpretation—that those who advance and fight on Honganji's behalf can look forward to an auspicious rebirth but those who flee can expect nothing but hell in the next life—seems more likely. Although this common understanding is already removed from orthodox Honganji doctrine because it promises salvation based on a person's own actions, it fits with what we know of popular beliefs. Occam's razor applies here.

Did Honganji members blindly obey a Patriarch's call to arms? In some cases, such as the Kaga or Mikawa uprisings, the Patriarch had no role to play in the decision to fight. Members chose whether or not to participate in *ikkō ikki*. In battles ordered by Honganji's leaders, though, there can be no doubt that some *monto* participated because they wanted to obey the Patriarch, not because they necessarily shared the specific aims of a given action. When the disruptions were spontaneous or local, however, a crowd mentality may have influenced individuals to participate without question. Furthermore, when I assert that members made a choice to fight, I do not mean that they necessarily consciously weighed the pros and cons of action. I mean, that they were aware of an option and were driven by a perception of their own interests, perhaps hazily conceived.

For many of the *ikki*, the choices made are obvious. In 1506, members in Kawachi and Settsu refused to comply with the Patriarch's wishes and contested his authority to order military activity. The 1531 *dai-shō ikki* required members to take sides. Most of Ieyasu's Mikawa retainers who followed Honganji rebelled when their temples were threatened but failed to rebel when they were later destroyed. This behavior is inexplicable if the retainers acted solely out of blind loyalty to their faith.

The war with Nobunaga provides still more evidence of choice. Followers in Ōmi first resisted Nobunaga but later effectively surrendered to him, pledging to behave. Had they supported their Patriarch and faith unconditionally, they would have continued to fight, even if it meant massacre and death. They chose to live. After the Patriarch concluded a peace with his enemy, his son and other sectarians continued to fight Nobunaga locally in Kaga and Kii. Evidently they had other reasons that compelled them to persist.

That said, when *ikki* fought to defend Honganji sect temples or the sect itself, the fighting became an expression of faith. Shōnyo and Kennyo appealed to the sectarians on the basis of their faith. When Shōnyo assured bereaved villagers that their loved ones had certainly been reborn in the Pure Land because they fought as allies of the founder, he certified their actions as acts of faith.

Kennyo's letters did not make the connection between fighting and rebirth in paradise so explicit, but he did close his letters with exhortations to his followers that it was most important to "settle their faith." At the same time that he preached the orthodoxy—an auspicious rebirth depends on Amida's power alone—he reminded the letters' recipients of the importance of faith and of the dire situation of Honganji and its teachings. In some letters, he also threatened expulsion for those who did not respond to his call. Even without that threat, however, anyone who believed the teachings would recognize the danger that loss of the sect would pose to the successful and continued attainment of faith.

It was also popularly believed that the Patriarch could guarantee rebirth in Amida's Pure Land. This was in line with some other sects' claims, explicit or implicit, that their leader had such power. As Jitsugo pointed out much later, no Buddhist text justifies the claim that the Patriarch could promise an auspicious rebirth. Further, no sectarian theologian derived it from Honganji doctrine. Starting with Shōnyo, they just failed to discourage it explicitly; it may have been so culturally entrenched that it would be fruitless to try to eradicate the belief, and it certainly was convenient to maintain during a war.

Kennyo never claimed that he could guarantee paradise for anyone who supported the sect in the wars against Nobunaga. The Honganji sectarians evidently just believed it, and they felt all the more courage for the comfort it gave them. It is unlikely that either Shōnyo or Kennyo could have been so effective a leader without the popular belief that they held the keys to paradise and hell, and less effective leaders would not have attained the heights that the two reached.

So the sect's eventual power owed more to the members and the times than it did to the Patriarchs. The members' initially disruptive behavior prompted Rennyo to make rules. The interpretations of the meaning of expulsion and its corollaries invested the Patriarch with more power than he officially claimed. The attribution to Shōnyo and Kennyo of the ability to grant rebirth in paradise gave them still more. Both of these notions appear to have grown in popular belief without a basis in the sect's official teachings, and both meant that followers ceded more and more power to the Patriarch. That enhanced Kennyo's ability to summon help from the members and helped make the *ikkō ikki* effective against Nobunaga for so long.

Honganji members, then, gave the Patriarch the power he exercised. *Ikkō ikki* arose from the disordered and changing political landscape of *sengoku* Japan. They emerged and could exist as phenomena independent of the Patriarch, as we have had ample opportunity to observe, as well as at his instigation. Why, then, did the leagues and their military activities cease?

The most basic answer is that they ceased because the unifiers took steps to ensure that they ceased. Perhaps the most consequential policies of the unifiers were those that redrew society: the separation of farmer and soldier, the removal of soldiers from the land, the relative disarmament of villagers, and the new edicts defining social classes as hereditary. All of these policies contributed to making military *ikkō ikki* unlikely, if not impossible, and that was part of the unifiers' goal. When Hideyoshi required *jizamurai* to choose between an agricultural life in the countryside and a military life in town, he effectively separated the *ikki* from most of their leaders. His sword hunt, which collected arms from the villages, deprived them and the remaining leaders of most if not all of their weapons. Finally, he and Nobunaga had redefined the place of religion in society, severing it from its independent economic and military base and confining it to a far narrower band of operation.

This does not mean that *ikki* of all kinds disappeared, of course. Villagers still found them to be effective organizations for attending to their needs, and hundreds occurred in the following centuries. The religious *ikki*, though, had no direct descendants.

The phenomenon of *ikkō ikki* surely contributed to the decision of Hideyoshi, Ieyasu, and his successors to isolate Europeans and root out Christianity. Ieyasu in Mikawa and Hideyoshi through the Nobunaga war both experienced the power that religious cohesion and loyalty could deliver. Ieyasu especially had seen, and had suffered from, retainers who placed loyalty to their co-religionists and religion above their loyalty to him. Japan's leaders were aware of the Europeans' imperialism and were led to believe that Christian missionaries were paving the way. They had reason to fear that Christian daimyo and samurai would side with the other Christians, especially if the Pope told them to, and the realm-builders' experience of *ikkō ikki* must have reinforced that fear. In the end, *ikkō ikki* had no direct heirs, but they contributed to the redrawing of society and probably to the decision of Japan's leaders to limit and regulate European activity in Japan. That is no trivial legacy.

Reference Matter

Notes

Introduction

1. *Echizen no kuni sōetsuki*, 4. Entry dated Tenshō 3 [1575]/8/29.

2. This is a broad generalization. In the twelfth century, the military government was limited, and worked with or through the imperial court.

3. Sometimes the phrase is translated "warring states," which emphasizes the independence of the different regions under the control of daimyo. It has also been translated as "the country at war," which emphasizes the unity of Japan more than I think is appropriate. In addition, there are many other historical periods that might just as easily be called "the country at war," perhaps most notably the 1930s and 1940s. "Warring provinces," by contrast, acknowledges the continued relevance of court—and shogunate, to a lesser degree—even though they could not exercise coercive power. Historians also disagree on the length of the period. Many accept 1467, the beginning of the Ōnin War, as the starting date, as do I, and I have used the ultimate fall of the Muromachi shogunate for its end.

4. There is no plural form in Japanese. The word remains the same whether it refers to one person or thing, or several.

5. Enryakuji, Kōfukuji, and Negoroji are some examples besides Honganji.

6. The sect leader's legitimacy rested on his status as a direct descendant of the True Pure Land sect's founder Shinran, and the hierarchy of the sect leadership paralleled that of the core family, much the way other monarchies do. Hence, I term the leader the

Patriarch. True Pure Land Buddhism was unique in its time for encouraging a married priesthood and requiring a married leader. This practice made hereditary (biological) succession possible. Not all of the groups whose teachings were based on Shinran's followed the same pattern; most still adhered to the more traditional teacher-disciple succession.

7. One such was Tondabayashi, near Osaka. Nobunaga expressed his gratitude by allowing it to maintain some special rights it had enjoyed as a temple town. McMullin, 198.

8. Davis, "The Kaga *Ikkō Ikki*"; Amstutz, "The Honganji Institution"; and Davis, "Ikki in Late Medieval Japan."

9. Especially Dobbins; Rogers and Rogers; Solomon, "Rennyo and the Rise of Honganji"; Solomon, "The Dilemma of Religious Power"; and Weinstein. For works that address member communities in the Jishū, a Pure Land sect, see also Thornton and Brown.

10. For Nobunaga, see McMullin and Lamers. Ira Michael Solomon also wrote of an *ikkō ikki* that took place in 1506, in "The Dilemma of Religious Power." As one can observe from Solomon's title alone, he too looks at *ikkō ikki* from an elite perspective, dealing with the Patriarch rather than looking at the *ikkō ikki* from the bottom up.

11. Sources include the writings of local priests, which sometimes reflect beliefs different from the sect's official teachings. One of the eighth Patriarch's sons, Jitsugo, also wrote criticizing notions he found abominable but that were nevertheless encouraged by his great-nephew, the tenth Patriarch. He also wrote of outsiders' popular conceptions of sect doctrine and practice.

12. A few sources are written from the *ikki* perspective, such as *Eiroku ikki yurai*, which tells of the Mikawa *ikkō ikki* from the perspective of one of the rebellious temples.

Chapter One

1. Quoted in Cooper, ed., 319.
2. Imai, 47.
3. Quoted in Imai, 1–2.
4. Dobbins, 31–38, examines Shinran's teachings as reflected in his major work, *Kōgyōshinshō*, in depth.
5. Of course, the child of a man's wife is not necessarily the child of the husband. In Honganji's case, however, the child of a Patriarch's wife or consort was deemed to be the Patriarch's child.
6. Kanda, *Ikkō ikki to shinshū shinkō*, 142–45.

7. Imai, 54, mentions no names but points out that many great priests in the Kamakura era made the same claim.

8. Some scholars emphasize the humble origins of Shinran's followers; others doubt that humbler villagers were free to exercise their own choice of religion and, thus, question the importance or even existence of peasant followers. Imai, 53–54.

9. Inoue, *Honganij*, 54. Inoue identifies the Shimotsuma as followers, though other sources call them "hereditary servants." The latter term designates a kind of unfree labor differentiated from retainers who might, in theory, leave for a new master. The bond between the Shimotsuma family and the Patriarch's household was as permanent as one of blood kinship, and perhaps stronger, and they performed vital roles within the sect. In this sense, a Shimotsuma was fully a member of the household.

10. Most scholars have interpreted this document to mean that Kakunyo was under special pressure from the Kantō congregations to be obedient, especially after the trouble his half-uncle had caused them. Kanda Chisato, however, points out that Yuizen had, at some point, also signed some kind of pledge, whose contents are unknown. Kanda argues that the congregations punished Yuizen because he violated his pledge. If so, Kanda reasons, the agreement simply shows that the caretaker was subordinate to the Kantō congregations, rather than reflecting Kakunyo's particular circumstances. Kanda, *Shinshū shinkō*, 22–28.

11. Inoue, *Honganji*, 54, 60. By "aristocratic mentality," Inoue seems to mean Kakunyo's perception of himself as being of courtier status, too important to be just a caretaker.

12. Honganji-shi hensanjo, *Honganji-shi*, 1: 179–81.

13. The earliest appearance of the name in an extant document is dated Genkō 1 [1321]. It was probably changed several years previously, possibly as early as 1312. Inoue, *Honganji*, 63.

14. Five main True Pure Land factions became organized: the Bukkōji, Kinshokuji, Senjuji, Sanmonto, and Honganji sects.

15. Kanda, *Shinshū shinkō*, 44–47.

16. Kanda, *Shinshū shinkō*, 223–26. Kanda links the acceptance of Honganji's bloodline argument to the spread of the household (*ie*) system to rural society. People with a concept of the household system may have accepted a hereditary argument more easily than those without. This may be so, but the *ie* system was dedicated to the preservation of the household, not to a specific biological line.

17. The Patriarchal line has more in common with the claims of imperial descent than with other families' practices. This observation and its implications may merit further investigation, but they are outside the bounds of the current study.

18. There were no social or religious impediments to a man having several wives at one time. There were, however, economic considerations that made this an option only for the wealthy as poorer men could not afford to support more wives and children.

19. For a recent contribution to the debate, see Butler.

20. For a more exhaustive treatment of this topic, see Tsang, "Marriage, Adoption, and Honganji."

21. *Hogo no uragaki*, 755.

22. *Hino ichiryū keizu*, 532–40.

23. At least one historian, Kinryū Shizuka, sees the increasing exclusivity as part of a larger process of sect differentiation affecting all, or nearly all, Amidist traditions. See Kinryū Shizuka, "Rennyo kyōdan no hatten," 710–16.

24. Imai, 53.

25. Inoue, *Yama no tami*, 114–17.

26. Most of these people also grew food and paid taxes, thus earning the label of *hyakushō*, which at the time meant something closer to "taxpayer" than it did to "peasant."

27. Minegishi, "Ikkō ikki," *Shimpojiumu Nihon rekishi*, 9: 157–60.

28. Chiba, *Honpukuji shi*, 132–33.

29. Chiba, *Honpukuji shi*, 48.

30. *Honpukuji yuraiki*, 324–25.

31. *Honpukuji yuraiki*, 334.

32. *Honpukuji atogaki*, 356.

33. Kitai, "Hirakata jinaichō," 34–35; Suitō, 92, 97–98.

34. Kitai, "Hirakata jinaichō," 35–36, argues persuasively that non-members also lived in *jinaichō* and were not even excluded from organizations that were at least superficially religious. There is still debate on the issue, but no rules barring non-members from the towns, or similar clear evidence, exist to support claims to the contrary.

35. Shōmanji, in the province of Mikawa, for instance, sheltered the women and children of a warrior involved in a rebellion against his overlord. *Mikawa monogatari*, 64.

36. Suitō, 95–96.

37. *Hogo no uragaki*, 747–48.

38. Kasahara, *Ikkō ikki no kenkyū*, 130–31.

39. *Shinpen Okazaki-shi shi*, 2: 477.

40. Kasahara, *Ikkō ikki no kenkyū*, 349–89. Kasahara's discussion of the *kō*'s role in the sect assumes that the *kō* mentioned in fifteenth- and early sixteenth-century documents were identical to the *kō* of the seventeenth century since both were called *kō*. The documents he used to understand what a *kō* was or what it did date from no earlier than the end of the 1500s, and most of them date from the last quarter of the seventeenth century. None of them relates to *ikkō ikki*. The *kō* mentioned in earlier documents appears to have been constituted quite differently from the one Kasahara discussed.

41. Fujiki, *Sengoku shi o miru me*, 97.

42. Endō, "Kaga ikkō ikki no rekishiteki zentei," 187–99.

43. Several of Rennyo's letters addressed to *kō* express his thanks for their gifts. Inaba, ed., *Rennyo shōnin ibun*, 492–504.

44. Fujiki, *Sengoku shi o miru me*, 97–101.

45. See Kinryū Shizuka, *Ikkō ikki ron*, 353–54, for some letters from Shimotsuma administrators acknowledging receipt of, and offering thanks for, money sent by the Kagoshima twentieth-day *kō*, dated [year unknown]/11/28.

46. *Kennyo shōnin bun'an*, 1166–78.

47. *Honpukuji atogaki*, 356, lists them as "Honpukuji mai-toshi jūni-ka-getsu nenbutsu no ongashira." Many were merchants or artisans, such as an oil-seller or a cooper, so financial sponsorship of some kind seems a likely explanation.

48. Dobbins, 15–16, translates the passage of the *Gukanshō* that discusses this suppression.

49. Quoted in Dobbins, 114. The translation is Dobbins's.

50. *Honpukuji atogaki*, 358. Unless otherwise noted, translations are mine.

51. Ira Michael Solomon points out that the concept of other power is hard to grasp. How does someone believe without willing the belief? By contrast, the concept of human power, especially when it took the form of ascribing special power to a priest, chanting the *nenbutsu*, or signing salvation registers, was much easier to grasp. Solomon, "Rennyo and the Rise of Honganji," 40–41. Kanda, *Ikkō ikki to Shinshū shinkō*, 50–52, draws on accounts of miracles at the deaths of True Pure Land religious figures to argue that people perceived true faith as difficult to achieve, and thus followers did not take rebirth in the Pure Land for granted, at least through most of the fifteenth century.

52. Jitsugo says that it was under the care of three or four members of the Shimotsuma family of Honganji temple officials. *Honganji sahō no shidai*, 584.

53. *Hogo no uragaki*, 744; *Honganji sahō no shidai*, 584; *Kenshin monogatari*, quoted in Kinryū Shizuka, "Rennyo kyōdan," 720–21.

54. Inoue, *Ikkō ikki no kenkyū*, 277–87.

55. Inoue, *Ikkō ikki no kenkyū*, 284.

56. Kinryū Shizuka, "Rennyo kyōdan," 719–23.

57. As mentioned earlier, the seventh shogun was eight when he took office and died two years later. His younger brother succeeded him, also at the age of 8.

58. See Minegishi, "Chūsei shakai," 48–50, for the multifaceted nature of *chūsei* status concepts and distinctions.

59. Most recently, see Amstutz.

60. Minegishi, "Chūsei shakai."

61. Fukuda Toyohiko described them as groups of warriors who were not direct vassals of a *shugo,* or not vassals of such a vassal, who nevertheless joined together in order to support the *shugo* in battle. Fukuda argued that after the battle ended, the *ikki* disbanded. Minegishi, "Chūsei shakai," 56, emphasizes the continuity of some of these *ikki* over time.

62. Minegishi, "Chūsei shakai," 57.

63. *Ichizoku* literally means one family but refers to all the branches of a family.

64. Shingyō, *Ikkō ikki no kiso kōzō*, 47–55, discusses a document that served, in part, the same purpose. It was not an *ikki* contract but rather a guarantee of protections for the Matsudaira family memorial temple and signed by the heads of several Matsudaira cadet branches in 1501. In brief, the document commemorated the recent death of the head of one branch of the family and thus served two purposes: to remind them that they were family members (by confirming their responsibilities to the family memorial temple) and to emphasize the subordinate position of the cadet branches (because by doing so, they all honored the head of the one branch).

65. Minegishi's article lists 31 warrior *ikki* contracts, most of them from Hizen but also including ones in Mutsu, Ōsumi, Mikawa, Ōmi, Kii, Aki, and elsewhere. Minegishi, "Chūsei shakai," 53–54.

66. See Keirstead, Chapter 4, "The Theater of Protest."

67. For a more detailed description of *tokusei ikki*, see Gay, 128–48.

68. Tanaka, 10–11, quoting *Gohōkōinki*, the diary of former imperial regent Konoe Masaie.

69. Ikegami, 98.

70. These were both factions of the Hatakeyama family, embroiled in a prolonged succession dispute.

71. Ikegami, 91, quoting *Daijōin jisha zōjiki*.

72. Literature on the Yamashiro *kuni ikki* is extensive; a useful introduction is Nihonshi kenkyūkai and Rekishigaku kenkyūkai, eds. See 230–37 for transcriptions of the primary sources relevant to study of the Yamashiro *kuni ikki*.

73. Ishida, "Yamashiro no kuni ikki," argues that the *ikki* members were vassals of Hosokawa Masamoto, who acted as *de facto shugo* of Yamashiro by letting them form an *ikki*. Without Masamoto's protection, he says, the *ikki* could not have survived for as long as it did. The other warriors finally destroyed the *ikki* because in 1493 Masamoto had focused his attention and forces elsewhere, that is, his coup d'état.

Chapter Two

1. Rogers and Rogers used this phrase as the subtitle in their biography of Rennyo.

2. The leader of the Takada sect, Shin'e, was another who also enjoyed considerable success in the middle of the fifteenth century.

3. See Introduction.

4. The facts of Rennyo's early life are few but available in many secondary accounts. Unless otherwise noted, in this section my account follows that found in Kinryū Shizuka, *Rennyo*, 6–34, the most recent authoritative biography of Rennyo. Kinryū incorporates recent scholarship and offers challenging new interpretations of documentary evidence.

5. She is known only by the Buddhist name Nyoen-ni, or Nyoen the nun.

6. Strictly speaking, Rennyo's sponsor was from the Hirohashi branch of the Hino family, which became the main branch in 1443, when the previous main branch ended. *Sonpi bunmyaku*, 2: 239, 260.

7. *Rennyo goichi kiki*, 511. Taking the tonsure, that is, shaving one's head, was part of the ritual of taking religious orders.

8. Kinryū Shizuka, *Rennyo*, 9–10.

9. Kanda, "Rennyo no jitsuzō," 121–22.

10. Kasahara, *Ikkō ikki no kenkyū*, 68–69. There is, however, no mention of this woman in the most complete genealogical charts available for Honganji, Jitsugo's *Hino ichiryū keizu*.

11. *Rennyo goichi kiki*, 529.

12. *Rennyo goichi kiki*, 511. For widows' roles, see Tabata, 95–98.

13. During Rennyo's life, he would have five wives, whom he married in succession. He practiced serial monogamy despite the lack of an institutional or moral obligation to do so because, it is said, he wished to avoid the position in which his father had been placed when he had to send Rennyo's mother away.

14. The first wife's religious name was Nyoryō, and the second one's was Renyū.

15. Kinryū Shizuka, *Rennyo*, 10. See also *Sonpi bunmyaku*, 3, pt. 2: 29.

16. *Hino ichiryū keizu*, 524, and *Sonpi bunmyaku*, 2: 244.

17. Kasahara, *Ikkō ikki no kenkyū*, 68.

18. Ashikaga Yoshinori's older brother was the fourth shogun Yoshimochi, and Yoshinori had become the leader of the Tendai sect. When Yoshimochi's son and successor Yoshikazu died, Yoshinori was chosen as the sixth shogun and thus returned to lay life in 1428.

19. *Hino ichiryū keizu*, 523–26. Kinryū Shizuka, *Rennyo*, 11–12. All of these temples were in Kyoto.

20. Rennyo had greater need of help with his children than previous Patriarchs had because so many of his survived to adulthood. The temple's fortunes improved so much under Rennyo and his successors that subsequent Patriarchs had no need to provide for their children in this way.

21. Minegishi, "Rennyo no jidai," 79–80.

22. *Kanegamori nikki batsu*, 701. The original of the letter no longer exists.

23. *Honpukuji yuraiki*, 329–30. The actual date of the attack is unclear. Most secondary accounts follow *Honpukuji yuraiki*, which says that attack occurred on the ninth day. So does *Honpukuji atogaki*, 364. *Kanegamori nikki batsu* suggests the tenth, 701. Others, more contemporary with the events described, give the date as the eleventh. See the diaries of two Kōfukuji priests: *An'ijidono gojiki*, quoted in Inoue, *Ikkō ikki no kenkyū*, 310; and *Daijōin jisha zōjiki*, 3: 478, entry dated Kanshō 6 [1465]/3/24.

24. *Kanegamori nikki batsu*, 701, says 300, but Myōshū's account is earlier and probably more accurate.

25. *Honpukuji yuraiki*, 330, only mentions the 80 men. *Honpukuji atogaki*, 364, says the 80 men led a total force of over 200.

26. *Honpukuji yuraiki*, 329–30, and *Honpukuji atogaki*, 364–65. The two accounts are very similar.

27. *Honpukuji yuraiki*, 330. The economic importance of Ōmi to Enryakuji can be easily grasped by looking at a chart listing all of Enryakuji's estate holdings as reflected in surviving documents. Out of a total of 270 holdings, nearly half—116—were located in the province of Ōmi, with 25 in the county of Shiga alone. The province with the next largest number was Yamashiro, in which there were a mere 15 holdings. *Kokushi daijiten*, 2: 430–32, s.v. Enryakuji.

28. *Kyōkaku shiyōshō*, Kanshō 6 [1465]/1/12, quoted in Kasahara, *Rennyo*, 112. According to *Honpukuji yuraiki*, the money itself came primarily from Mikawa, 330–31.

29. *Yasaka jinja monjo*, 1: 937.

30. *Inryōken nichiroku*, 2: 13–14, entry dated Kanshō 6 [1465]/3/24. It appears that this was not the first time such a letter went out. *Chikamoto nikki*, 1: 209, entry dated Kanshō 6 [1465]/2/21, also mentions an order that went out to warriors telling them not to respond to Enryakuji's orders to attack the Honganji followers in Ōmi.

31. *Honpukuji yuraiki*, 331, mentions the assistance of someone named Hyōgo, who is identified as an important person in Ōmi. He may be the same "Hyōgo" mentioned in *Daijōin jisha zōjiki*, 3: 478, entry dated Kanshō 6 [1465]/3/24. The *Daijōin jisha zōjiki*'s Hyōgo can be identified as Sadamune, the son of the shogunal official Ise Sadachika who was also head of the main branch of the Ise family. Rennyo's first two wives came from a collateral branch of the Ise family. See also the letter from Enryakuji complaining of this man's siding with Honganji against Enryakuji. *Yasaka jinja monjo*, 1: 936.

32. *Inryōken nichiroku*, 2: 20, 37, 45; entries dated Kanshō 6 [1465]/5/10, 8/5, and 9/15. *Kanegamori nikki batsu*, 702.

33. *Honpukuji yuraiki*, 331–33.

34. Inoue, *Ikkō ikki no kenkyū*, 316.

35. This translation for the term *mugekō* comes from Rogers and Rogers, 65.

36. *Honpukuji yuraiki*, 333.

37. See Chapter 1 on the Ōnin War.

38. *Honpukuji atogaki*, 367–69.

39. It is worth mentioning that Enryakuji also threatened other True Pure Land factions, like the Takada sect, claiming they too

spread the "unhindered light" heresy. The Takada sect leaders managed to convince Enryakuji that they were not guilty and so were spared both physical attacks and demands for cash payments. Inoue, *Ikkō ikki no kenkyū*, 153. Most of the Honganji leadership were already convinced this approach would not work for them. Perhaps the theological defense worked for the Takada sect because its successes did not come so close to Enryakuji's home. Enryakuji fought Honganji to win, if not the hearts and minds, then the rice and cash of the people of Ōmi.

40. This was actually done twice in different locations within Ōtsu. *Honpukuji atogaki*, 367–68.

41. *Honpukuji yuraiki*, 340.

42. Letter dated Bunmei 5 [1473]/10/3, Inaba, ed., *Rennyo shōnin ibun*, 129.

43. Hongakuji received an object of worship from Zonnyo, Rennyo's father, in 1451. Its dedication can be found in Kitanishi Hiromu, *Ikkō ikki no kenkyū*, 689. It may have been affiliated with Honganji for a generation before that, when a succession dispute within the temple resulted in a split congregation. The second congregation later accepted Zonnyo's uncle, Ton'en, and became Chōshōji. Asaka, 28–31.

44. Asaka, 37–39.

45. Chiba, "Sōsetsu," 25.

46. *Hogo no uragaki*, 750.

47. Inoue, *Ikkō ikki no kenkyū*, 283–84.

48. Most scholars say he received the official appointment of military governor in the fifth month of 1471, if not sooner. At least one scholar doubts this. Shigematsu, *Honganji hyakunen sensō*, 92. *Pace* Shigematsu, if control of Echizen was still contested at this time, Toshikage had the lion's share of it.

49. Kinryū Shizuka, *Rennyo*, 75–76, argues that Rennyo based his choice primarily on Yoshizaki's distance from the centers of power.

50. For a particularly informative discussion of the importance of reading the letters aloud, see Fujiwara, 279–90.

51. *Kanegamori nikki batsu*, 704.

52. Kinryū Shizuka, *Rennyo*, 83–85.

53. This collection contains 29 letters that could be considered business letters, acknowledging receipt of donations for example, rather than *ofumi* whose main purpose was exposition of doctrine. Since many of the business letters also include passages relating to doctrine, though, the distinction is somewhat artificial.

54. Forty of the canonical 80 letters are dated between the seventh month of 1471 and the eighth month of 1475, when Rennyo left Yoshizaki. Only 18 letters are dated later, though some 22 carry no dates at all.

55. The entire set of these 80 letters has been translated in Rogers and Rogers, 142–259.

56. Of the 80 letters in the canonical collection, 25 address heresies, of which 20 were sent from Yoshizaki, a total of 80 percent. Rogers and Rogers, 79, n. 24.

57. Kinryū Shizuka, *Rennyo*, 105–6. The Takada sect's main temple was Senjuji, and the sect is sometimes called by that name.

58. *Asakura shimatsuki*, 328.

59. *Rennyo shōnin ibun*, 104. Letter dated Bunmei 5 [1473]/8/2.

60. *Rennyo shōnin ibun*, 108–9. Letter dated Bunmei 5 [1473]/9, no day.

61. For Honganji and merchants, see Kitai, "Sengoku-ki no shūkyō to shōgyō," 157–86, although Kitai is more interested in Honganji temple towns in the second half of the sixteenth century. For Hida, one timber and mining area, see Mitsumoto, 171–73. For Noto, another, see Kigoshi, "Amine Honseiji," 266. In Echizen, many temples changed affiliation from other factions, like the Takada faction, as they did in Mikawa. See Koizumi, *Echizen ikkōshū*, 126–229.

62. Kinryū Shizuka, "Rennyo kyōdan no hatten," 726.

63. Kinryū Shizuka, *Rennyo*, 55–56.

64. Hamaoka Nobuya, "Rennyo to Kaga," 238–44.

65. For Rennyo's travels, see Kinryū Shizuka, *Rennyo*, 114–16. For villages and towns, see Yamamoto, "Chūsei nōmin no seikatsu no sekai," 131–66.

66. *Nyokō deshi chō*, 630–34.

67. Kitanishi, *Ikkō ikki no kenkyū*, 689–720, shows that Rennyo issued 32 objects of worship between his accession as Patriarch in 1457 and his retirement in 1489. In the next four years, 18 images were issued, 13 of them signed by Rennyo. During the last five years of Rennyo's life, he only signed 3 more objects, while Jitsunyo issued 29. During the remainder of Jitsunyo's tenure, he distributed another 123. The pattern holds for Etchū, Noto, and Kaga even using Kasahara Kazuo's method of relying on temple histories, despite the fact that histories written later have a tendency to exaggerate the length of time the temples were associated with the Honganji sect. Kasahara, *Ikkō ikki no kenkyū*, 228–61, 288–99, and 301–3.

68. *Rennyo shōnin goichidaiki kikigaki*, 529.

69. Kinryū Kyōei, for example, argues that in spite of this story, real growth did not begin until after 1489—that is, after Rennyo's retirement as Patriarch—and did not reach the villages in Etchū until after 1513. Kinryū Kyōei, "Etchū kyōdan," 206. Kinryū bases his findings on the dedications of sacred objects, but it is also possible that the dedication of these objects reflects formal institutionalization, which may have occurred after the number of believers had already begun to grow. It is undeniable that by 1488, there were enough Honganji believers in the Hokuriku to make a good deal of trouble.

70. *Hino ichiryū keizu*, 523.

71. For example, *Rennyo shōnin ibun*, 114–15.

72. Dobbins, 110–11.

73. *Rennyo shōnin ibun*, 109–11, letter dated Bunmei 5 [1473]/9/n.d.

74. The discussion that follows is centered more on the perception of the followers than on Rennyo's complex teachings on faith. For analysis of Rennyo's doctrines, see Dobbins, and Rogers and Rogers.

75. *Rennyo shōnin ibun*, 131–33, letter dated Bunmei 5 [1473]/11/n.d.

76. The phrase is *nenbutsu mono to shite*.

77. Rogers and Rogers, 87.

78. *Rennyo shōnin ibun*, 199–200, letter dated Bunmei 6 [1474]/7/3.

79. Dobbins, 143–44, treats the rules and the issue of Rennyo's vision of faith in detail. Although my argument diverges from his in some parts, my treatment is greatly indebted to his, and "articles of faith" is his phrase.

80. Kinryū Shizuka, *Rennyo*, 26, 105.

81. *Rennyo shōnin ibun*, 177–81, reprints the texts of three letters, one undated and two with the same date, whose contents show considerable overlap. All three contain the passages discussed in the text.

82. The two heresies most closely associated here are *ichiyaku hōmon* and *fuhai hiji*, the beliefs that one is a Buddha and that where one resides is itself the Pure Land, and the belief that since one is a Buddha, it is unnecessary to worship other deities, respectively. Presumably the latter belief would also leave one free to belittle or slander other deities as well as fail to worship them. Kinryū Shizuka, *Rennyo*, 105–7.

83. *Daijōin jisha zōjiki*, 5: 70, entry dated Bunmei 3 [1471]/2/29. Ostensibly, Toshikage became subordinate to Shiba Yoshitoshi, one of the contenders for headship of the house of Shiba, so in effect he offered support in exchange for one of the titles the Shiba had held.

84. Inoue, *Ikkō ikki no kenkyū*, 335; *Daijōin jisha zōjiki*, 5: 288, entry dated Bunmei 4 [1472]/8/20.

85. Koizumi, "Echizen ni okeru Shinshū no hatten," 295–96.

86. Toshikage won. *Hino ichiryū keizu*, 539.

87. Sources place the warrior families Yamagawa, Motoori, and Tsukinohashi in Masachika's camp, and Nuka, Sawai, Aso, Kanō, and Kosugi in Kōchiyo's. *Shirayamagū shōgon kōchū kiroku*, 110.

88. The outlines of the struggle for Kaga thus far are detailed with little variation in a number of secondary sources. This account draws on Kasahara, *Ikkō ikki no kenkyū*, 151–92; Inoue, *Ikkō ikki no kenkyū*, 334–35; and Inoue, *Honganji*, 154–55.

89. *Daijōin jisha zōjiki*, 5: 387–88, entry dated Bunmei 5 [1473]/8/15.

90. *Daijōin jisha zōjiki*, 5: 412, entry dated Bunmei 5 [1473]/10/16.

91. *Rennyo shōnin ibun*, 129, letter dated Bunmei 5 [1473]/10/3. Another undated letter first published by a historian in 1956, supposedly written by Rennyo, accuses the Takada followers of murder and arson directed against Honganji adherents and urges his followers to fight the "enemies of the [Buddhist] law," even if that should include the legally constituted authorities. Sasaki, 83. Some historians, notably Inoue, in *Ikkō ikki no kenkyū*, 342–43, and Kanda, *Ikkō ikki to shinshū shinkō*, 265–66, take the letter at face value. As Ishida Haruo has pointed out, however, the letter survives only in copy form, and many of the passages, including the one about "enemies of the law," sound distinctly unlike Rennyo, though other passages follow his writings closely. Ishida, "Sengokuki Kaga ni okeru 'gunchū' ni tsuite (jō)," 78–79. Kanda argues that, since there are passages that sound like Rennyo, the letter should be accepted as real. If one were to forge a letter, however, particularly one as formulaic as the pastoral letters were, it would make sense to start with a genuine one and make the necessary changes. Furthermore, in later years, a number of priests within the Honganji sect would have found it helpful to be able to quote Rennyo as supporting armed resistance, so there would have been a strong motive for creating a forgery of this type. Until further evidence supporting the authenticity of the letter emerges, it should be used with caution.

92. *Tenshō sannen ki*, 416.

93. Solomon argued that, "As far as the Ikki were concerned, there was no difference between Kōchiyo and Masachika, and a confrontation with the latter was only a matter of time." Solomon, "Rennyo and the Rise of Honganji," 220. Certainly there was no ideological or

programmatic difference between Kōchiyo and Masachika, except that Masachika promised to support the Honganji sect, and Kōchiyo had already allied with the Takada sect. This kind of connection based on self-interest, however, was the basis for most alliances of all kinds in *sengoku*. While it did turn out to be "only a matter of time" before Masachika and the Honganji followers clashed, the same could be said of Masachika and his warrior supporters, many of whom also turned on him in 1488.

94. *Konko dokugo*, 720. It goes on to credit Honganji members and Rennyo for settling affairs in Kaga.

95. *Daijōin jisha zōjiki*, 5: 479, entry dated Bunmei 6 [1474]/5/15.

96. *Daijōin jisha zōjiki*, 5: 488, entry dated Bunmei 6 [1474]/6/17. I have been unable to identify the Mino commander that Jinson mentions.

97. *Shirayamagū shōgon kōchū kiroku*, 110.

98. *Daijōin jisha zōjiki*, 6: 50, entry dated Bunmei 6 [1474]/11/1. Although Rennyo rejected the term of *ikkōshū* to describe his sect, outsiders consistently used the term to refer to the Honganji sect and its adherents.

99. Letter dated Bunmei 11 [1479]/11/2 from *Nakanoin monjo*, quoted in Kanda, *Shinshū shinkō*, 263–64.

100. Kinryū Shizuka, "Rennyo kyōdan no hatten," 749–50.

101. *Tenshō sannen ki*, 416.

102. *Shirayamagū shōgon kōchū kiroku*, 110.

103. For a thorough treatment, see Tanaka.

104. *Tenshō sannen ki*, 416.

105. *Tenshō sannen ki*, 415–17.

106. Kinryū Shizuka, *Rennyo*, 124–25.

Chapter Three

1. *Honpukuji yuraiki*, 341–42.

2. *Kanegamori nikki batsu*, 704. Rennyo's tenth son Jitsugo credits another priest, Junsei, with telling Rennyo about the site. *Yamashina gobō no koto narabi ni sono jidai no koto*, 543.

3. *Rennyo shōnin ibun*, 317, letter undated, but probably Bunmei 12 [1480] from internal evidence.

4. Rogers and Rogers, *Rennyo*, 107, n7.

5. *Rennyo shōnin ibun*, 306, letter dated Bunmei 11 [1479]/12/n.d. Rennyo, of course, uses Japanese count.

6. *Rennyo shōnin ibun,* 315–18, letter undated but probably Bunmei 12 [1480] from internal evidence.

7. *Yamashina gobō no koto,* 543.

8. *Rennyo shōnin ibun,* 336–38, letter dated Bunmei 15 [1483]/8/28.

9. *Yamashina gobō no koto,* 543.

10. *Hino ichiryū keizu,* 524.

11. Kinryū Shizuka, *Rennyo,* 138–41, says that after Rennyo's flight to Yoshizaki, Junnyo took over as Patriarch, as evidenced by his caring for Shinran's statue in Rennyo's absence. He also points out that Rennyo signed three letters, at different times, designating his heir. Each time, Kinryū argues, Rennyo actually resigned. The first letter was written after Enryakuji's 1465 attack on the Ōtani Honganji, when Kinryū says Junnyo succeeded him. A few years later, in 1468, he designated another son, Jitsunyo. The third letter was written in 1489, when he finally did retire, and Jitsunyo became the ninth Patriarch. Kinryū Shizuka, *Rennyo,* 63–64.

12. Inoue, *Honganji,* 178.

13. *Hino ichiryū keizu,* 530.

14. Although Ton'en is generally credited with founding Chōshōji, it is likely that the temple was formed because of a split within the Hongakuji congregation, and the new group that formed asked Ton'en to be their priest. Asaka, 28–30.

15. *Hogo no uragaki,* 755. The age is Japanese count. The woman was the child's great-aunt.

16. *Rennyo shōnin ibun,* 121–27.

17. *Hino ichiryū keizu,* 533. The young man's first wife was his father's cousin.

18. *Hino ichiryū keizu,* 524–27.

19. Kinryū Shizuka, "Rennyo kyōdan no hatten," 745.

20. *Kuni* is a vague term that could mean anything from a province to a county unless combined with a specific province's name.

21. Shigematsu, *Honganji hyakunen sensō,* 133–34.

22. Kinryū Shizuka, "Rennyo kyōdan no hatten," 745–46. Kinryū reports that the sect built one temple close to Ishiguro's castle, which could not have been done while Ishiguro remained in charge. If one accepts the war tale's version that an *ikkō ikki* destroyed Ishiguro rule, then his argument makes sense. If we reject the war tale, however, and its story about Ishiguro and Zuisenji, some other group may have caused the demise of the family. In that case, the existence of a Honganji temple near the castle may be insignificant. Other than

the war tale, no evidence exists of hostility between the Ishiguro family and Honganji members.

23. Shingyō, "Etchū ikkō ikki," 88.

24. Shingyō, "Etchū ikkō ikki," 89.

25. Kubo, *Shōkōji to Etchū ikkō ikki*, 30–31, points out that after 1481 the shogunate increasingly appealed to Honganji temples as well as to the constituted authorities to help carry out orders in Kaga. Kubo, citing Asaka Toshio, argues that this was necessary—that the shogunate and governor could not govern without the assistance of Honganji temples—because of the success of the Etchū conflict. After defeating Ishiguro, according to Kubo, the members who had fled to Etchū returned to Kaga, tipping the balance in Honganji's favor. As will become clear in the next section, I argue that this interpretation of the shogunate's letters requires a very narrow reading of the available documents about Kaga. Sending letters to the *shugo*, the *shugo-dai*, and Honganji sect temples, in addition to the villagers themselves, suggests an attempt to get help from anyone at all who might be able to compel the villagers to pay the rents and dues. Furthermore, since it was not Ishiguro Mitsuyoshi who kept them from returning to Kaga, if indeed they were so kept, Kubo's thesis fails to explain the connection between winning the fight in Etchū and being able to return to Kaga.

26. Indeed, the sources do not even agree on the year, though 1485 is the one most often used. Other possibilities are 1488 and 1475. Kasahara, *Ikkō ikki no kenkyū*, 532, n. 78. None of the sources is contemporary with the conflict, and the most important one dates from the eighteenth century. Mitsumoto, 157.

27. Kasahara, *Ikkō ikki no kenkyū*, 502–4.

28. Inoue, *Ikkō ikki no kenkyū*, 423–30.

29. Mitsumoto, 157–75, traces the recovery of Shinshū in Hida. See 170–73 especially for rebuilding of Shōrenji.

30. A letter quoted in Kasahara, *Ikkō ikki no kenkyū*, 155, is addressed to both Kōtokuji and the Kahoku-gun *ikki*, and Kasahara dates it around Bunmei 14 [1487]. The *Bugyōnin hosho*, which has the letter on 2: 87–88, expresses doubts about its authenticity.

31. For example in *Jūrin'in naifuki*, entry dated Bunmei 9 [1477]/2/29, quoted in Kanda, *Ikkō ikki to sengoku shakai*, 18. One undated letter purporting to be from the shogunate to the Kahoku-gun *ikki* is dated to 1482 by Kasahara Kazuo. See his *Ikkō ikki no kenkyū*, 155. The editors of a collection of the letters from shogunal

officials only date this letter tentatively to "before 1507?" and more importantly they consider the letter to be of doubtful authenticity because of its format. Hence, I have not included it as a reference to Kahoku-gun by name in the 1480s. *Bugyōnin hōsho*, 2: 87–88.

32. From proceedings of a meeting at Enryakuji in the eighth month of 1482, quoted in Kasahara, *Ikkō ikki no kenkyū*, 165.

33. *Bugyōnin hōsho*, 1: 283–84, letter dated Bunmei 8 [1476]/11/4, addressed to *ikki chū*. There is no way to determine if the league in question consisted largely of Honganji members or only partly. Since there were so many followers in the region, it is highly unlikely that it included none.

34. *Tenbun nikki*, entry dated Tenbun 13 [1544]/10/22, quoted in *Nihon rekishi chimei taikei*, 17: 346, s.v. Kuratsuki-no-shō. In 1544, at least two areas within the estate were being handled by *kumi* and the *gunjū*.

35. There is a wealth of secondary literature in Japanese devoted to arguments about the sectarian composition of Kaga *ikki* in both the fifteenth and sixteenth centuries. All the historians use the same documents to explore the issue and usually have incompatible solutions to the puzzle. Because of the ambiguity of many of the documents, the arguments often rest on grammatical issues and interpretations. The liveliest ongoing debate of the issue is between Kanda Chisato, who argues that all the Kaga leagues were composed solely of Honganji members, and Ishida Haruo, who argues instead that they were non-member vassals of the shogun. Kanda, "Kaga ikkō ikki no hassei," 214–45; Ishida, "Sengoku-ki Kaga ni okeru 'gunjū' ni tsuite (jō)," 70–100, and "(ge)," 106–32. For a general but by no means exhaustive idea of the range of the debate, see also Kinryū Shizuka, "Kaga ikkō ikki no keisei katei," 1–16; Yanagi, "Kaga ikkō ikki no tenkai," 20–56; Endō, "Kaga ikkō ikki no seiritsu ni tsuite," 160–213; Fujiki, *Sengoku shi o miru me*, 88–121, especially 97–110; and Kigoshi, "Bunmei/Chōkyō-ki no Kaga ni okeru 'gun' ni tsuite," 335–63.

36. *Bugyōnin hōsho*, 1: 392, letter dated Bunmei 17 [1485]/9/21.

37. *Bugyōnin hōsho*, 1: 187, letter dated Kanshō 4 [1463]/12/27.

38. *Jūrin'in naifuki*, entry dated Bunmei 9 [1477]/2/29, quoted in Kanda, *Ikkō ikki to sengoku shakai*, 18. This particular clause has an ambiguity in the original. To be precise, there is a grammatical particle missing between the "Honganji members" and "acting as the *ikki*" phrases. Ishida Haruo argues strongly that the missing particle is not a subject identifier but rather one that indicates direction. According to him, the section would be translated as "to the Honganji

members, the two *gun* Nomi and Enuma, acting as *ikki*," a reading that differentiates between the two groups. He says that is the only way that the second part of the letter makes sense. Ishida, "Sengoku-ki Kaga ni okeru 'gunchū' ni tsuite (jō)," 72–73. If Ishida is correct, however, the shogunate's response in wanting Rennyo to expel the members makes no sense. Other historians interpret the phrase as I have translated it.

39. *Rennyo shōnin ichigoki*, 463.

40. *Nihon rekishi chimei taikei*, 17: 235, s.v. Yatanoshō.

41. Letter dated Chōkyō 1 [1487]/10/2, quoted in full. Kasahara, *Ikkō ikki no kenkyū*, 156.

42. Letter dated Chōkyō 1 [1487]/10/18, quoted in full. Kasahara, *Ikkō ikki no kenkyū*, 156–57.

43. Letter from Yamagawa Takafuji (one of Kaga's deputy governors), dated Chōkyō 1 [1487]/11/6, quoted in full. Kasahara, *Ikkō ikki no kenkyū*, 157. Letter from other officials, same date. *Tatsunokuchi machi shi*, 473.

44. Letter dated Chōkyō 1 [1487]/12/2, quoted in full. Kasahara, *Ikkō ikki no kenkyū*, 158.

45. *Inryōken nichiroku*, 2: 377, entry dated Bunmei 18 [1486]/11/3. Note that the Enuma-gun *ikki* and Shōkōji were treated separately.

46. *Daijōin jisha zōjiki*, 6: 353, entry dated Bunmei 6 [1477]/12/10.

47. *Gohōkōin-ki*, 1: 215, entry dated Bunmei 11 [1479]/8/19.

48. *Sanetaka kōki*, 1: 213, entry dated Bunmei 9 [1477]/2/20, and *Chikanaga kyōki*, 1: 296, entry dated Bunmei 9 [1477]/2/20.

49. *Bugyōnin hōsho*, 1: 347, letter dated Bunmei 12 [1480]/10/2.

50. *Inryōken nichiroku*, 2: 391, entry dated Bunmei 18 [1486]/11/27.

51. *Inryōken nichiroku*, 2: 258, entry dated Bunmei 17 [1485]/10/24.

52. *Inryōken nichiroku*, 3: 152–53, entry dated Chōkyo 2 [1488]/5/6.

53. Davis, "*Ikki* in Late Medieval Japan," 221–47, especially 243–44.

54. *Daijōin jisha zōjiki*, 8: 239, entry dated Bunmei 16 [1484]/11/7.

55. Legitimacy, which derives from a legal definition of rights, and effectiveness, which in *sengoku* derived from military power, do not always go together, and a leader may have had one without the other.

56. Inoue, *Ikkō ikki no kenkyū*, 367.

57. *Inryōken nichiroku*, 2: 572, entry dated Chōkyō 1 [1487]/9/12.

58. *Rokuon nichiroku*, 1: 17–18, entry dated Chōkyō 1 [1487]/11/8.

59. The most widely used account of the problems in Kaga leading up to the rebellion against Masachika is *Kanchiron*, a war tale osten-

sibly written by the son of a man killed while fighting on Masachika's side. Scholars have been unable to identify the author or to date the tale, though much of what the tale says is supported by, or at least consistent with, more reliable sources contemporary with the events.

60. *Kanchiron*, 47–49.

61. *Inryōken nichiroku*, 3: 172, entry dated Chōkyō 2 [1488]/5/26.

62. *Inryōken nichiroku*, 3: 193, entry dated Chōkyō 2 [1488]/6/25, reported that the *ikki* had overwhelming numbers—as many as 200,000—so Toshikage had to retreat. *Kanchiron* claims that after an initial success, Toshikage was forced to retreat by an *ikki* counterattack. *Kanchiron*, 68. *Asakura shimatsuki* credits not Toshikage but another warrior related to Masachika with the attempted intervention and says that this man decided to leave when he learned of his relative's death. On the way back to Echizen, however, they were set upon by *ikki* fighters, and both sides dispersed after minor losses. *Asakura shimatsuki*, 328.

63. *Kanchiron*, 50–68.

64. Two usually reliable diaries disagree on the date. Rumors of the attack and of Masachika's death reached the capital on the ninth day. *Inryōken nichiroku*, 3: 182, entry dated Chōkyō 2 [1488]/6/9. Over the next few weeks, as more details were reported, *Inryōken nichiroku* reaffirmed that the debacle occurred on the ninth, the first day on which the rumor was reported. *Inryōken nichiroku*, 3: 193, entry dated Chōkyō 2 [1488]/6/25. Another diary contests that, giving the eighth as the date of Masachika's death. *Gohōkōin-ki*, 2: 214, entry dated Chōkyō 2 [1488]/6/15. The eighth, or even earlier, seems more plausible because of the time it would have taken for news of the defeat to travel the eighty or more miles from Kaga to Kyoto.

65. *Kanchiron*, 50–51. The four temples were Guganji, Senkōji, Shōanji, and Kōtokuji.

66. Very little is known of Kawara Gen'emon, and too little evidence exists to say more precisely when he organized the *kumi*.

67. Kasahara and Inoue, eds., 559, n3, s.v. Yasuyoshi Gen'emon-no-jō Ietsugu.

68. *Gohōkōin-ki*, 2: 214, entry dated Chōkyō 2 [1488]/6/15.

69. *Kanchiron*, 50–51.

70. These figures come from *Gohōkōin-ki*, 2: 214 (entry dated Chōkyō 2 [1488]/6/15) and *Inryōken nichiroku*, 3: 193 (entry dated Chōkyō 2 [1488]/6/25), respectively.

71. *Tenshō sannen ki*, 416. The word I have translated as "commoners" is *hyakushō*, which in later times would come to mean peasants. In the medieval period, however, it simply referred to those who were responsible for paying certain kinds of rents and taxes. Because of the later meaning of the word, however, coupled with a tendency to overlook the word "like," in this quotation, many writers have quoted this phrase as meaning that Kaga was a "province held by peasants." The full translation of what Jitsugo wrote is "Yasutaka became the governor, and since this Togashi was set up by the commoners, the commoners became stronger, so in recent years it [Kaga] was like a province held by commoners."

72. *Rennyo shōnin ichigoki*, 463.

73. *Dai hasso onmonogatari Kūzen kikigaki*, 431. At least two copies of the harsh letter survive, each with the same text but addressed to different temples in Kaga. One of these is printed in *Rennyo shōnin ibun*, 511.

Chapter Four

1. *Ōtani Honganji tsūki*, 368.

2. Inoue, *Ikkō ikki no kenkyū*, 375.

3. On Entoku 3 [1491]/5/6 alone, the shogunate sent out sixteen letters ordering the payment of rents due to Kitano shrine. The letters referred to thirteen separate holdings in ten different provinces and accused seven of the relevant *shugo* of seizing the shrine's holdings for themselves. *Bugyōnin hōsho*, 1: 473–78.

4. *Daijōin jisha zōjiki*, 11: 65, entry dated Meiō 5 [1496]/9/16.

5. *Bugyōnin hōsho*, 1: 436, letter dated Chōkyō 2 [1488]/11/3 confirms direct holding; 1: 448, letter dated Entoku 1 [1489]/10/2 to Shikichi Hikouemon-no-jō accuses him of taking over the shrine's holdings (*ōryō*) and orders him to leave and turn over the holding to the shrine's *daikan*.

6. For the shogunate's first orders, see *Bugyōnin hōsho*, 1: 449–50, four letters issued on the same date, Entoku 1 [1489]/10/2, two to warriors (Senshū Izu-no-kami and Shibayama Kurōzaemon), one to the *shōen* administrator (*shōshu*) of Nosaka-no-shō, and one to the taxpayers of Fukuda-no-shō, all urging them to cooperate with the new *daikan* and not with Shikichi. For the shogunate's next orders, after the shrine had tried appointing the warrior as its *daikan* but was still not receiving the rents, see *Bugyōnin hōsho*, 1: 473–74, letter dated Entoku 2 [1491]/5/6. Another letter went to the villagers

ordering them to send rents directly to the shrine again. *Bugyōnin hōsho,* 1: 474, letter dated Entoku 2 [1491]/5/6. Orders in 1491 refer to Shikichi as the shrine daikan, a title that had not been used for him earlier. These letters also accused him of misappropriating the rents and dues.

7. *Bugyōnin hōsho,* 2: 59–60, letter dated Eishō 2 [1505]/5/23.

8. *Bugyōnin hōsho,* 2: 119, letter dated Eishō 6 [1509]/8/15, orders villagers to send part of rents to Kitano shrine and part to Hatakeyama Ueno-no-suke; 140, letter dated Eishō 7 [1510]/12/17, returns full rule to Kitano shrine.

9. In records of Rinsenji's estate Ōno-no-shō, in 1493 groups connected with Honganji called *kumi* handled the rents for one of the villages. Muroyama, "Shiryō shōkai," 78. The tenth Patriarch's diary includes notations of donations sent to the main temple by several *kumi* in Kaga, indicating that these groups consisted solely of Honganji members.

10. *Kitano shake nikki,* 3: 30. Kankiji received the same appointment for Yamashiro, a town in Kaga Province, not the province in the Kinai. In 1490 the town had also been given an unsatisfactory warrior overseer.

11. *Bugyōnin hōsho,* 2: 171–72, letter dated Eishō 11 [1514]/7/5.

12. *Bugyōnin hōsho,* 2: 232–33, letter dated Eishō 16 [1519]/3/3.

13. *Bugyōnin hōsho,* 2: 252, letter dated Taiei 1 [1521]/11/16.

14. *Inryōken nichiroku,* 4: 205, entry dated Entoku 2 [1490]/10/27.

15. *Daijōin jisha zōjiki,* 10: 307–8, entry dated Meiō 2 [1493]/7/26.

16. *Daijōin jisha zōjiki,* 10: 407, entry dated Meiō 3 [1494]/10/15.

17. *Daijōin jisha zōjiki,* 10: 430, entry dated Meiō 2 [1493], end matter.

18. *Daijōin jisha zōjiki,* 11: 65, entry dated Meiō 5 [1496]/9/16.

19. Inoue Toshio suggests that after the 1493 *coup d'état,* Kaga allied with the ousted shogun, Ashikaga Yoshitane. Under his orders, they attacked Asakura Sadakage. Although the diarists of the time credited the Kai with attacking Echizen, Inoue argues that it was the Kaga forces, including the *ikki,* and not the Kai after all. The *ikki* then changed sides because of the close connection between Masamoto and the Honganji leadership. While Inoue's interpretation explains how the groups within Kaga came to pursue different alliances, it leaves gaps in other areas. The most perplexing is that Inoue has the Kaga forces attacking Echizen at the behest of the deposed shogun, but at the time, Asakura Sadakage supported Yoshitane. Inoue, *Ikkō ikki no kenkyū,* 387–90.

20. Junnyo had a daughter who married a son who was adopted into the family. In spite of the adopted son's own ancestry being traceable all the way to Shinran as well, apparently he was not seen as an appropriate heir. It is unclear why none of the intervening sons was chosen as heir.

21. The first indication that Jitsunyo might succeed Rennyo came as early as 1468, when Rennyo signed a letter naming the child, then only 11 years old, as heir. Kinryū Shizuka, *Rennyo*, 63–64. The significance of this document is unclear, however, because even after 1468, until his death in 1483, Junnyo served as guardian of Shinran's sacred image at the temple in Ōtsu, and he sometimes signed sacred objects that were given to member congregations. Both of these functions were usually performed only by the Patriarch or his recognized heir. It is not clear precisely when Jitsunyo was adopted into the Hino family or when he began study at Shōren'in. His preparation may have started as soon as 1468 or as soon as it appeared likely that Junnyo would not have a son of his own to succeed him.

22. *Hino ichiryū keizu*, 526.

23. *Hino ichiryū keizu*, 526; *Ōtani chakuryū*, 638. The Takakura were a relatively minor aristocratic family, but they were court nobility nonetheless. Evidently both sides hoped to gain from the linkage.

24. For example, the Honganji leadership distributed sacred objects to temples, marking their affiliation with the sect. As noted in Ch. 2 n. 63, between 1489 and 1495, Rennyo signed thirteen out of eighteen surviving objects.

25. Inoue, *Honganji*, 161.

26. *Konko dokugo*, 718–19.

27. *Tōji kakochō*. It is in scroll form with the names of the dead or entries like those quoted here written on the front of the paper and dates, sometimes with other details, written in the corresponding space on the back. All entries quoted here were dated Eishō 3 [1506].

28. *Tōji kakochō*. The dates given in brackets are those found on the backs of the entries.

29. *Tōji kōmyōkō kakochō*. This entry can also be found in print in *Nochi no kagami*, 132. Although *Nochi no kagami* identifies it as "*Tōji kakochō*," it is in fact this *Tōji kōmyōkō kakochō* and not to be confused with the *Tōji kakochō* mentioned above.

30. *Shiryō sōran*, 9: 162–79, entries from the year Eishō 3 [1506].

31. *Asakura shimatsuki* is written from this perspective. The editors tentatively date this work to around 1577. *Rennyo, ikkō ikki*, 657.

32. Shingyō, "Eishō sannen ikkō ikki." This argument has gained wide acceptance and can be found in many general histories of the *ikkō ikki*, such as Shigematsu, *Honganji hyakunen sensō*, 148–59. Shingyō's basic argument can also be found in English in Solomon, "The Dilemma of Religious Power." Solomon uses Shingyō's conclusions as a starting point for exploring the conflicting demands Jitsunyo faced as the leader of a large religious organization. Some scholars have criticized Shingyō's argument, however. Galen Amstutz points out that the Honganji sect was not an "orderly monolith" ready to carry out Jitsunyo's orders at once and that the members of the sect could have "pick[ed] up on . . . a trend" to attack Masamoto's enemies. Amstutz, 188–89.

33. After 1531, when Honganji exercised *shugo* power over Kaga, it used a wider range of sanctions related to the civil authority it wielded. Within the sect, however, expulsion was the sole punishment.

34. *Honganji sahō no shidai*, 586. Jitsugo found the idea "suspicious."

35. *Daijōin jisha zōjiki*, 12: 27–29, entries dated Eishō 1 [1503]/12/17, 22, 28. Most standard histories of this period in Japanese discuss the background of this rebellion; in English, Solomon, "The Dilemma of Religious Power," 60.

36. *Daijōin jisha zōjiki*, 10: 369, entry dated Meiō 3 [1494]/2/23. Also Kubo, "Muromachi jidai no Etchū," 447–48.

37. I use Shōjun, the Sinicized reading of his name, because I have come across too many other readings, including Hisanobu, Hisanori, and Naonobu. None of these choices (including Shōjun) enjoys general acceptance.

38. *Gohōkōinki*, 8: 235.

39. *Tōji kōmyōkō kakochō; Tamon'in nikki*, 1: 174, entry dated Eishō 2 [1505]/11/28.

40. *Yamashina gobō*, 555–56. Jitsugo's story is the only record of Honganji involvement in this case. This narrative is based on his work.

41. *Tōji kōmyōkō kakochō*, Eishō 3 [1506]/1/26. Also, *Tamon'in nikki*, 1: 178, Eishō 3 [1506]/1/26.

42. *Tamon'in nikki*, 1: 178, entry dated Eishō 3 [1506]/1/29.

43. Honganji itself moved to this now better-known location after the Yamashina site was destroyed in 1532.

44. *Yamashina gobō*, 555.

45. *Yamashina gobō*, 555–56. See also *Hogo no uragaki*, 745. Jikken was given a living at Shōtokuji temple in Ōmi and died in 1523 at the age of 34.

46. *Hogo no uragaki*, 745, written by her step-grandson, identifies her as the older sister of Hatakeyama Ietoshi, which would have made her the Noto governor's cousin. Other genealogies, however, offer conflicting information. For details, see Inoue, *Ikkō ikki no kenkyū*, 386–87.

47. *Yamashina gobō*, 556.

48. Kubo, "Echigo Nagao-shi," 466–67, for example, suggests that the Settsu and Kawachi followers believed Jitsunyo should support the Hatakeyama instead.

49. *Gohōjōji kanpaku ki*, 1: 26–27, entries dated Eishō 3 [1506]/4/16 and 4/18. Manuscript copies of this diary, kept by the courtier Konoe Hisamichi, appear under several variant titles, including *Gohōjōji kanpaku ki, Gohōjōji Gohōjōji kanpaku ki, Udaijin Gohōjōji kanpaku ki*, and *Konoe Gohōjōji kanpaku ki*.

50. *Daijōin jisha zōjiki*, 12: 72, entry dated Eishō 3 [1506]/5/8.

51. *Shinshū-shi gaisetsu*, 222.

52. Yoshikage's death is noted in several records, including the *Todera chōchō*, in *Toyama-ken shi, shiryō*, 2: 762, where it is dated incorrectly on the twenty-sixth, and *Hondoji kakochō*, in *Toyama-ken shi*, 2: 761. For deputy governor Jinbō Yoshimune's defection, see Kubo, "Echigo Nagao-shi," 472.

53. *Sanetaka kōki*, 4: 640, entry dated Eishō 3 [1506]/10/21.

54. Ishida, "Miyako, Kamakura-fu," 36–38.

55. *Asakura shimatsuki*, 329; *Nobutane kyōki*, 126, entry dated Eishō 3 [1506]/7/21.

56. *Honpukuji montoki*, 400, says only that the invasion occurred in 1506 and gives the size of the force as three hundred, but *Honpukuji atogaki*, 387, places it in the third month. Other sources fail to mention an invasion at that time. *Honpukuji montoki* also claims that a force sent to rescue the Settsu and Ōmi members when the attack failed involved "several hundred" boats, indicating a much larger expedition at that time.

57. Amstutz, 191.

58. *Anrakusan Sanfukuzenji nendaiki*, printed in Muroyama, "Anrakusan Sanfukuzenji," 1–6, entry dated Eishō 3 [1506]. *Yokōji nendaiki*, 52, reports *do-ikki* in Noto and Etchū in Eishō 2 [1505]; it seems likely

that the chronicler, who wrote it many years after the fact, was off by one year.

59. The younger brother was Hatakeyama Yoshimoto.

60. According to *Sengoku jinmei jiten*, 633, s.v. Hatakeyama Yoshimune, the *ikki* provided the reason for the brothers to heal the breach; they teamed up to defeat the *ikki* in Noto. Higashiyotsuyanagi, 42, concludes that the brothers reconciled in 1508, a year after Masamoto's death and shortly after Yoshitane's return to power.

61. *Tōji kakochō*, entries as noted.

62. *Yokōji nendaiki*, 52. Other sources also record famine and outbreak; see, for example, *Honkokuji nenpu*, entry dated Eishō 1 [1504].

63. See the ones in Kyoto in 1504 and Nara in 1505. Nakamura Kichiji, *Do-ikki kenkyū*, 527–30.

64. *Shinpen Okazaki-shi shi*, 6: 1047, doc. 10, dated Eishō 9 [1512]/2/1, giving land to a Jishū temple to pay for *nenbutsu odori* in memory of those killed in the wars from Eishō 3 to 6. Also see 6: 742, doc. 15, dated Eishō 10 [1513], which is a temple history that includes references to eight years of fighting, that is, since 1503, that left the temple badly damaged.

65. Matsudaira Nagachika, Tokugawa Ieyasu's great-great-grandfather. His great-grandfather Nobutada bore the brunt of the fighting against the Imagawa, and it is said that he used his success here to further his ambition of succeeding Nagachika. (The heir had not yet been determined and was not always the oldest son.)

66. The Matsudaira branch families gained a good deal of control in the 1530s by supporting the current Matsudaira hegemon. When he died in 1549 at the age of 24, his only son was 8 years old, and the Imagawa then took Mikawa under their direct control.

67. *Sanetaka kōki*, 4: 544, entry dated Eishō 3 [1506]/5/7.

68. The Saitō, who had intermarried with the Asakura.

69. Kinryū Shizuka, "Etchū ikkōshū kyōdan," 18–44, contains an extended discussion of the relationship of temples in Etchū and Noto with the Kaga conciliar temple Honsenji, for example.

70. *Toyama-ken shi shiryō*, 2: 762. The temple is Honsenji, headed by Rengo, Jitsunyo's brother.

71. Kinryū Shizuka, "Rennyo kyōdan," 760–61, points out the likelihood that these letters are forgeries but prefers to think of them as based on actual letters of similar import.

72. This is a famous letter that is reprinted in nearly every article that discusses the 1506 *ikki*. A photographic copy of the original, along

with a transcription of the text as written and one in *kakikudashibun*, that is, how the text would have been read aloud, can be found in *Honganji komonjo,* doc. 3 (pages are unnumbered). The phrase "people of good faith" is rendered as "men of principle" (for "*kokorozashi ninzu shūjū*") in Solomon, "The Dilemma of Religious Power," 62.

73. Inoue, *Ikkō ikki no kenkyū*, 394–95.

74. *Yamashina gobō no koto*, 555.

75. This is attributed by some to an involvement with Shugendō and by others to an exclusively homosexual orientation. The former interpretation often appears in books written for a general audience, while the latter is more generally accepted in scholarly circles.

76. *Sonpi bunmyaku*, 2: 251.

77. *Tamon'in nikki*, 1: 195, entry dated Eishō 4 [1507]/6/23, for the death itself, 6/24 for the description.

78. Takakuni was a cousin of the second-named heir, and Harumoto was the son of that same heir.

79. *Honpukuji atogaki*, 388.

80. Kinryū Shizuka, *Rennyo*, 79–81.

81. *Hogo no uragaki*, 746. The three exceptions were Jitsugen, Jitsue, and Jitsugo. Jitsugen was Jitsunyo's third son, Jitsue was Jitsujun's second son. Jitsugo was one of Jitsunyo's younger half-brothers, that is, one of Rennyo's sons, usually included in the *ichimon* level, but he had been adopted by another half-brother, Rengo, who was himself adopted by his father Rennyo's cousin Renjō and thus outside the *ichimon* circle as Jitsunyo defined it.

82. Kinryū Shizuka, "Rennyo kyōdan," 793–94.

83. *Konko dokugo*, 719.

84. *Hogo no uragaki*, 747.

85. *Hogo no uragaki*, 747–48.

86. *Niigata-ken shi, tsūshi*, 2: 543.

87. Kinryū Shizuka, "Rennyo kyōdan," 796.

88. *Niigata-ken shi tsūshi*, 2: 551.

89. Literally, "the school of unhindered light." Rennyo had used this phrase occasionally in the 1460s but ceased after Enryakuji associated the "unhindered light" with heresy.

90. *Toyama-ken shi shiryō*, 2: 826–27.

91. *Honganji komonjo,* doc. 3. As noted earlier, most historians treat this letter as if it were written fifteen years previously, during the Eishō 3 [1506] *ikkō ikki* episode, as noted earlier. Kasahara Kazuo, *Ikkō*

ikki no kenkyū, 441–42, also places it in 1521. For an earlier formulation of my argument, see Tsang, "The Development of Ikkō Ikki," 133–39.

92. Kinryū Shizuka, "Rennyo kyōdan," 803.

93. Quoted in Kinryū Shizuka, "Rennyo kyōdan," 803.

94. *Konko dokugo*, 719–20.

95. *Hino ichiryū keizu*, 526.

96. *Yamashina gobō*, 545.

Chapter Five

1. There was no functioning shogunate in Kyoto at the time. Harumoto had set up his base in Sakai, and his government ruled from there.

2. Inaba, ed., *Rennyo shōnin gyōjitsu*, 170, n. 465.

3. Jitsunyo's first-born son, Ennyo, died in 1521. The succession then passed to Ennyo's son, Shōnyo.

4. Genealogical information is taken from *Hino ichiryū keizu*, 522–29.

5. Inoue, *Ikkō ikki no kenkyū*, 443–45, also discusses the familial relationships within Honganji, particularly those of Renjun.

6. Davis, "The Kaga *Ikkō Ikki*," 106–7, regards the conflict between Takakuni and Harumoto as the real key to understanding the Kaga civil war, as he terms the *dai-shō ikki*. According to Davis, the main issue was the disposition of land that Takakuni had held. Shimotsuma Raishū's takeover threatened the interests of other temples. Many of Takakuni's officials were *ikki* members, and the Shimotsuma would replace them. Therefore, many of Takakuni's former officials sided with the *ikkeshū* temples against the former Echizen temples.

7. They were members of the Shimotsuma family, which served the Patriarch's family and Honganji temple. Some had administrative duties at the temple, some ritual, and still others were military generals.

8. *Hogo no uragaki*, 752, says that Honganji joined Jikken's side because another priest from Chōshōji, Jisshō, misrepresented the situation to the leadership. Then again, *Hogo no uragaki* was written by Jikken's enemy, and the text is strongly critical of the Chōshōji priest and his supporters.

9. *Shirayama-gū shōgon kōchū kiroku*, 112. Inoue, *Honganji*, 181, and some other secondary sources put this in the fifth month, but the original says "intercalary," and for that matter so does Inoue, *Ikkō ikki no kenkyū*, 452–53.

10. *Shirayama-gū*, 112. See also *Asakura shimatsuki*, 339. The former says the priests were captured and that nine people were killed; the latter says that everyone was killed. According to both *Konko dokugo*, 721, and *Hino ichiryū keizu*, 524–25, the Shōkōji main priest and his sons died later, on [1531]/11/18.

11. *Togashi-shi to Kaga ikkō ikki shiryō*, 511, doc. 63, is a letter from the Shimotsuma thanking members in Hida for their help against Honsenji; 538, doc. 134, addressed to priests and followers in Mikawa thanks them for their "long campaign" in Kaga. *Konko dokugo*, 721, also mentions Jitsuen, the *ichimon* priest from Mikawa, by name as supplying some of the reinforcements that arrived to help the Honganji side.

12. Forces from the Shirayama shrine also joined with the Honganji *ikki* for reasons that remain unclear.

13. *Shirayama-gū*, 112.

14. *Asakura shimatsuki*, 339.

15. *Asakura shimatsuki*, 339. In the chronicles Kensei wrote many years later—*Hogo no uragaki* and *Konko dokugo*—he does not mention this, but there is no particular reason why he should have. The story is plausible, at least in that Kensei found safety in Echizen when he had to escape Kaga, and so must have been on good terms with Asakura Norikage. *Konko dokugo*, 721.

16. *Asakura shimatsuki*, 339–40.

17. *Togashi-shi to Kaga ikkō ikki shiryō*, 509, doc. 59.

18. The Kahoku *gun ikki* is not mentioned specifically in the sources, so one cannot say with certainty on which side its members stood. They may well have been divided internally.

19. *Asakura shimatsuki*, 340–41; *Shirayama-gū*, 112. *Asakura shimatsuki* has this second battle take place on 10/29, but *Shirayama-gū* is more reliable.

20. *Shirayama-gū*, 112; *Asakura shimatsuki*, 341.

21. *Hino ichiryū keizu*, 524–25; *Shimotsuma keizu*, 684, for Raisen and Renkō; 686 for Raikei.

22. *Konko dokugo*, 721.

23. *Hino ichiryū keizu*, 533.

24. The *ichimon* temples outside of Kaga had supported Honganji in the *dai-shō ikki* conflict and would continue to do so in later battles.

25. Hatakeyama Yoshinobu, the son of Masamoto's rebellious subordinate, Hatakeyama Yoshihide.

26. *Gonjo ōnenki*, 368. The entry says Shōnyo took his "*naishū* and those below"; *naishū* refers to the Shimotsuma retainers.

27. Hino, *Settsu no kuni*, 41. Imatani, *Muromachi bakufu kaitai katei no kenkyū*, 408, has Hatakeyama Yoshinobu in Iimori castle and Kizawa besieging it, but other historians have Kizawa in the castle. In *Sengoku-ki Miyoshi ichizoku*, 89–91, Imatani also places Kizawa in the castle and Yoshinobu besieging it, so presumably this is correct. Berry, 148, apparently follows *Muromachi bakufu kaitai*.

28. *Nijōji shukaki*, part of *Zoku nangyō zatsuroku*, a collection of copies made in the Edo period of documents, many of which are no longer extant. *Zoku nangyō zatsuroku*.

29. Kinryū Shizuka, "Tenbun no Kinai ikkō ikki," 71, has this occurring on the eighteenth. *Nijōji shukaki* says the seventeenth. Hino, *Settsu no kuni*, 41, also dates Hatakeyama Yoshinobu's death on the seventeenth.

30. Imatani, *Sengoku-ki no Muromachi bakufu*, 180–81.

31. For nearly blow-by-blow details on the progress of the hostilities between Motonaga and Harumoto, see Imatani, *Sengoku-ki Miyoshi ichizoku*, 86–91.

32. *Gonjo ōnenki* reports on the twentieth that Harumoto has ordered Miyoshi Motonaga killed and that the Honganji has agreed to help. *Kōdaiji kakochō*, in *Shotera kakochō*, has his death on the twenty-third. Most histories take the twentieth to be the day of the successful attack, based on the diary of the courtier Yamashina Tokitsugu, *Tokitsugu kyōki*, 1: 191–92, entry dated Tenbun 1 [1532]/6/22.

33. The figure of 30,000 is possible, though unlikely. Kinryū Shizuka, "Tenbun no Kinai ikkō ikki," 71, regards this as the maximum number of fighters that could be raised. Just as a quick point of reference, the figure of 210,000 is more than twice the number of Union troops at the battle of Gettysburg, which occurred at a time when assembling, supplying, and moving large numbers of people was much easier. Kennedy, 117. A perhaps more relevant comparison might be the forces the French brought to the battle against the English king Henry V at Agincourt in 1380. They were variously estimated at anywhere from 10,000 to 200,000, with 25,000 seeming the most likely. Keegan, 87.

34. For an estimate of 100,000, for which the source is unclear, see Inoue, *Honganji*, 183. The figure of 30,000 is from *Hosokawa ryōkaki*, and 210,000 is from *Myohōjiki*, both cited in Kinryū Shizuka, "Tenbun

no Kinai ikkō ikki," 72. The figure of 210,000 is from *Tokitsugu kyōki*, 1: 191, entry dated 6/22, which cites the combined force and even uses the counter for horsemen. The deaths of 3,000 are also from *Tokitsugu kyōki*, 1: 191, entry dated 6/17.

35. See preceding chapter.

36. *Shimotsuma keizu*, 681.

37. *Yamashina gobō no koto to sono jidai no koto*, 556.

38. Kasahara, *Ikkō ikki no kenkyū*, 827–28.

39. The *shugo* authority adhered to the temple, and, no doubt, whoever served as head priest exercised the authority. The *ikki*'s attack was reported widely in courtier diaries and other records. *Nijōji shukaki* says the rioting began on the tenth, but nothing appears in other diaries until the seventeenth. *Gonjo ōnenki*, 368; *Nisuiki*, entry dated Tenbun 1 [1532]/7/17; and *Gohōjōji kanpakuki* 1: 306, entry dated same date. In the diary *Tokitsugu kyōki*, the entries from 7/14 to 7/22 are missing, and there is nothing about Nara in any of the surviving entries.

40. *Nijōji shukaki*, entry dated Tenbun [1532]/7/17; also *Nisuiki*, same date.

41. *Gohōjōji kanpakuki*, 306, entry dated Tenbun 1 [1532]/7/17.

42. *Gonjo ōnenki*, 368.

43. For two examples of this interpretation, see Imatani, *Sengoku-ki no Muromachi bakufu*, 182; Kinryū Shizuka, "Tenbun no Kinai ikkō ikki," 72.

44. Kinryū Shizuka, "Tenbun no Kinai ikkō ikki," 72.

45. *Aguchi jinja monjo*.

46. *Nijōji shukaki*, entry dated Tenbun 1 [1532]/8/9.

47. *Tsutsui kaki*, quoted in Nagashima, 25.

48. Akamatsu and Kasahara, eds., 139.

49. Nagashima, 25.

50. Their names are listed in *Nijōji shukaki*, entry dated Tenbun 1 [1532]/8/23.

51. Nagashima, 25.

52. Nagashima, 25; as for the *jinaichō*, according to Mizumoto, 380, they were both founded in 1495.

53. Mizumoto, 380.

54. Imatani, *Sengoku-ki no Muromachi bakufu*, 182.

55. Kinryū Shizuka, "Tenbun no Kinai ikkō ikki," 72.

56. Inoue, *Honganji*, 183, attributes Harumoto's opposition after Kōfukuji to his seeing the real power of the sect. Shigematsu, *Honganji*

hyakunen sensō, 169–71, argues that the Honganji members turned against Harumoto, which resulted in the attack on Nara.

57. *Shishinki*, 540, entries dated Tenbun 1 [1532]/8/11 and 8/12; also *Gonjo ōnen-ki*, 368, entry dated 8/12.

58. *Kyōkō hōin nikki*, 419, entry dated Tenbun 1 [1532]/8/10.

59. *Nisuiki*, entry dated Tenbun 1 [1532]/8/3.

60. *Shishinki*, 540, entry dated Tenbun 1 [1532]/8/14.

61. Imatani, *Tenbun hokke ikki no ran*, 63.

62. Imatani, *Tenbun hokke ikki no ran*, 63, summarizing an argument by Yamaori Tetsuo. Berry, 146, who may have used a source written in *kana*, bases her explanation of *uchi-mawari* on a reading of *uchi* as "interior." So it is, when written with one character, but the character used for *uchi* in the documents means "to strike."

63. Imatani, *Tenbun hokke ikki no ran*, 64.

64. Katsumata, 27–40.

65. Letters from Yoshiharu to the Nichiren temples Honmanji and Honnōji praise the sectarians for their assistance in the battle at Shirutani on 8/17. *Honmanji monjo, Honnōji monjo*. Several courtier diaries also note the battle. See, for example, *Nisuiki*, entry dated Tenbun 1 [1532]/8/16; *Kyōkō hōin nikki*, 419, entry dated Tenbun 1 [1532]/8/17; *Gohōjōji kanpakuki*, 312–13, entry dated Tenbun 1 [1532]/8/17.

66. *Shishinki*, 540, entry dated Tenbun 1 [1532]/8/23.

67. *Kyōkō hōin nikki*, 421, entry dated Tenbun 1 [1532]/8/23.

68. *Kyōkō hōin nikki*, 421, entry dated Tenbun 1 [1532]/8/23.

69. *Nisuiki*, entry dated Tenbun 1 [1532]/8/23. Of course, as always in such cases, the numbers may have been greatly exaggerated. Nevertheless, the anti-Honganji forces must have been formidable.

70. *Shishinki*, 540–41, entry dated Tenbun 1 [1532]/8/24.

71. *Kyōkō hōin nikki*, 421, entry dated Tenbun 1 [1532]/8/24.

72. *Kyōkō hōin nikki*, 421, entry dated Tenbun 1 [1532]/8/24.

73. *Nisuiki*, entry dated Tenbun 1 [1532]/8/25.

74. This vassal was Kōzai Motonaga, who tried to fight the seven villages alone at first but was defeated. Iikura, 409–10.

75. Shigematsu, *Honganji hyakunen sensō*, 170. The installation occurred in Tenbun 2 [1533]/7.

76. *Nisuiki*, entries dated Tenbun 1 [1532]/9/26 and 9/28; *Gohōjōji kanpakuki*, entry dated 9/28; *Shishinki*, 542, entry dated Tenbun 1 [1532]/9/28, reports the battle.

77. *Shishinki*, 546, entry dated Tenbun 2 [1533]/2/11, that Sakai has fallen. *Nisuiki*, entry dated Tenbun 2 [1533]/2/11, reports the same

news. *Honpukuji Myōshū atogaki*, 351, dates the defeat 2/9, which seems to be correct; it appears that news from Sakai usually took two days to reach the capital, or at least the Nisuiki diarist. *Sanetaka kōki*, 8: 394, entry dated Tenbun 2 [1533]/2/13, notes a rumor of a great defeat at Sakai on the ninth. Also see Imatani, *Sengoku-ki no Muromachi bakufu*, 187, for the flight to Awa.

78. *Shishinki*, 547, entry dated Tenbun 2 [1533]/4/6, states that Harumoto was back in Settsu. For Honganji's defeat, Honganji-shi hensanjo, *Honganji-shi*, 1: 414. *Shishinki*, 548, entry dated Tenbun 2 [1533]/4/26, only says that the Nichiren sect had camped at Osaka.

79. *Honpukuji Myōshū atogaki*, 351.

80. *Shishinki*, 548, entries dated Tenbun 2 [1533]/5/21 and 5/30. The *Honganji-shi* dates Harukuni's victory over the Nichiren sect on 5/11, but I have been unable to find corroboration. *Gohōjōji kanpakuki*, on 5/24, notes that Harukuni is on the march. Honganji-shi hensanjo, *Honganji-shi*, 1: 414.

81. The general was Yakushiji Kuninaga. *Gohōjōji kanpakuki*, entries dated Tenbun 2 [1533]/6/18 and 6/19, which says 400 to 500 people were killed; *Sanetaka kōki*, 8: 448, entry dated Tenbun 2 [1533]/6/18; *Shishinki*, 548, entry dated 6/18. Yakushiji Kuninaga's death is also reported in *Ganjō shinshū gekōki*, entry dated Tenbun 2 [1533]/7/13.

82. *Ganjō shinshū gekōki*, entry dated Tenbun 2 [1533]/7/13. Kinryū Shizuka, "Tenbun no Kinai ikkō ikki," 78.

83. *Gonjo ōnenki*, 370, entry dated Tenbun 2 [1533]/6/29.

84. Kinryū Shizuka, "Tenbun no Kinai ikkō ikki," 79; *Shishinki*, 550–51, entry dated Tenbun 2 [1533]/9/1, says that in the last day Kawarabayashi, Yakushiji, and others had entered Nakashima, a temple town not far from Osaka.

85. *Shishinki*, 553, entry dated Tenbun 2 [1533]/11/16. The text says "*uchi-mawashi-sōrō*," which is similar to an *uchi-mawari*. The former takes place on a battlefield and engages in provocative behavior. The latter occurs away from the battlefield and recruits or attracts participants.

86. *Shishinki*, 551, entry dated Tenbun 2 [1533]/10/6.

87. *Shishinki*, 558, entry dated Tenbun 3 [1534]/3/8, 3/10.

88. *Shishinki*, 550, entry dated Tenbun 3 [1534]/8/14. It says that the Kōshōji priest, originally the leader of a Bukkōji faction that had since joined the Honganji but retained some independence within the sect, had submitted a *wabigoto*. This word usually means some kind of apology, but here it is likely to have meant a kind

of resignation; he and the Honganji would eventually be reconciled in Tenbun 3 [1534]/11. The other possibility is that the two temples had already been estranged for a while and that this first attempt at reconciliation was rejected.

89. A transcribed copy of the letter can be found in Kinryū Shizuka, "Tenbun no Kinai ikkō ikki," 80. The letter bears no year, but, from other evidence, Kinryū concludes that 1534 is correct, and it certainly fits the circumstances existing in 1534/4. At least Mino and Owari responded at some point. *Shishinki*, 579, entries dated Tenbun 4 [1535]/11/23–28, states they were present the next year for services.

90. *Shishinki*, 560, entry dated Tenbun 3 [1534]/5/29.

91. For Motonobu, *Shishinki*, 556–57, entries dated Tenbun 3 [1534]/1/25 and 11/7. For the other, *Shishinki*, 557, entry dated Tenbun 3 [1534]/2/11. I have been unable to identify the name of the warrior from the Miyake family.

92. *Shishinki*, 560, entries dated Tenbun 3 [1534]/6/5 and 6/7.

93. *Shishinki*, 561–65, entries dated Tenbun 3 [1534]/6/26, 7/21, 8/11, and 10/20.

94. Kinryū Shizuka, "Tenbun no Kinai ikkō ikki," 84. Miyoshi Iga just drops out of the documents.

95. Kinryū Shizuka, "Tenbun no Kinai ikkō ikki," 83–84.

96. *Shishinki*, 567, entry dated Tenbun 3 [1534]/11/28. On Tenbun 3 [1534]/12/1, Jitsujū also records the gifts Renshu offered the Honganji in thanks for his pardon.

97. *Shishinki*, 572, entry dated Tenbun 4 [1535]/3/25.

98. *Shishinki*, 572, entry dated Tenbun 4 [1535]/4/9.

99. Kinryū Shizuka, "Tenbun no Kinai ikkō ikki," 85.

100. *Shishinki*, 574, entries dated Tenbun 4 [1535]/6/1, 6/2, 6/10, and 6/11.

101. *Go-Narain shinki*, quoted in Kinryū Shizuka, "Tenbun no Kinai ikkō ikki," 85.

102. *Shishinki*, 574–75, entries dated Tenbun 4 [1535]/6/17 and 6/25, for the reinforcements; for the defection, 7/26.

103. *Shishinki*, 576–77, entries dated Tenbun 4 [1535]/9/2, 9/3, 9/7, 9/10, and 9/11.

104. *Shishinki*, 576, entries dated Tenbun 4 [1535]/9/5 and 9/6. Inoue, *Honganji*, 185, suggests they were afraid the general would try to take over the Honganji.

105. *Shishinki*, 577, entry dated Tenbun 4 [1535]/9/14.

106. Shōren'in maintained long-standing ties with Honganji. This is where Shinran is believed to have taken the tonsure. Also, the Honganji was, formally at least, a branch of the Shōren'in until 1559. *Shishinki*, 579–80, entry dated Tenbun 4 [1535]/11/26, mentions Shōren'in in connection with peace negotiations, and on 12/1, a representative was to meet with Harumoto with thanks (and, presumably, gifts) for the peace.

107. Akamatsu and Kasahara, eds., 239.

108. Inoue, *Honganji*, 185.

109. Hino, 55.

110. Honganji-shi hensanjo, 416.

111. Inoue, *Honganji*, 185.

112. My discussion relies heavily on the most recent and extensive treatment of it in Japanese. Imatani, *Tenbun hokke ikki no ran*.

113. Imatani, *Tenbun hokke ikki no ran*, 119.

114. Imatani, *Tenbun hokke ikki no ran*, 132–34.

115. Imatani, *Tenbun hokke ikki no ran*, 165, and Imatani, *Sengoku-ki no Muromachi bakufu*, 188.

116. Imatani, *Tenbun hokke ikki no ran*, 208–9.

117. *Aguchi jinja monjo*; Kinryū Shizuka, "Tenbun no Kinai ikkō ikki," 72.

118. Quoted in Kinryū Shizuka, "Tenbun no Kinai ikkō ikki," 80.

119. *Shishinki*, 574, entry dated Tenbun 4 [1535]/6/25.

120. The priests of these temples, known as *jikisan* (lit., direct attendance) temples, had the right to obtain a direct audience with the Patriarch, as opposed to communicating with him through attendants. One such was the priest of Honpukuji in Ōmi, who supplied forces to the Osaka Honganji. *Honpukuji Myōshū atogaki*, 351.

121. *Honpukuji atogaki*, 381.

122. Kinryū Shizuka, "Tenbun no Kinai ikkō ikki," 87–88.

123. In his memoir, one priest wrote about the men who served as guards to the Yamashina Honganji and their role fighting in the Tenbun War. *Honpukuji Myōshū atogaki*, 350–51.

124. Letter quoted in full in Kinryū Shizuka, "Tenbun no Kinai ikkō ikki," 100–1.

125. Shingyō, *Kiso kōzō*, 224.

126. *Honganji sahō no shidai*, 586.

127. Imatani, *Sengoku-ki Muromachi bakufu*, 182. "Ishiyama" refers to a later name for the Osaka site of Honganji, and the war against Nobunaga is often called the Ishiyama War.

128. *Shishinki*, 579, entries dated Tenbun 4 [1535]/11/23–28, list priests and groups at services on days following the conclusion of peace, and all these provinces are represented.

129. *Honpukuji Myōshū atogaki*, 351.

130. *Kyōkō hōin nikki*, 421, entry dated Tenbun 1 [1532]/8/23.

131. See *Tenbun nikki*, 124–25, entry dated Tenbun 5 [1536]/6/22; 127, entry dated Tenbun 5 [1536]/8/5; and 131, entry dated Tenbun 5 [1536]/9/6, for fighting in Mino that Shōnyo says the priests know nothing about. Also, 262–63, entry dated Tenbun 9 [1540]/10/2, for an incident in Ise; 339, entry dated Tenbun 11 [1542]/8/6, in Kii and Yamato; 390–91, entry dated Tenbun 15 [1546]/12/16, in Kawachi; and 412, entry dated Tenbun 16 [1547]/9/5, for one in Kii that Shōnyo says involves *hyakushō*—not just Honganji members but everyone.

132. It might also testify to connections he had made. The connections might not have been made, however, had the power and wealth not been there.

133. Inoue, *Ikkō ikki no kenkyū*, 557; for membership request; *Ōtani chakuryū jikki*, 642, for marriage arrangement.

134. The timing of the marriage is the subject of some debate.

135. Katayama, 177.

136. *Bugyōnin hōsho*, 2: 359, letter from the shogunate addressed to Enuma-gun *kumichū*. Katayama, 178–79.

137. The estate was Ōno-no-shō, held by Rinsenji. Muroyama, "Shiryō shōkai," 78.

138. Inoue, *Ikkō ikki no kenkyū*, 519–20.

Chapter Six

1. There is some dispute about the year, and the *ikki* may have been in 1562–63. See discussion below.

2. The term is also an anachronism because the Honganji district was not given that name until after Honganji had left it.

3. Some historians have labeled both the Mikawa *ikkō ikki* and the anti-Nobunaga war as uprisings against unifiers. See, for example, Kitanishi. Leaving aside the question of what an uprising against a unifier (as opposed to a daimyo) entails, construing Ieyasu as a "unifier" before he had control of Mikawa province seems premature.

4. Trewartha, 491–92.

5. The following discussion of Mikawa's medieval geography is based on *Shinpen Okazaki-shi shi*, 2: 12–25.

6. Kubota, "Sengokuki Matsudaira kenryoku," 84–95, argues that the family head was only the chief of a coalition of Matsudaira branches. Tokoro, "Henkaku-ki Mikawa," 89–102, sees even Ieyasu in that light. Shingyō, *Kiso kōzō*, 49–53, may also be helpful in understanding the idea of an *ikki* of blood relatives versus a *kuni ikki*. In the pledges Shingyō uses as primary evidence to show a family *ikki*, though, family hierarchy is reflected in the signatures.

7. Shingyō, *Kiso kōzō*, 68.

8. Shingyō, *Kiso kōzō*, 181–93, argues the more direct control. Tokoro, review of *Ikkō ikki no kiso kōzō*, 53, expresses the doubts.

9. Shingyō, *Kiso kōzō*, 285–87.

10. See also Kasahara, *Nihon ni okeru nōmin sensō*, 139–40.

11. There are many accounts of Matsudaira history and Ieyasu's career. Mine relies heavily on *Shinpen Okazaki-shi shi*, 2: 652–807.

12. Nakamura Kōya, *Tokugawa Ieyasu kōden*, 105.

13. Sakai Tatsuo, "Sengoku jidai," in *Nishio-shi shi*, 2: 191.

14. Kitahara Masao, "Muromachi-ki Mikawa Kira-shi no ichi kenkyū," 32–49, gives the history of the family from the Kamakura period to just after the Ōnin war.

15. Sakai, "Sengoku jidai," 183–85. Sakai discusses the family's history through the *sengoku* period in detail, 173–91.

16. Nakamura Kōya, *Tokugawa Ieyasu kōden*, 108–9. See also Sakai, "Tokugawa-shi no ryōgoku shihai," 329–32.

17. Kubota, "Eiroku rokunen ikkō ikki," 13, and Shingyō, *Kiso kōzō*, 279.

18. Nakamura Kōya, *Ieyasu no shinryō*, 177.

19. Nakamura Kōya, *Tokugawa Ieyasu kōden*, appendix "Tokugawa Ieyasu-kō shōsai nenpu," 12. The appendix pages are numbered separately from the main text.

20. Nakamura Kōya, *Tokugawa ke*, 49.

21. Shingyō, *Kiso kōzō*, 268.

22. The first three were founded earlier as Takada branch temples. Jōgūji became affiliated with Honganji in 1461, when it received a ten-character invocation of Amida's name (*myōgō*) from Rennyo. Honshōji received a six-character *myōgō*, marking its affiliation with the sect, in 1468. Shōmanji changed its sect affiliation by 1478. Shingyō, *Kiso kōzō*, 213, 217. Honshūji, an *ichimon* temple, was founded by Rennyo in 1468. *Shinpen Okazaki-shi shi*, 2: 193–205 and 2: 455–85, contains a history of the temples based on a critical reading of primary sources. It differs in many details from standard treatments such as

those found in Kasahara, *Ikkō ikki no kenkyū*, or Dobbins. Also, see Oda Kenshin, "Honshūji kō," 29–42, for the early history of Honshūji and Oda, "Sasaki Nyokō (ichi)," 58–71, for Jōgūji.

23. For example, during a rebellion against Matsudaira Hirotada in 1543, the Ōkubo women and children were sent to Shōmanji's *jinaichō* for safety. The Ōkubo supported Hirotada, which left them open to attack by the rebels. *Mikawa monogatari*, 64.

24. *Shinpen Okazaki-shi shi*, 2: 810. Doc. 158, dated Eiroku 4 [1561], spells out the details of levies due for one particular donation of land to a temple.

25. Scholars offer numerous reasons for the Mikawa *ikkō ikki* apart from the economic and political ones. Kasahara, *Ikkō ikki no kenkyū*, 539–671, argues that it was a basic peasant uprising protesting their exploitation. Inoue, *Honganji*, 192–95, agrees that the peasants resisted taxes and that the warriors opposed Ieyasu for a variety of other reasons. Both take the "small samurai" mentioned in *Mikawa monogatari* and *Matsudairaki* to be peasants. In some sense, the small samurai were indeed peasants, but the two scholars portray the Mikawa *ikkō ikki* as following a European pattern of peasant uprisings. They attribute the peasants' militancy to Honganji's doctrine of equality. Nakamura Kōya, *Ieyasu no shinryō*, 87, and Totman, 33, see the basic issue as one of land, not commerce. Tokoro, "Henkaku-ki Mikawa," 89–104, sees the event as a clash of two *ikki* fighting for control of Mikawa. One side—the *ikkō* side—consisted of both villagers and warriors, whereas the other side, Ieyasu's, was an *ikki* of *kokujin*.

26. *Togashi-shi to Kaga ikkō ikki shiryō*, 538, doc. 134. *Konko dokugo*, 721.

27. Many scholars credit the Honganji sect in Mikawa with controlling *all* the commerce and transport of goods in the province. Aoki Yoshinori, "Mikawa ikkō ikki no kenkyū," 107–50. Others making similar arguments include Irimoto, *Bakuhan taisei*, 34–61, and Kitajima, 26–59. Nakano, 114–34. These arguments overlook the evidence of other economic activities in the province, like those of Daijuji, the Matsudaira family temple, which played an economic role similar to that of the Honganji temples.

28. *Matsudairaki*, 116. *Mikawa monogatari*, 83, says the *ikki* began in the first month of Eiroku 6 [1563]. For contemporary documents, *Shinpen Okazaki-shi shi*, Vol. 6. There are letters from Ieyasu rewarding vassals, 1134–35, docs. 19, 20, and 21; and 1147–48, doc. 57. More to the point, Ieyasu rewarded a debt cancellation to his relative Koretada, dated Eiroku 7 [1564]/1/28, freeing him from debts owed to "Toro, Harisaki,

and other enemies." Toro and Harisaki were the sites of two of the rebellious Honganji temples, Honshūji and Shōmanji, respectively; 1144, doc. 48. Another debt cancellation edict issued by Ieyasu's ally, Mizuno Nobumoto, dated Eiroku 7 [1564]/12/1, refers to "the *ikki* during this past year," 1210, doc. 4. Also, *Ieyasu no sho to ihin*, 74, has a similar one from Ieyasu to Matsudaira Sanzō, dated Eiroku 7 [1564]/2/3. In addition to these letters, the death register from Daijuji, the Matsudaira family temple, lists the deaths of three men, all from families known to have taken part in the fighting, in late 1563 and early 1564. *Daijuji kakochō*. It would seem, then, that the fighting took place in 1563 and 1564, whenever the provocation occurred.

29. Shingyō, *Kiso kōzō*, 264, points out the commonality of abrogated rights in otherwise conflicting accounts of the start of the uprising.

30. The warrior in question was Suganuma Sadaaki.

31. Sakai Masachika, who had sent the unfortunate messengers.

32. *Matsudairaki*, 116.

33. *Eiroku ikki yurai*, in *Shinpen Okazaki-shi shi*, 6: 666, doc. 31. This version of events finds some support from Ōkubo Hikozaemon. In his *Mikawa monogatari*, 83, he states only that there was a disturbance at Honshōji, which Ieyasu sent a warrior to investigate.

34. Irimoto, "Mikawa ikkō ikki no saikentō," 46–49. See also his *Bakuhan taisei*, 34–37.

35. *Mikawa monogatari* says that Kira Yoshiaki was encouraged by the Honganji members to lead them and become their lord, and that Arakawa Yoshihiro and Matsudaira Ietsugu followed Yoshiaki. *Mikawa monogatari*, 83. By contrast, *Matsudairaki* observes that the Honganji members were only protecting their temples and had no intention of seizing political control. *Matsudairaki*, 121. The *Matsudairaki* version is better supported by events than that of *Mikawa monogatari*.

36. He was at either Mutsuguri or Noba—the sources are unclear. *Matsudairaki*, 117, says Noba; *Mikawa monogatari*, 85, says Mutsuguri. As they are neighboring towns, with Noba lying to the north of Mutsuguri, it probably matters little which of the two it was. For Yoshinobu's father, see Yamamoto and Owada, eds., 402.

37. The Ōkusa leader was Matsudaira Masahisa, and the Sakurai branch head was Matsudaira Ietsugu. Masahisa's father had originally held Okazaki castle until Ieyasu's grandfather Kiyoyasu forced him out of it. Nakamura Kōya, *Ieyasu no zokuyō*, 85–86. Ietsugu's grandfather sat out Kiyoyasu's last campaign because he felt he had been unjustly criticized. Nakamura Kōya, *Ieyasu no zokuyō*, 134–35. He

also tried to supplant the adolescent Hirotada in 1543 after Kiyoyasu's death. *Mikawa monogatari*, 64. After the *ikki*, Ieyasu pardoned Ietsugu but not Masahisa. Nakamura Kōya, *Ieyasu no zokuyō*, 86.

38. At Honshōji there were "more than 100 [fighters], small samurai of unknown number." At Honshūji were "70 or 80 horsemen and more than 100 small samurai." *Mikawa monogatari*, 85–86.

39. Jōgūji counted 105 branch temples by 1484. *Shinpen Okazaki-shi shi*, 2: 477. Shōmanji probably had at least 36 branches. *Shinpen Okazaki-shi shi*, 2: 483. Figures are not available for Honshōji, but it seems likely that it had at least as many branches as Shōmanji.

40. Nakamura Kōya, *Ieyasu no shinryō*, 83; Shingyō, *Kiso kōzō*, 290; *Matsudaira ki*, 116–19; *Mikawa monogatari*, 84–89.

41. *Watanabe Chūemon oboegaki*, quoted in Shingyō, "Mikawa ikkō ikki ron ho-i (sono ichi)," 84.

42. Shingyō, *Kiso kōzō*, 291–92.

43. *Matsudairaki*, 118, 119; *Mikawa monogatari*, 86–87, 89. *Matsudairaki* provides a date for only one of these ventures: 11/25. It also specifies that it was the Ōkubo at Kamiwada who prevented the *ikki* forces from reaching Okazaki.

44. *Matsudairaki*, 120; *Mikawa monogatari*, 92.

45. *Eiroku ikki yurai*, 667.

46. *Mikawa monogatari*, 89.

47. *Matsudairaki*, 118. It also says that Sakai Tadanao was defeated on 1563/9/6 and fled into Suruga. *Matsudairaki*, 122.

48. See Ieyasu's letters of enfeoffment, which award lands formerly belonging to Yoshiaki to Honda Hirotaka, dated Eiroku 6 [1563]/11/7, Eiroku 6 [1563]/12 (no day); and to Matsui Tadatsugu, dated Eiroku 6 [1563]/12 (no day), assigning lands formerly belonging to Yoshiaki. *Shinpen Okazaki-shi shi*, 6: 1134, 1135, 1147.

49. *Matsudairaki*, 119–20; *Watanabe Chūemon oboegaki*, quoted in Shingyō, "Mikawa ikkō ikki ron ho-i (sono ichi)," 85; *Mikawa monogatari*, 90–92.

50. *Mikawa monogatari*, 92.

51. *Matsudairaki*, 117, and *Mikawa monogatari*, 85, both mention this without dating the incident. Shingyō, *Kiso kōzō*, 300, concludes it took place on 1/25; Nakamura Kōya, *Tokugawa ke*, 53, says 1/11.

52. Shingyō, *Kiso kōzō*, 300–1.

53. *Mikawa monogatari*, 93.

54. *Matsudairaki*, 121.

55. Shingyō, *Kiso kōzō*, 304.

56. *Matsudairaki,* 121; *Mikawa monogatari,* 93–94. *Matsudairaki* adds that the ringleaders promised to tell Ieyasu about his remaining enemies' movements.

57. *Mikawa monogatari,* 93.

58. *Matsudairaki,* 122.

59. Shingyō, *Kiso kōzō,* 306.

60. *Matsudairaki,* 122.

61. *Mikawa monogatari,* 95.

62. Kasahara, *Ikkō ikki no kenkyū,* 646.

63. Shingyō, *Kiso kōzō,* 326.

64. For the Kira, see Oda, "Mikawa ikkō shokiroku," 92. For the Arakawa, Sakai, "Tokugawa-shi no ryōgoku shihai," 349. For the Sakai, see Nakamura Kōya, *Ieyasu no shinryō,* 452.

65. The main Matsudaira family temple, Daijuji, was Jōdoshū. Matsudaira Iekiyo, for example, supported the founding of Tenkei-in, a Sōtō Zen temple in what is now Gamagōri, in 1503. It became his branch family's memorial temple. *Heibonsha chimei jiten,* 23: 1033, s.v. Tenkei-in. See also Kasahara, *Ikkō ikki no kenkyū,* 552.

66. Nakamura Kōya, *Ieyasu no shinryō,* 533, says that both branches are listed as main ones in Edo-period sources because it is unclear which of the branches' founders was the elder.

67. Nakamura Kōya, *Ieyasu no shinryō,* 537.

68. It has also been suggested that he sent his son to Okazaki not as a guarantee to Ieyasu but for his son's safety. As has been noted, their castle at Doi was involved with the heavy fighting between Kamiwada and the temples at Toro and Harisaki. Nakamura Kōya, *Ieyasu no shinryō,* 533–34.

69. Nakano, 119–20. It is now clear that the Imagawa, not the Honganji members, did.

70. *Okazaki-shi shi,* 6: 1013–19, doc. 8.

71. Shingyō, *Kiso kōzō,* 225–31.

72. Matsudaira Nobumitsu and his son Chikatada, third and fourth in the line of which Ieyasu was the ninth, founded the two temples central to the expansion of Jōdoshū in Mikawa, Shinkōmyōji (founded 1451) and Daijuji (founded 1475). *Shinpen Okazaki-shi shi,* 2: 447–48. Shingyō, *Daijuji no rekishi,* 14–23.

73. Information on Myōkokuji can be found in the *Shinpen Okazaki-shi shi,* 2: 419; *Nihon rekishi chimei,* 23: 831. For the time at which the Ōkubo became retainers of the Matsudaira, see Kubota, "Eiroku rokunen," 15.

74. *Shinpen Okazaki-shi shi,* 2: 457.

75. The Takada sect's spread owed little to the Matsudaira as they were founded in the mid-thirteenth century, well before the Matsudaira left their mountain village. *Nihon chimei daijiten,* 23: 1308, s.v. Myōgenji, suggests 1256 for Myōgenji; a copy of a land grant to Manshōji exists dated Shōan 3 [1301], *Nihon chimei daijiten,* 23: 1261, s.v. Manshōji. Furthermore, there is no evidence that they had any patronage relationships with the Matsudaira in later years. By contrast, the mutual enmity of the Honganji sect and the Takada sect is well known and had played a role in the 1473 Kaga struggle between Togashi Masachika and Kōchiyo, for example. See Chapter 2.

76. *Kennyo shōnin bun'an,* 139. The gifts included a long sword, at least one reddish bear (there is a lacuna where a number might have been), three Chinese robes, two tiger skins, and one horse.

77. *Kennyo shōnin bun'an,* 1143. For the New Year greeting, he sent one long sword and one horse. On the fifteenth, he sent ten loads of grains and five carpets made from treated animal skins (*mōsen*). Nobunaga had left Kyoto for his home base in Gifu after his initial entry with Ashikaga Yoshiaki. There, he continued fighting his many opponents and returned to Kyoto in the first month of 1569 after traveling through heavy snow. *Shinchō kōki,* 93–94.

78. Cooper, ed., 319.

79. Peace between Honganji and Asakura Yoshikage was achieved in the third month of 1569. In 1571, Kennyo's son and heir Kyōnyo was married to Yoshikage's daughter.

80. This was addressed to followers in Ōmi. According to Imada, 139, these letters were sent as far as Kyūshū and Shikoku. Kita-nishi, *Ikkō ikki no kenkyū,* 199–200, says that many copies of these letters still exist, but the one to Ōmi translated here is the only one that scholars seem to have used. Also, see Kasahara, *Ikkō ikki no kenkyū,* 674–75.

81. *Honganji komonjo,* doc. 23.

82. *Kennyo shōnin bun'an,* 1147–48 letters from the tenth month onward to Asai Hisamasa, his son Nagamasa, their retainer Asai Sukechika, Asakura Yoshikage, Asakura Kagetake, Takeda Motoaki (of the Wakasa Takeda), Maeba Kagemasa, Maeba Shichirōbe-no-jō, Yamazaki Naganori, Isono Tanba-no-kami, and Nakashima Hyūga-no-kami.

83. Notably in Neil McMullin's *Buddhism and the State* and more recently in Jeroen Lamers's biography of the warlord, *Japonius Tyrannus: The Japanese Warlord Oda Nobunaga Reconsidered.*

84. *Shinchō kōki*, 118–19.

85. Ōta Gyūichi uses this term—*mononokazu to mo sezu*, or *mononokazu ni arazu*—more than once to describe league members, for example, *Shinchō kōki*, 179.

86. *Shinchō kōki*, 160–63.

87. *Shinchō kōki*, 163, says 20,000 people, but figures were often wildly exaggerated in texts from that time.

88. Jishū priests did, however, have special battlefield rituals to help warriors attain rebirth in the Pure Land in spite of dying in such a state of sin.

89. For a recent example of this see Kanda, *Nobunaga to Ishiyama-gassen*, 163–66. Kanda argues that this idea arose from a popular interpretation (or misinterpretation) of the sect's principles. Kennyo capitalized on this belief because he had to make the most of whatever tools he had to mobilize the followers. I agree with him.

90. The Yugyō-ha of the Ji sect was one. Thornton, 6.

91. *Toyama-ken shi, shiryō*, 2: 1060. The letter is dated Genki 3 [1572]/5/17.

92. Imada, 158–59.

93. *Honganji komonjo*, doc. 40, and *Toyama-ken shi, shiryō*, 2: 1117–18. The *Toyama-ken shi* editors date this letter to 1575, but I have followed the dating in *Honganji komonjo*, which I find more convincing.

94. *Kennyo shōnin bun'an*, 1166; Kanda, *Nobunaga to Ishiyama-gassen*, 165.

95. *Honganji sahō no shidai*, 586.

96. See, for instance, Kennyo's letters accompanying New Year's gifts to the emperor.

97. *Hino ichiryū keizu*, 526–28.

98. Kanda, *Ikkō ikki to sengoku shakai*, 291–93.

Conclusion

1. This is, of course, only one possible definition. Some religions involve two but not all three elements. What we now call Shinto, for example, has institutions and rituals without a defined theology.

2. Also in some literature published by the East and West Honganji temples today. Higashi Honganji shuppanbu, ed., *Rokuji no toride*, under the supervision of Kitanishi Hiromu. This comic book includes a scene in which some peasants hear Rennyo preach and conclude that they are a samurai's social equal, 45–46.

Works Cited

Unless otherwise noted, place of publication is Tokyo.

Abe Takeshi and Nishimura Keiko. *Sengoku jinmei jiten*. Shinjinbutsu ōraisha, 1987.

Akamatsu Toshihide and Kasahara Kazuo, eds. *Shinshū-shi gaisetsu*. Kyoto: Heirakuji shoten, 1963.

Aguchi jinja monjo. Tokyo University Historiographical Institute, ms. facsimile.

Amstutz, Galen. "The Honganji Institution, 1500–1570: The Politics of Pure Land Buddhism in Late Medieval Japan." Ph.D. diss., Princeton University, 1992.

Anjō-shi shi. Vol. 2. *Shiryō-hen*. Ed. Anjō-shi shi hensan iinkai. Anjō: Aichi-ken Anjō shiyakusho, 1973.

Aoki Michio, Irumata Nobuo, Kurokawa Naonori, Satō Kazuhiko, Satō Shigerō, Fukaya Katsumi, Minegishi Sumio, and Yamada Tadao, eds. *Ikki*. 5 vols. Tōkyō daigaku shuppankai, 1981.

Aoki Yoshinori. "Mikawa ikkō ikki no kenkyū." *Shien* 9 (June 1934): 107–50.

Asaka Toshiki. *Komatsu Hongaku shi*. Komatsu-shi: Shinshū Ōtani-ha Hongakuji, 1982.

Asakura shimatsuki. In *Rennyo, ikkō ikki*. Ed. Kasahara Kazuo and Inoue Toshio. 326–426. Iwanami shoten, 1972.

Berry, Mary Elizabeth. *The Culture of Civil War in Kyoto*. Stanford, CA: Stanford University Press, 1994.

Brown, Jonathan Todd. "Warrior Patronage, Institutional Change, and Doctrinal Innovation in the Early Jishū." Ph.D. diss., Princeton University, 1999.

Bugyōnin hōsho. 2 vols. *Muromachi bakufu monjo shūsei*. Kyoto: Shibunkaku shuppan, 1986.

Butler, Lee. *Emperor and Aristocracy in Japan, 1467–1680: Resilience and Renewal*. Cambridge, MA.: Harvard University Asia Center, 2002.

Chiba Jōryū, ed. *Honpukuji kyūki*. Kyoto: Dōhōsha, 1980.

——. *Honpukuji shi*. Kyoto: Dōhōsha, 1980.

——. "Sōsetsu." *Kōza Rennyo*. Vol. 1. Ed. Jōdo Shinshū kyōgaku kenkyūjo and Honganji shiryō kenkyūjo. 15–46. Heibonsha, 1996.

—— and Kitanishi Hiromu, eds. *Honganji komonjo*. Kashiwa shobō, 1986.

Chikamoto nikki. Vol. 1. *Zoku shiryō taisei*. Vol. 22. Reprinted Kyoto: Rinsen shoten, 1967.

Chikanaga kōki. Vol. 1. *Zōho shiryō taisei*. Vol. 41. Reprinted Kyoto: Rinsen shoten, 1965.

Cooper, Michael, ed. *They Came to Japan: An Anthology of European Reports on Japan, 1532–1640*. Berkeley, CA: University of California Press, 1965.

Dai hasso onmonogatari Kūzen kikigaki. In *Shinshū shiryō shūsei*. Vol. 2. *Rennyo to sono kyōdan*. Ed. Katada Osamu. 419–38. Kyoto: Dōhōsha, 1977.

Daijōin jisha zōjiki. 12 vols. Ed. Tsuji Zennosuke. Sankyō shoin, 1935–37.

Daijuji kakochō. Tokyo Historiographical Institute, ms. facsimile.

Davis, David L. "*Ikki* in Late Medieval Japan." In *Medieval Japan: Essays in Institutional History*. Ed. John W. Hall and Jeffrey Mass. 221–47. New Haven, CT: Yale University Press, 1974.

——. "The Kaga Ikkō Ikki, 1473–1580." Ph.D. diss., University of Chicago, 1978.

Dobbins, James C. *Jōdo Shinshū*. Bloomington, IN: Indiana University Press, 1989.

Echizen no kuni sōetsuki. Fukui shiritsu kyōdo rekishi hakubutsukan kanpō, supplement no. 1 (n.d.): 1–18.

Eiroku ikki yurai. In *Shinpen Okazaki-shi shi*. Vol. 6. *Kodai, chūsei shiryō*. 666–67. Okazaki: Okazaki shiyakusho, 1989.

Endō Hajime. "Kaga ikkō ikki no rekishiteki zentei." In *Honganji, ikkō ikki no kenkyū*. Ed. Minegishi Sumio. 117–59. Yoshikawa kōbunkan, 1984.

———. "Kaga ikkō ikki no seiritsu ni tsuite." *Ryūkoku shidan* 85 (December 1984): 43–80.

Fujiki Hisashi. *Sengoku shi o miru me*. Azekura shobō, 1995.

———, ed. *Shūkan Asahi hyakka Nihon no rekishi 26: Ikkō ikki to Ishiyama-gassen*. Asahi shinbunsha, 1986.

Fujiwara Masami. "'Kataru' Rennyo to 'katareta' Rennyo: sengoku shinshū shinkō no kosumorojii." In *Kōza Rennyo*. Vol. 1. Ed. Jōdo shinshū kyōgaku kenkyūjo and Honganji shiryō kenkyūjo. 275–306. Heibonsha, 1996.

Gonjo ōnenki. In *Kaitei shiseki shūran*. Vol. 25. Ed. Kondō Heijō. 346–406. Kondō kappansho, 1902. Reprinted Kyoto: Rinsen shoten, 1984.

Gonjo Shinshū gekōki. Tokyo University Historiographical Institute, ms. facsimile.

Gay, Suzanne. *The Moneylenders of Late Medieval Kyoto*. Honolulu, HI: University of Hawai'i Press, 2001.

Gohōkōinki. Vol. 4. *Zōho zoku shiryō taisei*. Vols. 5–8. Ed. Takeuchi Rizō. Kyoto: Rinsen shoten, 1967. Reprinted 1985.

Gohōjōji kanpakuki [*Hisamichi kōki*]. 2 vols. Kyoto: Shibunkaku shuppan, 1985.

Hall, John W. and Jeffrey Mass, eds. *Medieval Japan: Essays in Institutional History*. New Haven, CT: Yale University Press, 1974.

Hamaoka Nobuya. "Rennyo to Kaga." In *Kōza Rennyo*. Vol. 6. Ed. Jōdo shinshū kyōgaku kenkyūjo and Honganji shiryō kenkyūjo. 229–54. Heibonsha, 1998.

Higashi Honganji shuppanbu, ed. *Rokuji no toride: gekiga ikkō ikki*. Supervised by Kitanishi Hiromu. Kyoto: Shinshū Ōtani-ha shūmu, 1982.

Higashiyotsuyanagi Fumiaki. "Noto Hatakeyama-shi karyō ni tsuite no saikentō." *Kokugakuin zasshi* 73: 7 (July 1972): 35–46.

Hino ichiryū keizu. Jitsugo. In *Shinshū shiryō shūsei*. Vol. 7. *Denki, keizu*. Ed. Hiramatsu Reizō. 504–45. Kyoto: Dōhōsha, 1975.

Hino Shōshō. *Settsu no kuni Shinshū kaitenshi*. Kyoto: Dōhōsha, 1986.

Hogo no uragaki. Kensei. In *Shinshū shiryō shūsei*. Vol. 2. *Rennyo to sono kyōdan*. Ed. Katada Osamu. 740–57. Kyoto: Dōhōsha, 1977.

Honganji komonjo. Ed. Chiba Jōryū and Kitanishi Hiromu. Kashiwa shobō, 1986.

Honganji sahō no shidai. Jitsugo. In *Shinshū shiryō shūsei*. Vol. 2. *Rennyo to sono kyōdan*. Ed. Katada Osamu. 559–87. Kyoto: Dōhōsha, 1977.

Honganji-shi hensanjo. *Honganji-shi*. Vol. 1. Kyoto: Jōdo Shinshū Honganji-ha shūmusho, 1961.

Honkokuji nenpu. Tokyo University Historiographical Institute, ms. facsimile.

Honmanji monjo. Tokyo University Historiographical Institute, ms. facsimile.

Honnōji monjo. Tokyo University Historiographical Institute, ms. facsimile.

Honpukuji atogaki. Myōsei. In *Honpukuji kyūki*. Ed. Chiba Jōryū. 356–94. Kyoto: Dōhōsha, 1980.

Honpukuji montoki. In *Honpukuji kyūki*. Ed. Chiba Jōryū. 396–403. Kyoto: Dōhōsha, 1980.

Honpukuji Myōshū atogaki. In *Honpukuji kyūki*. Ed. Chiba Jōryū. 346–53. Kyoto: Dōhōsha, 1980.

Honpukuji yuraiki. Myōshū. In *Honpukuji kyūki*. Ed. Chiba Jōryū. 324–44. Kyoto: Dōhōsha, 1980.

Iikura Harutake. "Yamashiro no kuni Yamashina shichigō to Muromachi bakufu." In *Nihon kodai chūsei shi no chihōteki tenkai*. Ed. Toyoda Takeshi kyōju kanreki kinenkai. 387–415. Yoshikawa kōbunkan, 1973.

Ikegami Hiroko. "Sengoku-ki no ikki." In *Ikki*. Vol. 2. *Ikki no rekishi*. Ed. Aoki Michio et al. 91–136. Tōkyō Daigaku shuppankai, 1981.

Imada Hōyū. *Ishiyama sensō rimenshi no kenkyū*. Kyoto: Nagata bunshōdō, 1989.

Imai Masaharu. *Kamakura shin bukkyō no kenkyū*. Yoshikawa kōbunkan, 1991.

Imatani Akira. *Muromachi bakufu kaitai katei no kenkyū*. Iwanami shoten, 1985.

———. *Sengoku-ki Miyoshi ichizoku*. Shinjinbutsu ōraisha, 1985.

———. *Sengoku-ki no Muromachi bakufu*. Kadokawa shoten, 1975.

———. *Tenbun hokke no ran: busōsuru machishū*. Heibonsha, 1989.

——— and Takahashi Yasuo, eds. *Muromachi bakufu monjo shūsei: Bugyōnin hōsho*. 2 vols. Kyoto: Shibunkaku shuppan, 1986.

Inaba Masamaru, ed. *Rennyo shōnin gyōjitsu*. 1928. Reprinted Kyoto: Hōzōkan, 1990.

———, ed. *Rennyo shōnin ibun*. 1937. Reprinted Kyoto: Hōzōkan, 1990.

Inoue Toshio. *Honganji*. Shibundō, 1966. Reprinted 1988.

———. *Ikkō ikki no kenkyū*. Yoshikawa kōbunkan, 1968.

———. *Yama no tami, kawa no tami: Nihon chūsei no seikatsu to shinkō*. Heibonsha, 1981.

Inryōken nichiroku. Vols. 2–4. Ed. Takeuchi Rizō. Kyoto: Shiseki kankōsha, 1954. Reprinted in *Zōho zoku shiryō taisei*. Vols. 23–24. Kyoto: Rinsen shoten, 1980.

Irimoto Masuo. *Bakuhan taisei seiritsushi no kenkyū*. Yūzankaku, 1979.

——. "Mikawa ikkō ikki no saikentō—Tokugawa-shi no Mikawa ryōgokuka to no kanren de." *Shigaku zasshi* 78: 8 (1969): 45–67.

Ishida Haruo. "Miyako, Kamakura-fu taisei no hōki." In *Sengoku, Shokuhō*. Vol. 5. *Komonjo no kataru Nihon-shi*. Ed. Minegishi Sumio. 17–66. Chikuma shobō, 1989.

——. "Sengokuki Kaga ni okeru 'gunchū' ni tsuite (jō)." *Bukkyō shigaku kenkyū* 31: 1 (June 1988): 70–100.

——. "Sengokuki Kaga ni okeru 'gunchū' ni tsuite (ge)." *Bukkyō shigaku kenkyū* 31: 2 (November 1988): 106–32.

——. "Yamashiro kuni ikki no kaitai." *Shindai shigaku* 6 (January 1982): 39–54.

Jōdo Shinshū kyōgaku kenkyūjo and Honganji shiryō kenkyūjo, eds. *Kōza Rennyo*. 6 vols. Heibonsha, 1996–98.

Kanchiron. In *Ikkō ikki to Togashi-shi*. Ed. Heki Ken. 47–70. Kanazawa: Ishikawa-ken toshokan kyōkai, 1934.

Kanda Chisato. *Ikkō ikki to sengoku shakai*. Yoshikawa kōbunkan, 1998.

——. *Ikkō ikki to Shinshū shinkō*. Yoshikawa kōbunkan, 1991.

——. *Nobunaga to Ishiyama-gassen: chūsei no shinkō to ikki*. Yoshikawa kōbunkan, 1995.

——. "Kaga ikkō ikki no hassei." In *Honganji, ikkō ikki no kenkyū*. Ed. Minegishi Sumio. 214–45. Yoshikawa kōbunkan, 1984.

——. "Rennyo no jitsuzō." In *Kōza Rennyo*. Vol. 1. Ed. Jōdo shinshū kyōgaku kenkyūjo and Honganji shiryō kenkyūjo. 119–46. Heibonsha, 1996.

Kanegamori nikki batsu. In *Shinshū shiryō shūsei*. Vol. 2. *Rennyo to sono kyōdan*. Ed. Katada Osamu. 701–8. Kyoto: Dōhōsha, 1977.

Kasahara Kazuo. *Ikkō ikki no kenkyū*. Yamakawa shuppansha, 1962.

——. *Nihon ni okeru nōmin sensō*. Kokudosha, 1949.

——. *Rennyo*. Yoshikawa kōbunkan, 1963. Reprinted 1986.

—— and Inoue Toshio, eds. *Rennyo, ikkō ikki*. *Nihon shisō taikei*, vol. 17. Iwanami shoten, 1972.

Katayama Shin. "Kaga ikkō ikki to Honganji shugo-ken—'sankajō okite' o meguru kōsatsu." In *Chūsei shakai to ikkō ikki*. Ed. Kitanishi Hiromu sensei kanreki kinenkai. 175–98. Yoshikawa kōbunkan, 1985.

Katsumata Shizuo. *Ikki*. Iwanami shoten, 1982.

Keegan, John. *The Face of Battle*. New York: Viking Press, 1976. Reprinted Harmondsworth, Eng.: Penguin, 1978.

Keirstead, Thomas. *The Geography of Power in Medieval Japan*. Princeton, NJ: Princeton University Press, 1992.

Kennedy, Frances H., ed. *Civil War Battlefield Guide*. Boston: Houghton Mifflin, 1990.

Kennyo shōnin bun'an. In *Shinshū shiryō shūsei*. Vol. 3. *Ikkō ikki*. Ed. Kitanishi Hiromu. 1133–78. Kyoto: Dōhōsha, 1979.

Kigoshi Yūkei. "Amine Honseiji monjo ni miru Noto Honganji-ha ni tsuite." In *Kōza Rennyo*. Vol. 6. Ed. Jōdo shinshū kyōgaku kenkyūjo and Honganji shiryō kenkyūjo. 255–76. Heibonsha, 1998.

———. "Bunmei/Chōkyo ki no Kaga in okeru 'gun' ni tsuite." In *Kōza Rennyo*. Vol. 1. Ed. Jōdo Shinshū kyōgaku kenkyūjo and Honganji shiryō kenkyūjo. 335–63. Heibonsha, 1996.

Kinryū Kyōei. "Etchū kyōdan." In *Kōza Rennyo*. Vol. 6. Ed. Jōdo shinshū kyōgaku kenkyūjo and Honganji shiryō kenkyūjo. 187–228. Heibonsha, 1998.

Kinryū Shizuka. *Ikkō ikki ron*. Yoshikawa kōbunkan, 2004.

———. *Rennyo*. Yoshikawa kōbunkan, 1997.

———. "Etchū ikkōshū kyōdan no seiritsu to kōzō." *Bukkyō shigaku kenkyū* 26: 1 (November 1983): 18–44.

———. "Kaga ikkō ikki no keisei katei." In *Honganji, ikkō ikki no kenkyū*. Ed. Minegishi Sumio. 117–59; originally published in *Rekishigaku kenkyū* 436 (September 1976): 1–16.

———. "Rennyo kyōdan no hatten to ikkō ikki no tenkai." In *Tsūshihen, chūsei*. Vol. 2. *Toyama-ken shi*. 704–918. Toyama: Toyama-ken, 1984.

———. "Tenbun no Kinai ikkō ikki." In *Sengoku, Shokuhō*. Vol. 5. *Komonjo no kataru Nihon-shi*. Ed. Minegishi Sumio. 67–110. Chikuma shobō, 1989.

Kitahara Masao. "Muromachi-ki Mikawa Kira-shi no ichi kenkyū." *[Aichi kyōiku daigaku] Rekishi kenkyū* 27/28 (January 1983): 32–49.

Kitai Toshio. "Hirakata jinaichō no kōsei to kinō." *Kokugakuin zasshi* 86: 8 (August 1985): 29–43.

———. "Sengoku-ki no shūkyō to shōgyō: Honganji kyōdan no baai." In *Kōza Rennyo*. Vol. 3. Ed. Jōdo shinshū kyōgaku kenkyūjo and Honganji shiryō kenkyūjo. 157–86. Heibonsha, 1998.

Kitajima Masamoto. *Edo bakufu*. Vol. 16. *Nihon no rekishi*. 26–59. Shōgakukan, 1975.

Kitanishi Hiromu *Ikkō ikki no kenkyū*. Shunjūsha, 1981.

Kitanishi Hiromu sensei kanreki kinenkai, ed. *Chūsei shakai to ikkō ikki*. Yoshikawa kōbunkan, 1985.

Kitano shake nikki. Vol. 3. Zoku gunsho ruijū kanseikai, 1972.

Koizumi Yoshihiro. *Echizen ikkōshu no kenkyū*. Kyoto: Hōzōkan, 1999.

——. "Echizen ni okeru Shinshū no hatten." In *Kōza Rennyo*. Vol. 6. Ed. Jōdo shinshū kyōgaku kenkyūjo and Honganji shiryō kenkyūjo. 277–316. Heibonsha, 1998.

Kokushi daijiten. Vol. 2. Ed. Kokushi daijiten henshū iinkai. Yoshikawa kōbunkan, 1980.

Konko dokugo. In *Shinshū shiryō shūsei*. Vol. 2. *Rennyo to sono kyōdan*. 717–25. Ed. Katada Osamu. Kyoto: Dōhōsha, 1977.

Kubo Naofumi. *Shōkōji to Etchū ikkō ikki*. Toyama: Katsura shobō, 1986.

——. "Echigo Nagao-shi to Etchū shinkō." In *Tsūshi-hen, kodai, chūsei, kinsei*. Vol. 2.1. *Toyama-ken shi*. 463–519. Toyama: Toyama-ken, 1975.

——. "Muromachi jidai no Etchū." In *Tsūshi-hen, chūsei*. Vol. 2. *Toyama-ken shi*. 418–62. Toyama: Toyama-ken, 1984.

Kubota Masaki. "Eiroku rokunen ikkō ikki to Matsudaira-shi—kenryoku kōzō henyō no ichi sokumen." *Chihōshi kenkyū* 24: 3 (June 1974): 13–23.

——. "Sengokuki Matsudaira kenryoku to tokuseirei." *Komazawa daigaku shigaku ronshū* 10 (1980): 84–95.

Kyōkō hōin nikki. In *Kaitei shiseki shūran*. Vol. 25. Ed. Kondō Heijō. 416–28. Kondō kappansho, 1902. Reprinted Kyoto: Rinsen shoten, 1984.

Lamers, Jeroen P. *Japonicus Tyrannus: The Japanese Warlord Oda Nobunaga Reconsidered*. Leiden: Hotei Publishing, 2001.

Matsudairaki. In *Mikawa bunken shūsei, chūsei-hen*. Ed. Kyūsojin Hitaku. 101–61. Toyohashi: Aichi-ken Hoi chihōshi hensan iinkai, 1966.

McMullin, Neil. *Buddhism and the State in Sixteenth-Century Japan*. Princeton, NJ: Princeton University Press, 1984.

Mikawa monogatari. Ōkubo Hikozaemon Tadataka. *Nihon shisō taikei*, vol. 26. Ed. Saiki Kazuma et al. 10–212. Iwanami shoten, 1974.

Minegishi Sumio, ed. *Honganji, ikkō ikki no kenkyū*. Yoshikawa kōbunkan, 1984.

——, ed. *Komonjo no kataru Nihon-shi*. Vol. 5. *Sengoku, shokuhō*. Chikuma shobō, 1989.

——. "Ikkō ikki." In *Iwanami kōza Nihon rekishi 8 chūsei 4*. 128–73. Iwanami shoten, 1976.

———. "Ikkō ikki." In *Shinpojiumu Nihon rekishi 9 doikki*. 149–200. Gakuseisha, 1974.

———. "Rennyo no jidai: sono shakai to seiji." In *Kōza Rennyo*. Vol. 1. Ed. Jōdo Shinshū kyōgaku kenkyūjo and Honganji shiryō kenkyūjo. 67–91. Heibonsha, 1998.

Mitsumoto Masayuki. "Sengoku-ki Hida Shinshū no dōkō: Shorenji saikō to Shinran eizō no imi ni tsuite." In *Kōza Rennyo*. Vol 6. Ed. Jōdo Shinshū kyōgaku kenkyūjo and Honganji shiryō kenkyūjo. 157–85. Heibonsha, 1998.

Mizumoto Kunihito. "Kinai jinaichō no keisei to tenkai ni tsuite." In *Honganji, ikkō ikki no kenkyū*. Ed. Minegishi Sumio. 377–403. Yoshikawa kōbunkan, 1985.

Muroyama Kō. "'Anrakusan Sanfukuzenji nendaiki' ni tsuite." *Kano chiiki shi* 11 (June 1986): 1–6.

———. "Shiryō shōkai: Rinsenji-ryō Kaga no kuni Ōno-no-shō nengu sanyōjō ni tsuite." *Kano shiryō kenkyū* 4 (November 1989): 66–90.

Nagashima Fukutarō. "Honganji to Nara chōnin." *Nihon rekishi* 46 (March 1952): 24–26.

Nakamura Kichiji. *Do ikki kenkyū*. Azekura shobō, 1974.

Nakamura Kōya. *Ieyasu no shinryō: bushō-hen*. Jinbutsu ōraisha, 1955.

———. *Ieyasu no zokuyō*. Kōdansha, 1965.

———. *Tokugawa Ieyasu kōden*. Kōdansha, 1965.

———. *Tokugawa ke: Ieyasu o chūshin ni*. Shinbundō, 1955.

Nakano Kazuyuki. "Sengokuki Mikawa Honganji montodan ni okeru 'ikkō ikki.'" *Bukkyōshi kenkyū* 19/20 (December 1984): 114–34.

Nangyō zatsuroku. Tokyo University Historiographical Institute, ms. facsimile.

Nihon chimei daijiten. Vol. 23. Kadokawa shoten, 1989.

Nihon rekishi chimei taikei. Vols. 17, 23. Heibonsha, 1981–91.

Nihonshi kenkyūkai and Rekishigaku kenkyūkai, eds. *Yamashiro no kuni ikki*. Tōkyō Daigaku shuppankai, 1986.

Niigata-ken shi tsūshi-hen. Vol. 2. *Chūsei*. Ed. Niigata-ken. Niigata: Niigata-ken, 1987.

Nijōji shukaki. See *Zoku nangyō zatsuroku*.

Nishio-shi shi. Vol. 2. *Kodai, chūsei, kinsei*. Ed. Nishio-shi hensan iinkai. Nishio: Nishio-shi hensan iinkai, 1974.

Nisuiki. Tokyo University Historiographical Institute, ms. photocopy.

Nobutane kyōki. Vol. 2. *Zōho shiryō taisei*. Vol. 45. Ed. Zōho shiryō taisei kangyōkai. Kyoto: Rinsen shoten, 1965.

Nyokō deshi chō. In *Shinpen Okazaki-shi shi*. Vol. 6. *Kodai, chūsei shiryō*. Ed. Shinpen Okazaki-shi shi henshū iinkai. 630–34. Okazaki: Okazaki shiyakusho, 1983.

Oda Kenshin. "Honshūji kō." *Shinshū kyōgaku kenkyū* 3 (November 1979): 29–42.

———. "Mikawa ikkō ikki ni kansuru shokiroku ni tsuite—Shingyō Norikazu chō *Ikkō ikki no kiso kōzō—Mikawa ikki to Matsudaira-shi* o yonde." *Bukkyō shigaku kenkyū* 20: 1 (February 1978): 91–96.

———. "Sasaki Nyokō to sono shūhen (ichi)." *Shinshū kenkyū* 10 (October 1965): 58–71.

Ōtani chakuryū jikki. In *Shinshū shiryō shūsei*. Vol. 7. *Denki, keizu*. Ed. Hiramatsu Reizō. 601–76. Kyoto: Dōhōsha, 1975.

Ōtani Honganji tsūki. In *Shinshū shiryō shūsei*. Vol. 8. *Jishi, iseki*. Ed. Hosokawa Yukinobu. 342–584. Kyoto: Dōhōsha, 1974.

Rennyo shōnin goichidaiki kikigaki. In *Shinshū shiryō shūsei*. Vol. 2. *Rennyo to sono kyōdan*. Ed. Katada Osamu. 504–40. Kyoto: Dōhōsha, 1977.

Rennyo shōnin ichigoki. In *Shinshū shiryō shūsei*. Vol. 2. *Rennyo to sono kyōdan*. Ed. Katada Osamu. 444–69. Kyoto: Dōhōsha, 1977.

Rogers, Minor Lee and Ann T. Rogers. *Rennyo: The Second Founder of Shin Buddhism*. Berkeley, CA: Asian Humanities Press, 1991.

Rokuon nichiroku. Vol. 1. Ed. Tsuji Zennosuke. Zōho zoku gunsho ruijū kanseikai, 1934. Reprinted 1961.

Sakai Tatsuo. "Sengoku jidai." In *Nishio-shi shi*. Vol. 2. 152–326. Nishio: Nishio-shi shi hensan iinkai, 1974.

———. "Tokugawa-shi no ryōgoku shihai." In *Nishio-shi shi*. Vol. 2. 329–400. Nishio: Nishio-shi shi hensan iinkai, 1974.

Sanetaka kōki. Vols. 1, 4, and 8. Zoku-gun shoruijū kansei-kai, 1958–61.

Sasaki Motomi. "Shinshutsu gobunshū ni tsuite." *Shinshū kenkyū* 2 (September 1956): 77–92.

Shibano Yasuyuki. "Muromachi-ki Ka-shū ni okeru ichi zaikyō ryūshu ni tsuite." In *Chūsei shakai to ikkō ikki*. Ed. Kitanishi Hiromu sensei kanreki kinenkai. 323–45. Yoshikawa kōbunkan, 1985.

Shigematsu Akihisa. *Honganji hyakunen sensō*. Kyoto: Hōzōkan, 1986.

———. *Rennyo to Echizen ikkō ikki*. Fukui: Fukui-ken kyōdoshi kondankai, 1975.

Shimotsuma keizu. In *Shinshū shiryō shūsei*. Vol. 7. *Denki, keizu*. Ed. Katada Osamu. 677–91. Kyoto: Dōhōsha, 1977.

Shinchō kōki. *Sengoku shiryō sōsho*. Vol. 2. Ed. Kuwada Tadachika. Jinbutsu ōraisha, 1965.

Shingyō Norikazu. *Daijuji no rekishi*. Okazaki: Daijuji, 1983.

———. *Ikkō ikki no kiso kōzō – Mikawa ikki to Matsudaira-shi*. Yoshikawa kōbunkan, 1975.

———. "Eishō sannen ikkō ikki no seijiteki seikaku." *Shichō* 77 (November 1961): 21–38.

———. "Etchū ikkō ikki no sho zentei." *Nihon rekishi* 141 (March 1960): 83–94, 36.

———. "Mikawa ikkō ikki ron ho-i (sono ichi)." *Chūsei shi kenkyū* 2 (1977): 83–94.

Shinpen Okazaki-shi shi. Vol. 2. *Chūsei*. Ed. Shinpen Okazaki-shi shi iinkai. Okazaki: Okazaki shiyakusho, 1989.

———. Vol. 6. *Kodai, chūsei shiryō*. Okazaki: Okazaki shiyakusho, 1989.

Shirayamagū shōgon kōchū kiroku. In *Hakusan shiryō shū*. Vol. 1. *Nihonkai bunka sōsho*. Ed. Kanazawa Daigaku hōbungakunai nihonkai bunka shiryō shitsu. Kanazawa: Ishikawa-ken toshokan kyōkai, 1979.

Shiryō sōran. Vol. 9. Ed. Tōkyō Daigaku shiryō hensanjo. Heibonsha, 1966.

Shishinki. In *Shinshū shiryō shūsei*. Vol. 3. *Ikkō ikki*. Ed. Katada Osamu. 539–964. Kyoto: Dōhōsha, 1979.

Shotera kakochō. Tokyo University Historiographical Institute, ms. facsimile.

Solomon, Ira Michael. "The Dilemma of Religious Power: Honganji and Hosokawa Masamoto." *Monumenta Nipponica* 33: 1 (Spring 1978): 51–65.

———. "Rennyo and the Rise of Honganji in Muromachi Japan." Ph.D. diss., Columbia University, 1972.

Sonpi bunmyaku. Shintei zōho kokushi taikei. Vols. 59–60. Ed. Kokushi taikei henshūkai. Yoshikawa kōbunkan, 1962. Reprinted 2001.

Suitō Makoto. "Ōsaka jinaichō no hibi: *Tenbun nikki* kara." *Kokuritsu rekishi minzoku hakubutsukan kenkyū hōkoku* 39 (March 1992): 81–118.

Tabata Yasuko. *Nihon chūsei joseishi ron*. Kaku shobō, 1994.

Tamon'in nikki. 5 vols. Ed. Tsuji Zennosuke. Kadokawa shoten, 1968.

Tanaka Katsuyuki. "Mura no 'hanzei' to senran/tokusei ikki – sengokuki Kyōto kinkō sonraku no rentai to buryoku dōin." *Shigaku zasshi* 102: 6 (June 1993): 1–36.

Tatsunokuchi-chō shi. Vol. 2. *Zenkindai-hen*. Ed. Asaka Toshiki. Tatsunokuchi-chō: Ishikawa-ken Nomi-gun Tatsunokuchi-chō yakusho, 1987.

Tenbun nikki. In *Shinshū shiryō shūsei.* Vol. 3. *Ikkō ikki.* Ed. Kitanishi Hiromu. Kyoto: Dōhōsha, 1979.

Tenshō san-nen ki. In *Shinshū shiryō shūsei.* Vol. 2. *Rennyo to sono kyōdan.* Ed. Katada Osamu. 411–19. Kyoto: Dōhōsha, 1977.

Thornton, Sybil. *Charisma and Community Formation in Medieval Japan: The Case of the Yugyō-ha (1300–1700).* Ithaca, NY: East Asia Program, Cornell University, 1999.

Togashi-shi to Kaga ikkō ikki shiryō. Ed. Tate Zan'ō. Kanazawa: Ishikawa shisho kankōkai, 1973.

Tōji kakochō. Tokyo University Historiographical Institute, ms. facsimile.

Tōji kōmyōkō kakochō. Tokyo University Historiographical Institute, ms. facsimile.

Tokitsugu kyōki. Vol. 1. Ed. Ōta Tōshirō. Taiyōsha, 1941.

Tokoro Rikio. "Henkakuki Mikawa ni okeru teikō no ronri to shihai no ronri." *Shichō* new series 1 (November 1976): 89–104.

——. Review of Shingyō Norikazu's *Ikkō ikki no kiso kōzō. Rekishigaku kenkyū* 435 (August 1976): 50–53.

Tokugawa Bijutsukan and Gotō Bijutsukan, eds. *Ieyasu no sho to ihin.* Nagoya: Tokugawa bijutsukan, 1983.

Totman, Conrad. *Tokugawa Ieyasu: Shogun.* San Francisco, CA: Heian International, 1983.

Toyama-ken shi, shiryō-hen. Vol. 2. *Chūsei.* Toyama: Toyama-ken, 1975.

Toyama-ken shi, tsūshi-hen. Vol. 2. *Chūsei.* Toyama: Toyama-ken, 1984.

Trewartha, Glenn T. *Japan: A Geography.* Madison, WI: University of Wisconsin Press, 1965.

Tsang, Carol Richmond. "The Development of Ikkō Ikki, 1500–1570." Ph.D. diss., Harvard University, 1995.

——. "Marriage, Adoption, and Honganji." *Japanese Journal of Religious Studies,* 31: 1 (2005): 53–83.

Weinstein, Stanley. "Rennyo and the Shinshū Revival." In *Japan in the Muromachi Age.* Ed. John W. Hall and Toyoda Takeshi. 331–58. Berkeley, CA: University of California Press, 1977.

White, James W. *Ikki: Social Conflict and Political Protest in Early Modern Japan.* Ithaca, NY: Cornell University Press, 1995.

Yamamoto Takeshi. "Chūsei nōmin no seikatsu no sekai." In *Ikki.* Vol. 4. *Seikatsu, bunka, shisō.* Ed. Aoki Michio et al. 131–66. Tōkyō Daigaku shuppankai, 1981.

—— and Owada Tetsuo, eds. *Sengoku daimyō kashindan jiten.* 2 vols. Shinjinbutsu ōraisha, 1981.

Yamashina gobō no koto narabi ni sono jidai no koto. Jitsugo. In *Shinshū shiryō shūsei*. Vol. 2. *Rennyo to sono kyōdan*. Ed. Katada Osamu. 541–57. Kyoto: Dōhōsha, 1977.

Yanagi Chizuru. "Kaga ikkō ikki no tenkai—naibu kōzō no henshitsu o chūshin ni." *Nihonshi kenkyū* 106 (July 1969): 20–56. Also *Honganji, ikkō ikki no kenkyū*. Ed. Minegishi Sumio. 66–116. Yoshikawa kōbunkan, 1984.

Yasaka jinja monjo. Vol. 1. Kyoto: Yasaka jinja shamusho, 1939.

Yokōji nendaiki. "Yokōji shozō Yokōji nendaiki ni tsuite." Ed. Ishikawa kenritsu toshokan kano shiryō hensanshitsu. *Kano shiryō kenkyū* 105 (March 1986): 35, 51–53.

Zoku nangyō zatsuroku. Tokyo University Historiographical Institute, ms. facsimile.

Character List

Aguchi jinja monjo 開口神社文書
Akamatsu Masanori 赤松政範
Aki 安芸
Amida 阿弥陀
An'ijidono gojiki 安位寺殿御自記
Anrakusan Sanfukuzenji nendaiki 安楽山産福禅寺年代記
Arakawa Yoshihiro 荒川義広
Asai Hisamasa 浅井久政
Asai Nagamasa 浅井長政
Asai Sukechika 浅井亮親
Asakura Kagetake 朝倉景健
Asakura Norikage 朝倉教景
Asakura Sadakage 朝倉貞景
Asakura shimatsuki 朝倉始末記
Asakura Takakage 朝倉孝景
Asakura Toshikage 朝倉敏景
Asakura Yoshikage 朝倉義景
Ashikaga Yoshiaki 足利義昭
Ashikaga Yoshiharu 足利義晴
Ashikaga Yoshihisa 足利義尚
Ashikaga Yoshikazu 足利義量
Ashikaga Yoshimasa 足利義政
Ashikaga Yoshimochi 足利義持
Ashikaga Yoshinori 足利義教
Ashikaga Yoshitane 足利義稙
Ashikaga Yoshizumi 足利義澄
Aso 阿曾
Awa (Kantō) 安房
Awa (Shikoku) 阿波

Bingo 備後
Biwa 琵琶
Bugyōnin hōsho 奉行人奉書
Bukkōji 仏光寺
Bunmei 文明
buppō 仏法
buppōryō 仏法領

Chin'ei 鎮永
Chinzai 鎮西
Chōkyō 長享
Chōshōji 超勝寺

Dai hasso onmonogatari Kūzen kikigaki 第八祖御物語空善聞書
Daijōin 大乗院
Daijōin jisha zōjiki 大乗院寺社雜事記
Daijuji 大樹寺
Daijuji kakochō 大樹寺過去帳
daikan 代官
dai-shō ikki 大小一揆
Deguchi 出口
Doi 土井
do ikki 土一揆
dōjō 道場
domin 土民
Dōsai 道西

Ebina 海老名
Echigo 越後
Echizen 越前
Eiroku 永禄
Eiroku ikki yurai 永禄一揆由来
Eishō 永正
Ennyo 円如
Enryakuji 延暦寺
Enuma-gun 江沼郡
Entoku 延徳
Etchū 越中

fuhai hiji 不拝秘事
Fujishima 藤島
fuju fuse 不受不施
Fukama 福釜
Fukōzu 深溝
Fukuda-no-shō 福田荘
Fukumitsu 福光
funyū 不入

Gamagōri 蒲郡
Ganshōji 願証寺
Gantokuji 願徳寺
Genkō 元享
Gion 祇園
gō 郷
gobō 御坊
Gohōjōji kanpakuki 後法成寺関白記
Gohōkōinki 後法興院記
Go-Narain shinki 後奈良院宸記
Gonjo ōnenki 厳助往年記
Gonjo shinshū gekōki 厳助信州下向記
goshō gomen 後生御免
Guganji 弘願寺
Gukanshō 愚管抄
gun 郡
gun ikki 郡一揆
gunjū 郡中
Gyōnyo 巧如

Hachiya Hannojō Sadatsugu 蜂屋半之丞貞次
Hakui 羽咋
Hakusan 白山
hanzei 半済
Harima 播磨
Harisaki 針崎
Hasadani 波佐谷
Hatakeyama Motonobu 畠山基信
Hatakeyama Shōjun 畠山尚順

Hatakeyama Yoshihide 畠山義英
Hatakeyama Yoshimoto 畠山義元
Hatakeyama Yoshimune 畠山義宗
Hatakeyama Yoshinobu 畠山義宣
Heisenji 平泉寺
Hida 飛驒
Hiei 比叡
Hino ichiryū keizu 日野一流系図
Hino Katsumitsu 日野勝光
Hino Tomiko 日野富子
Hirohashi 広橋
Hizen 肥前
Hōchi 法智
Hogo no uragaki 反古裏書
Hōjū 法住
Hōki 伯耆
Hokuriku 北陸
Honda Hirotaka 本多広孝
Honda Masanobu 本多正信
Honda Tadakatsu 本多忠勝
Hōnen 法然
Hongakuji 本覚寺
Honganji 本願寺
Honganji sahō no shidai 本願寺作法之次第
Honkokuji nenpu 本圀寺年譜
Honmanji monjo 本満寺文書
Honnōji monjo 本能寺文書
Honpukuji 本福寺
Honpukuji atogaki 本福寺跡書
Honpukuji montoki 本幅寺門徒記
Honpukuji Myōshū atogaki 本福寺明宗跡書
Honpukuji yuraiki 本福寺由来記
Honrenji 本蓮寺
Honsenji 本泉寺
Honshōji 本證寺
Honshūji 本宗寺
honzan 本山
hōonkō 報恩講
Hosokawa Harukuni 細川晴国
Hosokawa Harumoto 細川晴元
Hosokawa Masamoto 細川政元
Hosokawa ryōkaki 細川両家記
Hosokawa Takakuni 細川高国
Hosorogi-gō 細呂木郷
hyakushō 百姓

Ibaraki Nagataka 茨木長隆
ichimon 一門
ichiyaku hōmon 一益法門
ichizoku ikki 一族一揆
Iigai 飯貝
Iimori 飯盛
ikkeshū 一家衆
ikki 一揆
ikkō ikki 一向一揆
ikkōshū 一向衆, 一向宗
Imagawa Ujichika 今川氏親
Imagawa Ujizane 今川氏真
Imagawa Yoshimoto 今川義元
Ima-Katata 今堅田
Inryōken nichiroku 蔭涼軒日録
Ise 伊勢
Ise Sadachika 伊勢貞親
Ise Sadafusa 伊勢貞房
Ise Sadamune 伊勢貞宗

Ishiguro Ukon Mitsuyoshi 石黒右近光義
Ishikawa-gun 石川郡
Ishiyama 石山
Isono Tanba-no-kami 磯野丹波守
Isshiki Masahiro 一色政熙
Iwanari Tomomichi 岩成友通
Izu 伊豆
Izumi 和泉

jikisan 直参
Jikken 実賢
Jikkyō 実慶
jinaichō 寺内町
Jinbō Yoshimune 神保慶宗
Jinson 尋尊
jiriki 自力
Jishū 時宗
jitō 地頭
Jitsue 実慧
Jitsuen 実円
Jitsugen 実玄
Jitsugo 実悟
Jitsujun 実淳
Jitsunyo 実如
jizamurai 地侍
Jōdo Shinshū 浄土真宗
Jōdoshū 浄土宗
Jōgūji 上宮寺
Junnyo 順如
Jūrin'in naifuki 十輪院内府記

Kaga 加賀
Kagaki 加賀記
Kahoku-gun 河北郡
Kai 甲斐
kakikudashibun 書き下し文
Kakue 覚恵
Kakunyo 覚如
Kakushin 覚信
kakutagai ikki 角違一揆
Kamakura 鎌倉
Kamiwada 上和田
kan 貫
Kanazawa 金沢
Kanchiron 官地論
Kanegamori 金森
Kanegamori nikki batsu 金森日記拔
Kankiji 勧帰寺
Kanō Hikoshichirō 狩野彦七郎
kanpaku 関白
Kanroji Chikanaga 甘露寺親長
Kanshō 寛正
Kantō 関東
Kariganeya Minbu 雁金屋民部
Kariya 刈谷
Kasama Ietsugu 笠間家次
Kashima 鹿島
Kasuga 春日
Katata 堅田
Kawachi 河内
Kawara Gen'emon 河原源衛門
kawara-mono 河原者
kawara-shū 河原衆
Kenninji 建仁寺
Kennyo 顕如
Kennyo shōnin bun'an 顕如上人文案
Kensei 顕誓
Kii 紀伊
Kinai 畿内
Kinshokuji 錦織寺
Kira Yoshiaki 吉良義昭

Kitano shake nikki
北野社家日記
Kizawa Nagamasa 木沢長政
kō 講
Kōfukuji 興福寺
Kōgyōji 興行寺
kokujin 国人
kokujin ikki 国人一揆
Kōkyōji 光教寺
Konda 金田
Konko dokugo 古今独語
Konoe Hisamichi 近衛尚通
Konoe Masaie 近衛政家
Kōshōji 興正寺
Kosugi 小杉
Kōtokuji 光徳寺
Kōzai Motonaga 香西元長
Kōzenji 光善寺
Kōzu 高津
Kujō Hisatsune 九条尚経
kumi 組
kuni ikki 国一揆
Kuratsuki-no-shō 倉月荘
Kyōkaku 慶覚
Kyōkō hōin nikki
経厚法印日記
Kyōnyo 教如

Maeba Kagemasa 前波景当
Maeba Shichirōbe-no-jō
前波七郎兵衛尉
Makino 牧野
mappō 末法
Matsudaira Chikatada
松平親忠
Matsudaira Chikatoshi
松平親俊
Matsudaira-gō 松平郷
Matsudaira Hirotada
松平広忠
Matsudaira Iekiyo
松平家清
Matsudaira Ietsugu
松平家次
Matsudairaki 松平記
Matsudaira Kiyoyasu
松平清康
Matsudaira Masahisa
松平昌久
Matsudaira Motoyasu
松平元康
Matsudaira Nagachika
松平長親
Matsudaira Nobumitsu
松平信光
Matsudaira Nobutada
松平信忠
Matsui Tadatsugu 松井忠次
mikata 御かた
Mikawa 三河
Mikawa monogatari 三河物語
Mikuriya 御厨
Mino 美濃
Miyoshi Motonaga 三好元長
Miyoshi Naganao 三好長直
Mizuno Nobumoto
水野信元
monto 門徒
monzenmachi 門前町
Mōri 毛利
Morikawachi 森河内
mōsen 毛氈
Motoori 本折
mugekō 無碍光
Muromachi 室町
Mutsu 陸奥
Mutsuguri 六栗
Myōgenji 妙源寺
myōgō 名号
Myohōjiki 妙法寺記

Myōkokuji 妙国寺
Myōsei 明誓
Myōshū 明宗

Nagao Tamekage
長尾為景
Nagao Yoshikage
長尾能景
Nagashima 長島
naishū 内衆
Nakanoin Michihide
中院通秀
Nakashima 中島
Nakashima Hyūga-no-kami
中島日向守
Namu Amida butsu
南無阿弥陀仏
Nanzenji 南禅寺
Nara 奈良
Natsume Yoshinobu
夏目吉信
Negoroji 根来寺
nenbutsu 念仏
nengu 年貢
Nichiren 日蓮
Nijōji shukaki
二条寺主家記
Nishio 西尾
Nisuiki 二水記
Niwata Shigeyasu
庭田重保
Noba 野場
Noda 野田
Nodera 野寺
Nomi-gun 能見郡
Nomura 野村
Nosaka-no-shō 野坂荘
Noto 能登
Nuka 額
Nukata-no-shō 額田荘

Nyoen 如円
Nyojō 如乗
Nyoryō 如了
Nyoshin 如信

Oda Nobunaga 織田信長
Oda Nobuoki 織田信興
ofumi 御文
Ogie 小木江
Ōhira 大平
Okazaki 岡崎
Okehazama 桶狭間
Ōkubo Hikozaemon Tadataka
大久保彦左衛門忠教
Ōkusa 大草
Ōmi 近江
Ōnin 応仁
Ōno-no-shō 大野荘
ōryō 横領
Ōsumi 大隅
Ōta Gyūichi 太田牛一
Ōtani 大谷
Ōtani chakuryū jikki
大谷嫡流実記
Ōtani Honganji tsūki
大谷本願寺通記
Ōtsu 大津
Owari 尾張

Rengo 蓮悟
Renjō 蓮乗
Renjun 蓮淳
Renkō 蓮綱
Renkyō (also read as Renkei)
蓮慶
Rennō-ni 蓮能尼
Rennyo 蓮如
Rennyo shōnin goichidaiki kikigaki 蓮如上人御一代記聞書

Rennyo shōnin ichigoki 蓮如上人一語記
Rensei 蓮誓
Ren'yū 蓮祐
Rinsenji 臨川寺
Rinshōji 隣松寺
Rokkaku Sadayori 六角定頼
Rokkaku Takayori 六角高頼
Rokuon nichiroku 鹿苑日録
ryōke 領家
ryōshu 領主

Saitō 斎藤
Saitōin 西塔院
Sakai 堺
Sakai Masachika 酒井正親
Sakai Tadanao 酒井忠尚
Sakurai 桜井
Sanetaka kōki 実隆公記
Sanjōnishi Sanetaka 三条西実隆
Sanmonto 三門徒
Sasaki 佐々木
Sawai 沢井
seken 世間
sekkanke 摂関家
sengoku 戦国
Senjuji 専修寺
Senkōji 専光寺
Settsu 摂津
Shakunyo 綽如
Shiba Yoshihiro 斯波義寛
Shiba Yoshikado 斯波義廉
Shiba Yoshitoshi 斯波義敏
Shibata Katsuie 柴田勝家
Shiga 滋賀
Shikichi Hikouemon-no-jō 敷地彦右衛門尉
Shimoichi 下市
Shimotsuma keizu 下間系図
Shimotsuma Raijō 下間頼盛
Shimotsuma Raikei 下間頼慶
Shimotsuma Raishū 下間頼秀
Shimotsuma Rensō 下間蓮崇
Shimotsuma Shōzen 下間性善
Shinano 信濃
Shinchō kōki 信長公記
Shin'e 真慧
shinjin 信心
Shinkōmyōji 信光明寺
Shinran 親鸞
Shirayama 白山
Shirayama-gū shōgon kōchū kiroku 白山宮荘厳講中記録
Shirutani 湿谷
Shishinki 私心記
Shōanji 聖安寺
shōen 荘園
Shōgoji 照護寺
shō ikki 荘一揆
Shōkōji (Etchū) 勝興寺
Shōkōji (Kaga) 松岡寺
Shōmanji 勝鬘寺
Shōnyo 証如
Shōren'in 青蓮院
Shōrenji 照蓮寺
shōshu 荘主

Shōtoku 聖徳
Shōtokuji 称徳寺
Shugendō 修験道
shugo 守護
shugo-dai 守護代
shugo funyū 守護不入
sōgō 総郷
Sōkaiji 惣海寺
sōkoku ikki 惣国一揆
Sonpi bunmyaku 尊卑分脈
Suganuma Sadaaki 菅沼定顕
Sugawara 菅原
Suruga 駿河
Suzaki Keigaku 洲崎慶覚

Taiheiki 太平記
Takada 高田
Takakura 高倉
Takao 高尾
Takechiyo 竹千代
Takeda Motoaki 武田元明
Takeda Shingen 武田信玄
Tamon'in nikki 多聞院日記
Tanba 丹波
Tango 丹後
tariki 他力
Tenbun 天文
Tendai 天台
Tenkei-in 天桂院
Tennōji 天王寺
Tenryūji 天龍寺
Tenshō 天正
Togashi Kōchiyo 富樫幸千代
Togashi Masachika 富樫政親
Togashi Yasutaka 富樫泰高
Tōji kakochō 東寺過去帳
Tōji kōmyōkō kakochō 東寺光明講過去帳
Tōkaidō 東海道
Tokitsugu kyōki 言継卿記
Tokugawa Ieyasu 徳川家康
Tokuhime 徳姫
tokusei ikki 徳政一揆
Tondabayashi 富田林
Ton'en 頓円
Toro 土呂
Tōsōki 闘争記
Tōtōmi 遠江
Toyotomi Hideyoshi 豊臣秀吉
Tsukinohashi 槻橋
Tsushima 津島
Tsutsui kaki 筒井家記

uchi-izu 打出
uchi-mawari 打廻
Ueno 上野
Uesugi Fusayoshi 上杉房能
Uramatsu 裏松

wabigoto 詫び言
Wakasa 若狭
Washizuka 鷲塚
Watanabe Chūemon oboegaki 渡辺忠右衛門覚書
Watanabe Genzō Sadatsuna 渡辺源蔵真綱
Watanabe Hanzō Moritsuna 渡辺半蔵守綱

Yakushiji Kuninaga 薬師寺国長
Yamada 山田
Yamagawa 山川
Yamana 山名
Yamanouchi 山内
Yamashina 山科
Yamashina gobō no koto narabi ni sono jidai no koto 山科御坊事並其時代事

Yamashina Tokitsugu
山科言継
Yamashiro 山城
Yamato 大和
Yamazaki Naganori
山崎長徳
Yasuyoshi Gen'emon-no-jō Ienaga 安吉源衛門尉家長
Yatsuomote 八ツ面
Yōkōji nendaiki 永光寺年代記
Yoshino 吉野
Yoshizaki 吉崎
Yugyō-ha 遊行派
Yuizen 唯善
Yuwakudani 湯涌谷

zaichi ryōshu 在地領主
Zenkōji 善光寺
Zoku nangyō zatsuroku
続南行雑録
Zonnyo 存如
Zuisenji 瑞泉寺

Index